The Struggle for Quebec

The Struggle for Quebec: From Referendum to Referendum?

ROBERT A. YOUNG

McGill-Queen's University Press
Montreal & Kingston • London • Ithaca

© McGill-Queen's University Press, 1999
ISBN 0-7735-1851-7 (cloth)
ISBN 0-7735-1874-6 (paper)

Legal deposit first quarter 1999
Bibliothèque nationale du Québec

Printed in Canada on acid-free paper

Publication of this book has been assisted by a grant
from the J.B. Smallman and Spencer Memorial Fund,
University of Western Ontario.

McGill-Queen's University Press acknowledges the
financial support of the Government of Canada
through the Book Publishing Industry Development
Program for its activities. We also acknowledge the
support of the Canada Council for the Arts for our
publishing program.

Canadian Cataloguing in Publication Data

Young, Robert Andrew
    The struggle for Quebec : from referendum to
    referendum?

    Includes bibliographical references and index.
    ISBN 0-7735-1851-7 (bound)
    ISBN 0-7735-1874-6 (pbk.)

    1. Quebec (Province) – History – Autonomy and
    independence movements. 2. Quebec (Province) –
    Politics and government – 1994–   . 3. Referendum –
    Quebec (Province) 4. Canada – Politics and govern-
    ment – 1993–   . I. Title.

    FC2926.9.R4Y68 1999   971.064'8   C98-901358-8
    F1053.2.Y68 1999

For Gordon Alexander Young –
keen student, great teacher

Contents

Abbreviations ix

Acknowledgments xi

Introduction 3

1 The 1995 Referendum and the Yes That Wasn't 13

2 The Logic of the Referendum Campaign 39

3 Had the Yes Side Won ... 60

4 The Fallout of the Referendum 72

5 Manoeuvring towards the Next Referendum 87

6 What Would Happen after a Yes in a
Future Referendum? 123

Postscript 145

Notes 151

Bibliography 193

Index 205

Abbreviations

ADQ	Action démocratique du Québec
BQ	Bloc québécois
EU	European Union
FTA	Canada – U.S. Free Trade Agreement
GATT	General Agreement on Tariffs and Trade
MNA	Member of the (Quebec) National Assembly
MP	Member of the (Canadian) Parliament
NAFTA	North American Free Trade Agreement
PQ	Parti québécois
QLP	Quebec Liberal Party
ROC	rest of Canada
UDI	unilateral declaration of independence

Acknowledgments

This study is the latest in a series of works on Canadian federalism and Quebec secession that has occupied me for most of the past decade. Over such a span of time, one accumulates a very large number of academic and editorial debts, not all of which can be acknowledged here. But I do wish to thank the institutions that have supported my work: the University of Western Ontario, the Institute of Intergovernmental Relations and the School of Policy Studies at Queen's University, and the Social Sciences and Humanities Research Council of Canada. Thanks are due as well to the kind colleagues who have afforded me the opportunity to discuss this work and the issues it raises, in sessions at universities, academic conferences, and research institutes, as well as at meetings of political parties, government agencies, and firms. Other colleagues have taken the time to read this material and make helpful comments; for this contribution over many years, I am especially grateful to Tom Courchene, John McDougall, and Peter Neary. I have also benefited from the work of fine research assistants, and for their help in assembling the material covered in this book I thank Andrew Goldstein, Richard Haigh, Laura Watton, and Mark Scott. This text was much improved by the expert and sympathetic editing of Carlotta Lemieux, while important support on the production side has been provided by Yvonne Adams, Valerie Jarus, and Mark Howes. I am also grateful for the interest and encouragement of Joan McGilvray and Philip Cercone at McGill-Queen's University Press. My greatest debt, of course, is to my dear wife, Louise Gadbois, who has sustained me through this and every other effort.

The Struggle for Quebec

Introduction

The biggest threat to the integrity of the Canadian state and the well-being of all Canadians is the possible secession of Quebec. In the struggle for its future that is being carried on within the province, the sovereigntists form a powerful movement with bases in many social institutions, while the federalists, who often seem to be on the defensive, count on support from their allies in the federal government. This is a grinding struggle. The two sides confront each other in every quarter, continually seeking to extend their support. The struggle intensifies during provincial elections as the parties representing the sovereigntists and federalists square off, and it peaks during referendum campaigns. In the first referendum, held in 1980, Quebecers rejected a proposal to negotiate "sovereignty-association" with Canada. In the second, in 1995, the federalist side won a very narrow victory. It is at this point that this book begins.

For a political scientist, this is an unusual type of book to set before readers, because it is a sequel. Scholarly students of politics rarely write such things, but doing so now seems justified because of the nature of the book it succeeds and the arguments that were presented there. This book follows *The Secession of Quebec and the Future of Canada*, which I wrote during the summer and autumn of 1994, aiming squarely at the referendum that was likely to take place in Quebec in 1995. On the assumption that a majority of Quebecers might vote Yes in that referendum (an assumption shared by very few at the time) and that separation would then occur (a contention which the book supported but which was hotly contested as the referendum approached), my purpose was "to assess what the long-term future of Canada would be in the event of Quebec's secession and also to explore the political and economic relationships that would exist between Canada and Quebec."[1]

The ultimate purpose of this book is similar, but it is also intended to bring us up to date on what has occurred since mid-1994. Thus it provides a history of what did in fact happen in the 1995 referendum and what has taken place since, both in Quebec and in the rest of Canada. It then uses this material as a basis for new predictions about what a Yes vote in yet another referendum might bring. Unlike *The Secession of Quebec and the Future of Canada* (and the revised and expanded edition of it, containing most of the six chapters that follow), which was intended for scholars and university students, this book is aimed at concerned citizens, many of whom became interested in this issue precisely because the 1995 Quebec referendum was so shocking. In order to make it more accessible to the general reader, I have dropped the long and detailed analysis that formed the core of the original book. But I give below a brief summary, since some context is necessary for the chapters that follow.

The first part of *The Secession of Quebec* dealt with the "grand alternatives" that might result from a Quebec secession. I showed that a Canada-without-Quebec could well be a viable economic and political unit but that many configurations were open to ROC (the Rest of Canada).[2] The country could become more centralized, could have a constitution rather like the present one, could become more decentralized, or could even fall apart. Similarly, the possible economic relations between ROC and Quebec were open, ranging from close integration to the type of relationship that exists between any pair of sovereign states in the international trading system. Political relations, in theory, could range from a system of joint legislative and executive bodies to an almost complete absence of common institutions or even of bilateral treaties. Further analysis of the general relationship between political and economic integration, and of the factors determining how centralized political systems are likely to be, showed that none of the results on the menu of possibilities was strictly dictated by the history or characteristics of Canada and Quebec.

These introductory chapters were dry, but they set up an important contention – the long-term outcomes of a Quebec secession from Canada would depend on how the transition to sovereignty unfolded. This was a critical part of the argument. Secessions are historic events. They are affected by conjunctural factors, and are characterized by a high level of uncertainty; they offer much latitude for political leadership, and many choices made during the process are irreversible. Hence, the long-term outcomes of a secession depend on the process through which it takes place.

Consequently, the study focused on how the transition to Quebec sovereignty might occur. First, I examined existing analyses of the Quebec-Canada case. The economic studies showed that the cost of separation could be either very large or rather limited, with the magnitude depending on the degree of political cooperation that existed through and after the transition. The legal studies were intricate and sometimes clever, but they were also highly indeterminate because the fundamental questions were whether Quebec could exercise control over its territory and whether other states would recognize it, and each is a political issue. I then examined the political scenarios that had been constructed in the past, but these were little help in predicting what might happen if there were to be a Yes vote in 1995. Political scientists' predictions ranged from civil war to a rather smooth disengagement of Quebec from ROC, and I concluded that although politics rather than economics or law would dominate the process of any Quebec secession, there was "a striking lack of consensus about questions that would critically determine the outcome of negotiations with Quebec and the way in which ROC would be reconstituted."[3]

Comparative analysis offered one possible way out, so the study looked at several other cases where secession had occurred peacefully. These included Norway-Sweden, Singapore-Malaysia, Austria-Hungary, several less notable cases, and the recent split between Slovakia and the Czech Republic. This last case deserved a separate chapter, one that highlighted the process of gradual polarization between the Czechs and the Slovaks.[4] Close examination of the political dynamics that accompanied – and drove – all of these secessions revealed a common pattern, a logic of secession, and this basic framework helped in approaching the Quebec-Canada case.[5] Of course, my predictions about what would follow a Yes vote in a 1995 referendum were also informed by standard political and economic literature, an appreciation of Canadian history, economics, and politics, and all the previous studies of a possible Quebec secession.

These predictions made up the third (more exciting) part of the original book. I tried to lay out how the 1995 campaign would unfold and, assuming a Yes vote for sovereignty, what would follow. A Yes vote would take Canadians by surprise, I predicted, it would produce enormous economic uncertainty across the country, and, I argued, if the question and campaign were fair, then the Yes verdict would be accepted by ROC, "for all other courses of action appear to produce inferior results."[6] (Some space was devoted to showing why other moves would be inferior.)[7] In this unprecedented crisis, power and authority would flow to the central government in Ottawa, which would accept in principle that secession would take place and, in conjunction with the Parti québécois government in Quebec City, would take immediate steps to settle the most pressing issues: the disposition of the armed forces and the public service, Quebec's borders, the national debt, and access between Ontario and the Atlantic provinces. The study also predicted what the outcomes would be on the other major dossiers of negotiation. These include the division of assets, environmental issues, citizenship, the First Nations, other minority rights, Quebec's secession to treaties, commercial and economic relations between Canada and Quebec, the currency and monetary policy, mobility and immigration, and social entitements. Rather boldly, the book laid out what would be agreed in these matters, and why. Readers interested in the substance of these issues might still profitably examine those discussions.[8]

As for ROC itself, I argued that concern about its future would gradually supersede Canadians' preoccupation with the ROC-Quebec negotiations. But partly because of how recent history had unfolded, there would be no massive changes in the constitutional configuration of what would surely continue to be called Canada. Instead, Quebec would be excised from the Constitution Acts with the minimal concomitant changes in the Canadian constitution, according to the proper amending formula, and this event – this secession – would be ratified by some form of popular consultation in ROC.[9]

Over the short term, given the nature of this disengagement, Canada would endure some substantial economic costs, but it should be politically stable, I concluded. Quebec would suffer larger transition costs, and these would very likely be compounded by political instability as the party system realigned. Relations between the two states would involve little political cooperation, and close economic relations "would erode as their policy framework gradually settled to the level of integration prevailing among the countries of North America."[10]

AN OVERVIEW OF THIS BOOK

This book continues the story, outlining the events that have occurred since *The Secession of Quebec* was written, and offering further analysis based on these developments. Chapter 1 simply updates the historical record. A straightforward account of the events leading up to the 1995 referendum on Quebec sovereignty, it begins by tracing the strategies of the sovereigntist and federalist sides from the autumn of 1994 to September 1995, when the official campaign began. The referendum campaign itself is then covered much more closely, with analyses of the actors involved, their tactics, the shifts in public opinion – especially in favour of the Yes side during the last part of the contest – and the results. My objective here is simply to provide a concise history of these remarkable events.

The next chapter analyses the logic of the campaign. It attempts to show why the sovereigntists gained ground and almost won the referendum. This is much more speculative, because it does not deal with many of the elements that produce political victory, such as grassroots organization and the strategic deployment of money, advertising, volunteers, and so on. Instead, the focus is on the political discourse of the two sides and how this was structured. My contention, in brief, is that the sovereigntists made their gains on the economic front, with arguments that a Yes vote would not produce material losses for Quebecers, and that the federalists could not counter these without acknowledging that secession might actually occur – which they were unable or unwilling to do.

Next, I consider an issue that was hotly debated in the run-up to the October 1995 referendum, one that *The Secession of Quebec* was designed to address. What would happen after a Yes vote? In 1994, all the answers to this question were speculative, but now, with the benefit of hindsight, it is possible to assess more precisely what would have happened, given the real nature of the campaign and the actual results. In this chapter, I argue that the sovereigntists could not have consolidated a narrow Yes victory in 1995 to produce the decisive split that I had earlier envisioned. They would have lacked the legitimacy required to do so, not because the question was unclear or the margin of victory slim but because of the unanticipated irregularities in the counting of ballots.

Chapter 4 moves on to consider the fallout of the referendum. This is in line with the basic argument that secessions are historic events. So too are near secessions. The events of 1995 and the very narrow No victory had enormous impact – on political parties and leaders, on minorities within Quebec, on public opinion in ROC as a whole, and on foreign powers. All of these effects are assessed, and I draw the conclusion that predictions about what would have followed a Yes vote in 1995 cannot be applied to a future Yes vote. Too much was changed by the shock of the October referendum.

The next chapter assesses the strategies of federalists and sovereigntists in "manoeuvring towards the next referendum." The sovereigntists, of course, are still committed to their objective of an independent Quebec, while the federalists in both Quebec and Ottawa are struggling to defeat them in the next provincial election or in a subsequent referendum. There is a brief examination here of the policies of the Quebec government led by Lucien Bouchard, and this is followed by a longer analysis of the federal Liberals' dual strategy, which incorporates Plan A (measures to accommodate Quebecers' traditional demands and to demonstrate the federation's virtues) and Plan B (measures to challenge the sovereigntists' assumptions about secession and to clarify some of its unpleasant implications). As well, this chapter treats the 1997 federal election campaign, because the issue of national unity came to dominate it, and there is also an account of the provincial premiers' effort to recognize Quebec symbolically in the Calgary Declaration.

Finally, chapter 6 takes up the old inevitable question. What will happen after a Yes in a future referendum? Of course, another referendum on Quebec sovereignty may never take place; and even if it does, the Yes side may not prevail. The first part of the chapter discusses these possibilities. But the sovereigntists could carry another referendum, and therefore it is important to think about what might then occur. Prediction is hard, though. In 1994, it was relatively straightforward to foresee what would happen if the sovereigntists won a referendum in 1995. In 1998, however, for reasons traced throughout this book, prediction is much more difficult, so I do not offer a single post-Yes projection. Instead, I sketch several possible scenarios – six in all – and the analysis concentrates on their preconditions and the series of events that could bring each of them about. The results of this survey of what could lie in store should be disquieting for both Quebecers and citizens in ROC. Nevertheless, the sovereigntists could still win the struggle for Quebec.

SOME BACKGROUND

For readers who are unfamiliar with the Canada-Quebec case or who wish to read more about it, I give here a brief background sketch to help set the scene.

During the 1960s the sovereignty movement in Quebec jelled in the form of the Parti québécois, which took power in 1976 and held a referendum in 1980 requesting a mandate to negotiate "sovereignty-association" with Canada.[11] The majority of Quebecers voted against this, but even before the referendum the pressure of Quebec nationalism had been the main force driving a series of attempts to reform the Canadian constitution.[12] Change did occur in 1982, when the constitution was "patriated" (from being an act of the British parliament). It was also enlarged to include processes for amending it and a new Canadian Charter of Rights and Freedoms. These changes were rejected by the sovereigntist Quebec government and a majority in the National Assembly of Quebec, though the Quebec MPs in Ottawa, led by Pierre Trudeau, supported them overwhelmingly. To satisfy Quebec's core demands, further amendments were proposed in the

1987 Meech Lake Accord, which recognized the province's distinctiveness and provided for greater protection against constitutional amendments and spending programs with which the provincial government disagreed. But these constitutional amendments failed to pass in 1990.[13] Public opinion in favour of sovereignty then soared in Quebec, and the moderate Liberal government of Robert Bourassa established the Bélanger-Campeau Commission to investigate the province's options.[14] In 1992 further negotiations produced the Charlottetown Accord, a much broader set of constitutional proposals that balanced Quebec's demands with those of other interests, but this too failed to be ratified by referendums in both Quebec and ROC.[15] It was against this constitutional background that the 1995 referendum on sovereignty took place.[16]

Public opinion about constitutional options has been thoroughly charted in Quebec, and several elements are clear and enduring.[17] First, the electorate is rather evenly divided on the issue. Analysts often distinguish between committed sovereigntists, committed federalists, and moderate nationalists. The last occupy the centre of the constitutional spectrum and are the swing voters. During the 1992 Charlottetown referendum, for instance, one team of researchers found that 39 per cent of the electorate were "firm sovereigntists," 8 per cent were "diffident sovereigntists," and 15 per cent were non-francophone and federalist; the 38 per cent who were non-sovereigntist francophones were "clearly on the battleground."[18] Another team used an eleven-category scale in 1991 to categorize francophone Quebecers. They found 29 per cent firmly in favour of independence, 21 per cent to be firm federalists, and 50 per cent ranging across the various shadings of support for sovereignty-association.[19] The voters in the centre are the "soft nationalists," and they are the battleground in any referendum on Quebec's future. They can shift towards sovereignty or federalism depending on several factors.

One factor is language – any perceived threat to linguistic security. Stéphane Dion has argued that "a linguistic crisis has been at the root of each new outburst of nationalism in Quebec since the 1960s."[20] A second factor is any sense among francophone Quebecers of rejection, contempt, or humiliation.[21] These two factors were combined when the Supreme Court of Canada struck down sections of Bill 101, the Quebec language law, and when the Meech Lake Accord failed to pass; support for sovereignty then rose dramatically, to peak at 58 per cent, with only 30 per cent opposed.[22] Another factor is the actual wording of the question, as many studies and polls have shown. There are substantial differences between support for "sovereignty," "independence," and "separation," and there is good evidence that these concepts have different connotations in Quebec. In a straightforward question about these terms, for example, 69 percent of Quebecers agreed that "sovereignty" and "independence" meant different things.[23] The substance of a referendum question is important at the margin, for when more information about the implications of sovereignty is provided to respondents, opinion shifts significantly. During the 1992 referendum campaign on the Charlottetown Accord, respondents to one survey were randomly asked either for their opinion on Quebec sovereignty per se or on Quebec sovereignty – "that is, Quebec is no longer a part of Canada." The proportion that was very favourable was 47 per cent on the first question and only 39 per cent on the second.[24] This shows the scope for political argument about the nature of "sovereignty" to move the Quebec electorate through the course of a referendum campaign. Another important factor is the perceived economic effect of the transition to independence. One analyst has shown that support for sovereignty drops by 6 to 7 per cent when survey questions specify that this means the ending of political and economic ties with the rest of Canada.[25] More pointedly, others have identified economic expectations as a major influence shaping the votes of soft nationalists: "Everything else being equal, support for sovereignty is 19 points lower among those who expect their standard of living to go down."[26]

Finally, support for sovereignty is affected by the political leaders involved in the debate, and by the political formations engaged in the struggle. At the outset of the period described here, the Parti québécois (PQ) held power in Quebec city. This is a strongly institutionalized party, with a large membership base and established links with powerful organizations of workers and teachers, and with deep roots in the cultural milieux and small business. In 1995 the party was more popular than its leader, Jacques Parizeau, a brilliant economist but a man regarded by some as rather antiquated and devious. Nevertheless, Mr Parizeau had an unwavering commitment to sovereignty and was prepared to lead a unified party into a referendum campaign. He had a strong ally in the Bloc québécois, the federal counterpart of the PQ. Although the Bloc rests largely on the PQ organizational base, it possessed some autonomy in the referendum campaign, because of its status as official opposition in the House of Commons, because of its elected members, and above all because of its leader, Lucien Bouchard, the most popular politician in Quebec. Mr Bouchard had resigned from the federal cabinet over modifications to the Meech Lake Accord and had created the Bloc as the federal vehicle to help Quebec's evolution towards sovereignty. It won almost 50 per cent of the Quebec vote in the 1993 federal election, and took 54 of Quebec's 75 seats. Mr Bouchard is a charismatic leader with great rhetorical skill, whom Quebecers regard as both strong and trustworthy. In 1994 his overall approval rating was high even among non-sovereigntist francophones.[27] The third nationalist leader was Mario Dumont, the young *chef* of the Action démocratique du Québec (ADQ), a party formed when Dumont and other provincial Liberals could not accept the Charlottetown Accord. The ADQ took about 10 per cent of the vote in the ridings it contested in the 1994 provincial election, though Mr Dumont was the sole member elected to the National Assembly.

On the federalist side, the firm position of the federal Liberal Party was that there should be no reopening of constitutional issues. The party's veteran leader, Jean Chrétien, had received a mandate in the 1993 election – 176 of the 301 seats – to provide good government and economic growth, and in any referendum campaign the Liberals would be the main federal defenders of the constitutional status quo. The Progressive Conservative Party was rebuilding after its massive defeat in the 1993 election. Its leader, Jean Charest, was a young, dynamic Quebecer who was credible in defending federalism and had a substantial incentive to improve his fortunes and those of his party by doing so. The third relevant party at the federal level was Reform, a classic populist party with a weak organizational structure and a dominant leader, Preston Manning. Based in the western provinces, Reformers made common cause with Quebec nationalists by supporting decentralization, but the party threatened Quebecers with other policies, such as equality of the provinces and opposition to bilingualism, group rights, and redistribution.[28] Finally, there was the Quebec Liberal Party, which is organizationally distinct from the federal Liberals. Although it lost power in September 1994, its unexpectedly strong showing in that election confirmed the leadership position of Daniel Johnson, who was a serious and hard-working campaigner, though regarded as too stolid by some. Mr Johnson at times appeared prepared to defend the existing federal constitution as being supple enough to accommodate Quebec's evolution; but the party's long association with demands for formal constitutional change made its position difficult and would be likely to weaken its unity if no offers of renewed federalism were forthcoming before or during a referendum campaign.[29]

It is against this history, in this context, and through these partisan formations and leaders that the 1995 Quebec referendum was played out. Let us turn to that chapter in the struggle for Quebec.

CHAPTER ONE

The 1995 Referendum and the Yes That Wasn't

As the new Parti québécois government began its referendum planning in October 1994, public support for sovereignty stood at around 45 per cent. Despite Premier Parizeau's "astute" tactics, including the deployment of regional commissions to spread the PQ vision, this figure budged little over the next six months. In the face of a probable No vote, the drive towards a June referendum stalled, and authority within the sovereigntist forces slid towards Lucien Bouchard, the most popular and trusted politician in Quebec. His full engagement in the campaign would be essential to attract those marginal, "soft-nationalist" voters who were uncommitted to either federalism or sovereignty. In April 1995, Mr Bouchard made his *virage* – offering a post-secession economic and political association with Canada – and drew the government towards a new referendum strategy. This position was cemented in a June alliance between Mr Bouchard, Mr Parizeau, and Mario Dumont, party leader of the Action démocratique du Québec (ADQ).

The campaign began in earnest in September. At the outset, the federalist forces seemed comfortably ahead, but their lead dwindled as the sovereigntists focused on the politics of identity, emphasized the federation's inflexibility, and successfully attacked the credibility of threats about economic damage. The No leadership, panicked by the polls, finally offered constitutional change in the last week of the campaign and mobilized hard. The final result was 50.6 per cent No and 49.4 per cent Yes.

The first section of this chapter describes the run-up to the referendum. The second section is an account of how the campaign itself unfolded. The next chapter presents an explanation of why the Yes forces gained ground and almost won the referendum.

PREPARING FOR THE REFERENDUM

The highly centralized PQ government began its referendum planning upon taking office. Most of its policy positions were subordinated to the goal of winning a June 1995 vote. For example, there were no unpopular actions taken to reduce the budget deficit, despite a downgrading of Quebec bonds.[1] Other initiatives were specifically designed to prepare the ground for the referendum. Notably, the government aimed to defuse the Aboriginal issue. Cancelling the contentious Great Whale hydroelectric project helped this, and a special assistant to the premier entered negotiations to reach comprehensive self-government agreements with separate First Nations.[2] These ultimately failed.[3] The government also aimed to placate the anglophone community by pledging that a sovereign Quebec's constitution would protect their rights.[4] As well, sovereigntist leaders quickly disciplined adherents who stressed ethnic divisions and the obstacle posed to a Yes referendum result by the massively pro-federalist anglophone and allophone communities.[5] Bernard Landry, the deputy premier, worked hard to emphasize the inclusive, modern, and pluralistic nature of the sovereignty movement, but this official line continued to have little appeal among suspicious non-francophones.

Externally, the PQ government aimed to secure commitments from the French about recognition, and it did achieve some success among the candidates in the presidential race.[6] Mr Parizeau also tried to reassure American investors and political leaders about sovereignty, stressing the mutual economic interest of the United States and Quebec in NAFTA; politically, he hoped to ensure non-involvement in the coming campaign.[7] With respect to ROC, the sovereigntist leaders eschewed the tactic of polarization – though Mr Parizeau provoked considerable dismay when he declared, in his first speech outside Quebec as premier, that the sovereignty drive would continue whatever the referendum outcome. For ROC, he said, the Quebec problem was "like a never-ending visit to the dentist."[8] But the fundamental message was that Quebec sovereignty was inevitable. Moreover, once Quebecers voted Yes, reason would prevail in ROC, so the hard issues would be settled and the costs of transition minimized, out of a logical appreciation of ROC's self-interest.[9]

These same messages were consistently deployed within Quebec. The basic objective was to increase support for secession by appealing to the undecided "soft nationalists." As Quebecers waited for the government's referendum plans to be unveiled, the PQ stressed that the sovereignty project had momentum. Second, its leaders emphasized the frustrations of federalism – the resources wasted through duplication, the interference by Ottawa in the province's affairs, and the lack of sufficient powers to realize Quebecers' objectives. A third message was that secession would create no significant disruption. While the PQ made no explicit promises about formal economic or political cooperation after a Yes vote, its leaders maintained that the rational self-interest of ROC would inhibit any damage to existing relations of trade, investment, procurement, and labour mobility; as well, the Canadian dollar would remain Quebec's currency. Finally, the government aimed to appeal positively to the bright future and new opportunities that sovereignty would bring. It was this vision that its initial referendum plan aimed to amplify and promulgate.[10]

The PQ government had allies. The most powerful was Lucien Bouchard, who, on Wednesday, 30 November 1994, was diagnosed as infected with streptococcus A bacteria – the "flesh-eating disease" – which normally is fatal. As rumours swirled throughout the province and the country, and as anxiety mounted, most Quebecers went to bed on Thursday night expecting to hear the next day that Mr Bouchard was dead. Instead, it was announced that he would recover (though much of one leg was amputated). His heroic struggle won sympathy throughout Canada. In Quebec, it reinforced the affection and reverence he attracted, and his survival was discussed with divine undertones.[11] It also had political overtones in the form of a highly publicized note which the stricken Bloc québécois leader had passed to his doctors: "Que l'on continue. Merçi."[12]

In fact, the Bloc had already been included in referendum planning, because the option of outright sovereignty remained low in the polls and victory would require the full commitment of Mr Bouchard to attract the soft nationalists. So the PQ national council endorsed a "rainbow coalition" strategy that would not only include other parties in the Yes organization but would also be open to competing visions of what "sovereignty" meant.[13] Soon after the initial referendum plans were released, the PQ and Bloc forces met to combine their organizations into "one big machine" for the referendum campaign.[14]

On 6 December, Mr Parizeau unveiled the referendum strategy. There were three elements. First was a bill introduced into the National Assembly, An Act Respecting the Sovereignty of Quebec.[15] Section 1 declared, "Quebec is a sovereign country." The remaining substantive sections provided for negotiating an economic association with Canada, agreeing on debt and asset division, and drafting a Quebec constitution. As well, there were provisions laying out the sovereigntist position on other issues: the integrity of Quebec territory; Quebec citizenship (and dual citizenship); use of the Canadian currency; succeeding to treaties and acceding to alliances and treaties (including NAFTA); and maintaining the continuity of law (including pensions, the courts, and the public administration).

The second element of the plan was the referendum question included in the bill. It was "Are you in favour of the Act passed by the National Assembly declaring the sovereignty of Quebec? Yes or No." The timing of the event followed from this. As the bill provided, the act would be passed by the assembly after consultation, but it would not come into force until it was approved by a majority in a referendum. Even then, only the sections providing for negotiation with Canada and the drawing up of a new constitution would come into effect immediately. The rest, including the statement of sovereignty, would become effective after one year (unless accelerated by the assembly).

The third element was public consultation. The government was to establish a set of regional commissions to hold hearings throughout the province, as well as a national commission made up of the regional chairs. Each commission would consist of several MNAs and MPs, along with appointed members representing various interests within the region. The commissions would discuss the draft bill and the whole sovereignty project. They would also receive submissions to fill in the bill's blank preamble, the Declaration of Sovereignty, which would set forth "the fundamental values and main objectives the Quebec nation wishes to make its own" once sovereignty was achieved.

The strategy was transparent. The bill's provisions about continuity were clearly intended to reassure undecided voters, while the vast exercise in public participation would generate support for sovereignty, especially in *Québec profond* (outside metropolitan Montreal).[16] As the consensus grew during February 1995, the sovereigntists' momentum would build, gaining further strength through meetings of the PQ and the Bloc's first national congress in April, after which the bill would be passed, and the ground would be ready for a Yes victory in a June referendum.

The federalist forces fought back, however. Of course, there had been intense activity throughout this period. One basic problem was how to reach a consensus on organization, strategy, and message when so many disparate actors and partisan organizations were involved. Relations were especially strained between the federal Liberals and the Quebec Liberal Party. Mr Johnson, for example, aware of the demand for constitutional change within the province, continually argued that Canada must make such a commitment, because then a No vote was not a vote in favour of the status quo: "It is a statement for Canada and in favour of the Canadian union. It is also a statement in favour of evolution."[17]

In the run-up to the referendum, Prime Minister Chrétien and members of the federal cabinet adopted several core positions. The most basic was that there was no danger that Quebecers would vote to secede. The polls confirmed that a majority of the public wanted to remain in Canada, and Mr Chrétien proclaimed, "I'm not scared. There's no reason to be scared. I have the best product to offer – Canada."[18] Second, because most Quebecers were concerned about jobs and the economy rather than sovereignty or the constitution, it was not necessary to reopen the constitutional dossier. Third, the federal Liberals denounced the sovereigntists, sometimes in contemptuous and bitter terms (which were reciprocated). In particular, the PQ referendum strategy was denounced as undemocratic, manipulative and misleading – in the prime minister's words, "a farce." The real question, he said, was simple: "Do you want to separate from Canada? That is the only question."[19] Or, as Deputy Prime Minister Sheila Copps put it, "Are you in or out of Canada?"[20]

The fourth consistent element was to keep options open. This fitted well with the position that any talk of a Yes majority was hypothetical, but at times it involved an awkward stonewalling of questions from the Reform Party, the Bloc, and the media. Asked whether Ottawa might organize its own referendum on sovereignty, Minister of Intergovernmental Affairs Marcel Massé answered, "Si je ne vous réponds pas, c'est parce que je ne veux pas vous répondre, et si je ne veux pas vous répondre, c'est parce qu'actuellement ce n'est pas la question."[21] Finally, warnings were issued about the dangers of secession and especially about the degree of cooperation to be expected from ROC. Mr Massé suggested that Canada might prohibit dual citizenship, and the prime minister pointed out that separation was "nonconstitutional," that Canada alone would decide on monetary policy and an economic union, and that the NAFTA partners could veto Quebec's admission to the treaty.[22]

The toughest reaction to the sovereignty plan was Mr Johnson's. He flatly refused to have the Quebec Liberal Party take part in the regional commissions. Calling the exercise a "parody of popular consultation," he argued that participants would be "placed in the position of accepting separation in a tacit way."[23] On the other hand, the federalist arguments could not remain unvoiced before the commissions, so the No forces began to coalesce through organizations such as the Council for Canadian Unity, Alliance Québec (representing anglophones), and the Conseil du patronat du Québec (representing major business interests), as well as ad hoc groups like the Quebec Business Council for Canada and others.[24]

Beyond this, the federalists adopted several tactics. The federal Liberals recruited new talent in the person of Lucienne Robillard, who was appointed minister of labour and was expected to be a powerful advocate of unity and a competent organizer of the No campaign.[25] Throughout early 1995 they drastically expanded the bureaucratic power of the national unity group in the Privy Council Office. They aimed to reassure the provincial premiers and to deflect criticism by the Reform Party in order to reduce the chance of intemperate, polarizing rhetoric. As well, the government moderated several policies that might alienate Quebec voters; for example, national unity concerns dictated that social policy reform be scaled back and delayed.[26] The 1995 federal budget contained relatively modest cuts in transfers to persons and provinces in the short term, and the distribution of block grants to provinces, which favoured Quebec somewhat, was not to be changed for one year.[27] Finally, the No side put its organization in place. The No campaign was to be led by Daniel Johnson, assisted by Michel Bélanger, head of the Quebec Liberal Party referendum committee. They were to coordinate strategy with Mme Robillard – the Ottawa liaison – and Jean Charest of the federal Progressive Conservative Party.[28]

By early March 1995, it was clear that Mr Parizeau's strategy had borne no fruit. His commissions had begun their hearings in February, with a massive program planned.[29] But the sessions had generated little drama or passion for independence; they were not closely covered by the media, and they produced as many troubling questions as reassurances.[30] Quebecers demanded more information about the purpose and implications of sovereignty. The first commission report that was released, from La Chaudière-Appalaches, stated, "La Commission croit avoir décelé ici la plus grande source d'inquiétudes à l'égard du projet souverainiste: le pain et le beurre après un changement politique aussi important."[31] Moreover, the polls showed no rise in support for sovereignty; the Yes was stalled below 45 per cent.[32] Given the widely shared expectation that the sovereigntists would lose support over the course of a campaign, along with the assumption that polls underreported federalist support, the prospect of a smashing defeat loomed.

In this context, divisions soon emerged in the sovereigntist ranks. While some hardliners continued to follow the December script,[33] others debated whether the referendum's timing and the question to be posed were appropriate. The premier himself admitted early on that the question might have to be changed, though he was insistent that the referendum would be held in 1995.[34] But this barely preceded the return to public life of Lucien Bouchard, who cut short his recuperation because of the urgency of the situation. The Bloc leader insisted that a lost referendum would be ruinous: "if we ever said No to the societal project that is the sovereignty of Quebec, which would signify a Yes to the status quo, we would pay dearly for that. Ottawa would allow itself every temptation."[35]

The debate about the referendum question concerned whether it should refer explicitly to economic association with Canada – or even political association, as Mr Dumont demanded.[36] On timing, the issue was whether to defer the referendum to the autumn or even beyond. A great many strategic variations were under discussion.[37] Despite meeting a dispirited caucus in early March, the premier continued to insist that the referendum would be about sovereignty and that a June vote was possible.[38] Nevertheless, the confusion grew and the pressure continued, not least when the deputy premier likened an early, losing vote to the Charge of the Light Brigade.[39] Finally, isolated, Mr Parizeau announced that the referendum would not be held before the autumn.[40]

This set the stage for more turmoil when Mr Bouchard made his *virage* at the first convention of the Bloc québécois. In his opening address, while insisting on the need for sovereignty, he referred at much greater length to the main concerns of the public as revealed by the PQ's consultative exercise. One was to decentralize the governance of Quebec; another was to design a *projet de société* for a sovereign Quebec. Mr Bouchard committed himself to the first but argued that the second depended on inclusiveness and solidarity, and that no specific guarantees could be provided in advance: "La souveraineté est d'abord et avant tout affaire de confiance."[41]

The core of his speech concerned a Yes vote. This would be an act of self-affirmation as a people, he said, and it would force ROC to recognize the fact. The two peoples would then discuss their mutual interests, the foremost of which was an economic union. Maintaining an economic union – *un nouveau partenariat économique* – through a global treaty could require common political institutions along the lines of the European Union. These structures might include a parliamentary conference, a ministerial council, a secretariat, a court, and administrative commissions.[42] The new notion of partnership flowed ineluctably from Quebecers' hesitations about sovereignty: "Aussi, ne souhaitent-ils dire NON à la souveraineté, dans un référendum qui brusquerait leurs hésitations et ne répondrait pas à leurs interrogations. Ils sont prêts à dire OUI à un projet rassembleur. Le projet souverainiste doit prendre rapidement un virage qui le rapproche davantage des Québécois et des Québécoises et qui ouvre une voie d'avenir crédible à de nouveaux rapports Québec-Canada, répondant à leurs légitimes préoccupations."[43] This bombshell was inscribed in a motion and pushed through the convention, though not without resistance.[44] The task of preparing proposals about Canada-Quebec institutions was conferred upon a committee headed by the lawyer Daniel Turp.[45]

As the *virage* reverbrated, Mr Bouchard was attacked as a perennial quitter and as being self-aggrandizing.[46] Others saw the move as a step in unblocking the sovereigntists' impasse by opening a way for Mr Dumont and the soft nationalists to engage in the movement.[47] In any case, the Bloc leader threatened not to campaign in a losing effort.[48] And Mr Parizeau eventually gave way. When it finally appeared, the report of the National Commission on the Future of Quebec proposed that the draft bill be amended to include an offer of Quebec-Canada political institutions, and the premier agreed.[49] The stage was now set for an autumn referendum on a new question.

This development provoked consternation among federalists, who had anticipated winning a June referendum on a fairly clear question about sovereignty. One reaction was ridicule. As Jean Paré, editor of *L'Actualité*, put it, Mr Bouchard had issued a "unilateral declaration of association."[50] Less pithily, some premiers and Reform Party spokespeople were moved to declare that common institutions were unlikely to be negotiated after a separation and that there was no middle way between federalism and independence.[51] On the strategic front, federalists could take some comfort in the thought that if common institutions were to be preserved, it would be harder for the sovereigntists to argue for the necessity of secession. However, the *virage* appealed to a conception of Canada widespread in Quebec – that the country is composed of two nations that must deal with each other *égal-à-égal*. A Yes vote could be depicted as forcing negotiations on this basis. Another source of anxiety for the federalists was that the new strategy put more pressure on them to define what would happen after a Yes. On the one hand, they were loath to admit that cooperation might be possible, for this could allay fears of economic loss and thus increase support for sovereignty. On the other hand, to deny flatly that a partnership was conceivable could be interpreted as an insulting rebuff, or at least as denying the history of accommodation and the sense of inclusion and respect in Canada to which the federalists appealed. In sum, the *virage* made the federalists' campaign more difficult. The No side had raised enough doubts to stop Mr Parizeau's drive towards sovereignty, but as one official later confided, "We did our job too well."

The new direction of the sovereignty movement was formalized in an agreement signed on 12 June 1995 by Mr Parizeau, Mr Bouchard, and Mr Dumont. This bound the PQ, the Bloc, and the ADQ to coordinate their efforts in the referendum that would be held in the autumn of 1995. Its essence was to combine a vote for sovereignty with "a formal proposal for a new economic and political partnership with Canada."[52] Sovereignty was defined as the power of Quebec "to levy all of its taxes, pass all of its laws, [and] sign all of its treaties." The partnership proposal was to reflect "the wish of Quebecers to maintain equitable and flexible ties with our Canadian neighbours so that we can manage our common economic space together, particularly by means of joint institutions, including institutions of a political nature."

A critical issue was what a positive referendum result would mean. The agreement specified that a Yes victory would empower the National Assembly to proclaim the sovereignty of Quebec; at the same time, the government would "be bound" to propose to Canada "a treaty on a new economic and political Partnership." Should an agreement on the partnership treaty be reached, it stated, the assembly "will" declare the sovereignty of Quebec; then the treaty would be ratified. If the negotiations proved "fruitless," the assembly "will be empowered to declare the sovereignty of Québec without further delay." The negotiations were to take no more than one year, "unless the National Assembly decides otherwise."

The partnership was to take the form of a general framework treaty. The agreement declared that despite the fact that a sovereign Quebec would maintain access to markets and could keep the Canadian dollar, "given the volume of trade between Québec and Canada and the extent of their economic integration, it will be to the evident advantage of both States to sign a formal treaty of economic and political Partnership." The treaty would cover a very wide range of economic activity. As well as dividing assets and providing for the "management of the common debt," it would permit the partnership to act with respect to a customs union (along with the free movement of goods, individuals, services and capital), monetary policy, labour mobility, and citizenship. Further provisions might concern internal trade, international trade, international representation, transportation, defence, financial institutions, fiscal and budgetary policies, environmental protection, crime, postal services, and other matters.

To manage all of this, joint institutions were proposed. These bore a close resemblance to those of the European Union. There would be a council made up of an equal number of ministers from each state, who would have the power to make decisions about the implementation of the treaty. Each state would have a veto. There would also be a parliamentary assembly composed of delegates from the legislatures of each state, which could pass resolutions and hear reports from joint administrative commissions. The assembly would be based on population, with Quebec having 25 per cent of the seats. The last body was a tribunal, which would have binding powers to settle disputes; its composition was unspecified, though the agreement suggested that it might work like the dispute resolution panels under NAFTA.

Perhaps the most remarkable elements of the 12 June agreement were its provisions on how the Canada-Quebec negotiations would be supervised. Obviously, there was some suspicion that the Government of Quebec, armed with a referendum mandate to declare sovereignty, might not negotiate in good faith to arrive at a partnership arrangement. Hence the agreement provided for an "orientation and supervision committee" made up of "independent personalities," who would be agreed on by the PQ, the BQ, and the ADQ. It would take part in the selection of the chief negotiator for Quebec, would have an observer at the negotiations, would advise the government about the talks, and, most important, would "inform the public on the procedures and on the outcome of the negotiations." Mr Bouchard, obviously aware of many Quebecers' doubts about the PQ government's commitment to the partnership (and perhaps sharing them), declared that the agreement embodied "a sacred commitment of sovereigntists that good faith negotiations will be conducted to achieve the goal."[53]

Altogether, this agreement melded the drive towards sovereignty with a set of partnership proposals designed to maintain very high levels of economic and political integration between Canada and Quebec. Potentially, it could minimize economic disruption and transition costs (while, obviously, constraining Quebec's policy autonomy and leaving vast areas of common policy open to veto and *immobilisme*). More important, it was designed to reassure Quebecers that the many areas of economic, political, and social life about which they had expressed concern before the regional commissions might continue undisturbed after a Yes vote. But of course the partnership was an offer only. There were no guarantees that such a comprehensive arrangement could be reached. The 12 June agreement even stated this: "We are convinced that this proposal is in the interests of both Québec and Canada, though we cannot of course presume to know what Canadians will decide in this regard." The federalist response was played out throughout the course of the whole referendum debate. But the core of that response emanated immediately from prime minister Chrétien: "They are not changing the substance of the problem. They still want to separate but they don't have the guts to say so."[54]

With the stage set for the referendum, there was little overt activity during the summer of 1995. The one punctuation of the period occurred when Mr Parizeau, in an unguarded moment, suggested that a Yes vote would plunge Quebecers into sovereignty as inescapably as lobsters that found themselves in a pot of boiling water – or (the words reported vary) in a trap. This seemed to substantiate many people's suspicions about the premier's weak commitment to the partnership, but the impact of the event was lost in disputes about translation and, more important, in the summer vacation from public politics.[55] Generally this was a period in which the two sides firmed up their organizations and worked on financing. The parameters for these efforts were established by Quebec's referendum law, which forced supporters of each side into one of two umbrella committees and strictly limited fundraising and spending.[56]

The summer was also a time for setting strategy and preparing for its tactical implementation through decisions about advertising, campaign tours, the division of leaders' responsibilities, the engagement of various groups, the mobilization of electors, and so on. The details of all of these matters are not public; they were manifest only as the campaign unfolded. Their most important strategic manifestation was the arguments deployed by the two sides. Politicians in critical contests have many weapons, including money, organization, force, and loyalty, but the basic tool in a democracy remains words. It is the superior deployment of arguments that ultimately produces victory. The 1995 referendum campaign involved an exceedingly rich and complex array of discourse. As will be shown, the play of argument and counterargument tilted gradually towards the Yes side and almost produced victory for the sovereigntists.

THE REFERENDUM CAMPAIGN

In late August the federalists and the sovereigntists were almost tied in public support, according to a poll that asked, "If the referendum were being held today, would you vote for or against the sovereignty of Quebec with an offer of economic and political partnership with Canada?" Respondents answering No totalled 45.3 per cent, those answering Yes were 44.4 per cent, 6.5 per cent were undecided, and 3.8 per cent refused to answer.[57] However, the No voters were firmer in their intentions than those inclined to vote Yes. As well, on harder questions that asked about Quebec becoming an independent country or that failed to mention association, Yes support sank to around 40 per cent or even lower.[58] On the other hand, large majorities of voters favoured federal offers of constitutional change, and the credibility of the three principal sovereigntist leaders was significantly higher than that of all the prominent federalists.[59] Mr Bouchard was, by far, the leader perceived as most competent (32 per cent among francophones versus 9 per cent for Mr Chrétien and 6 per cent for Mr Johnson), even though a clear majority of the electorate (52 per cent) identified the economy rather than sovereignty (6 per cent) as the main priority.[60]

In this context, the federalist side stuck to its basic strategy, confident that the sovereigntists would lose ground over the campaign and that the undecided voters would split predominantly towards the status quo in the end.[61] The strategy involved placing on the sovereigntists the burden of showing that their option was superior, appealing to Quebecers' sense of attachment to Canada, stressing the disruption that "separation" would cause, and showing that the federal system could provide good government while flexibly accommodating many voters' desire for change without making constitutional amendments.[62] For their part, the sovereigntists aimed to appeal to Quebecers' sense of national identification, to portray the existing order as inflexible and even threatening, and to show that sovereignty would bring gains on several fronts while the partnership would protect voters from short-term economic losses and eventual isolation from Canada.

The PQ government recalled the National Assembly on 7 September 1995. This timing allowed for a 30 October referendum date after the mandatory thirty-five hours of debate on the question to be put to the electorate and after the eighteen days that had to elapse before the writ was issued (which actually occurred on 1 October). The official campaign would last four weeks from the dropping of the writ.

Into the assembly, the government introduced Bill 1, An Act respecting the Future of Québec. The long preamble to the bill consisted of the Declaration of Sovereignty, which had been assembled by a committee over the preceding months. The declaration appealed to history and common values, to future goals, and to the various communities comprising modern Quebec. It also contained a litany of historic constitutional grievances (which might help legally to justify secession), and it led to three declarations:

1 We, the people of Québec, declare that we are free to choose our future.
2 We, the people of Québec, declare it is our will to be in full possession of all the powers of a state: to vote all our laws, to levy all our taxes, to sign all our treaties, and to exercise the highest power of all, conceiving, and controlling, by ourselves, our fundamental law.
3 We, the people of Québec, through our National Assembly, proclaim: Québec is a sovereign country.

The actual substance of the bill closely followed the framework of the 12 June agreement (which was attached to it as a schedule). Section 1 authorized the National Assembly "within the scope of this Act, to proclaim the sovereignty of Québec." But it also stipulated that "the proclamation must be preceded by a formal offer of economic and political partnership with Canada." The partnership treaty to be proposed was to be as described in the 12 June agreement, and it was to require ratification by the National Assembly. However, the assembly was empowered by the bill to make effective the Declaration of Sovereignty, at which time, according to section 2, "Québec shall become a sovereign country." This would take place after negotiations on the partnership treaty had been concluded (which had to be before 30 October 1996 "unless the National Assembly decides otherwise"). Then, according to section 26, "the proclamation of sovereignty may be made as soon as the partnership treaty has been approved by the National Assembly or as soon as the latter, after requesting the opinion of the orientation and supervision committee, has concluded that the negotiations have proved fruitless." Bill 1, in short, provided for a unilateral declaration of independence.

The rest of the bill provided for arrangements designed to appeal to various segments of the electorate. For example, the government would endeavour to locate the partnership institutions in the Outaouais region, where many federal public servants resided. The new constitution would be drawn up by a commission with equal gender representation (and it would be submitted to a referendum). The constitution would state that Quebec "is a French-speaking country," but it would "guarantee the English-speaking community that its identity and institutions will be preserved." Aboriginal nations would have their existing constitutional and self-government rights protected (but "in a manner consistent with the territorial integrity of Québec"). Significantly, given the persistent complaints from the regions about overcentralization, Bill 1 provided that the constitution would allocate powers and fiscal resources to local and regional authorities. Beyond this, the bill made four central promises: Quebec would maintain its existing boundaries; Quebec citizenship would be acquired by all residents holding Canadian citizenship and by all born within Quebec, and this could be held concurrently with Canadian citizenship; Quebec would have the Canadian dollar as its legal currency; and Quebec would assume its treaty obligations and rights, particularly with respect to the North American Free Trade Agreement.

The rest of the bill provided for the continuity of permits, contracts, courts, and laws (all existing Canadian laws would be deemed laws of Quebec until changed), of benefits (including unemployment insurance, child tax benefits, and pensions), and of public-service employment (for Quebec residents employed by Canada). The bill also provided for an interim constitution, if necessary, to bridge the period between the declaration of sovereignty and the entry into force of the new constitution. It further authorized the government to conclude with Canada "any other agreement to facilitate the application of this Act," especially about "the equitable apportionment of the assets and liabilities of the Government of Canada" – phrasing which suggested that the 12 June language about "management of the common debt" might be too constraining in the circumstances of a vote for sovereignty.

The bill was not intended to be passed by the assembly before the referendum. It was the referendum that would trigger its passage, negotiations with Canada, and all the rest. On 7 September the PQ government also unveiled the referendum question (which was eventually adopted by the assembly on 20 September). It read:

Do you agree that Québec should become sovereign, after having made a formal offer to Canada for a new Economic and Political Partnership, within the scope of the Bill respecting the future of Québec and of the agreement signed on June 12, 1995? YES or NO?[63]

A copy of the bill was sent to every household in the province.

At the outset of the campaign, the federalist side was confident, almost to the point of complacency. In his first address on the issue, Mr Chrétien argued that the sovereigntists' question was duplicitous because a Yes vote was really "a one-way ticket to separation," but he was certain that Quebecers would choose Canada: "It's the best country in the world, and you all know that Canada will win."[64] Even before the campaign began, the prime minister said, "I'm not losing any sleep. I'm extremely confident. We're way ahead of where we were two months before the referendum last time."[65] Indeed, the sovereigntists appeared to be making little headway, despite the publicity surrounding the launch of the campaign. While some early polls showed the voters evenly divided, with the Yes support softer, others placed the No clearly ahead, a trend that seemed to grow slightly (although the difference was often within the polls' margin of error, and much depended on how the undecided and non-respondents were allocated).[66] By the end of September there were rumours that the vote might be delayed, and Mr Bouchard admitted, "I'm not saying the campaign is going marvellously well. I say that we are in a tight spot, that we will have to brace ourselves for a tough fight."[67]

One tactic of the Yes side that had failed was the release of economic studies of sovereignty, commissioned under the leadership of Restructuring Minister Richard Le Hir. On topics such as the division of the debt, a sovereign Quebec's fiscal situation, and monetary policy, most of the more than forty studies produced little public reaction. A few failed to lend credibility to the sovereigntist position, all were assailed by competing experts, there were allegations of patronage in their commissioning, and the whole exercise collapsed rather ignominiously.[68] Later in the campaign, Mr Bouchard declared that the studies were irrelevant.

Another possibility for the sovereigntists was to provoke polarization between Quebecers and Canada. The Yes side made some early moves in this direction, and clearly there was deep animosity between some leaders in the two camps. In May 1995, as the *virage* was being consolidated, Mr Chrétien accused the sovereigntists of trying to "trick" Quebecers: "There is now a very cynical and very transparent attempt to confuse Quebecers, to mislead them, to suggest that you can separate from Canada and still be Canadian." In contrast to the federalists' frankness, he insisted, "the other way of governing shows – and I measure my words carefully – a contempt for democracy."[69] Mr Parizeau lashed back immediately, accusing the prime minister of betraying his fellow Quebecers: "This man is sabotaging the economy of Quebec, and in the exact way he sabotaged the powers of Quebec in 1981 ... One day we will have to understand this method of using Quebecers in Ottawa to carry out designs, to achieve things that anglophones would not dare try on their own. These affairs are nauseating."[70] Apart from such personal attacks, polarization could be increased by focusing on how the federal system had failed Quebec and, more powerfully, by suggesting that a No vote would unleash upon Quebecers the centralizing tendencies of Ottawa and the homogenizing propensities of English Canada.

These themes did persist in the discourse of the campaign,[71] but they were not major ones; the drive towards the referendum was not marked by the polarization that could have occurred, as it did in the

Czech-Slovak split. Along with structural constraints such as democratic norms and a free media, other factors limited the capacity to polarize (or diminished the political rewards to be realized through this strategy). First was the fact that reaction in ROC to all such accusations – indeed, to the whole content of the campaign – was very muted. The provincial premiers largely kept quiet throughout the campaign, respecting it as an internal Quebec debate and remaining confident, until very near the end, in Ottawa's lead. The media behaved similarly. Second, the Bloc had conducted itself responsibly in Ottawa. With few exceptions, it had not impeded federal business, and the governing Liberals had tended to reserve their nastiest attacks for the Reform Party.[72] Third, a polarizing strategy would have alienated those voters with strong attachments to Canada (who were presumably more numerous among the undecided voters, the real objects of the campaign), and it would have flown in the face of many Quebecers' objective experiences of Canada.[73] Further, polarization would have deeply contradicted the fact that the partnership was fundamentally positive in its attitude towards Canada – and indeed was designed to attract voters who felt that way. Finally, it would have sharply divided Quebecers, denying the position that sovereignty represented a *projet rassembleur*, open and inclusive, with promise for all, and undermining the civility that characterizes democratic politics in that province. Essentially, the great majority of Quebecers regarded both federalism and sovereignty as legitimate options; while one's opponents could be misguided and uninformed, they were not treasonous.

These features of the campaign, and the norms impeding polarization, were clearly shown in late September when a prominent federalist businessman addressing a No rally stated, "We can't just win on October 30; we have to crush them." This gaffe provoked a storm of outrage, and the federalist leaders were quick to distance themselves from such language. It was a gaffe not only because it appeared overconfident and arrogant, but more basically because it denied the other side a legitimate existence within the community. Mr Johnson reacted quickly, stating, "I'm asking everyone to lower the volume because it is everyone in Quebec who will still be here the morning after the vote."[74] Neither the Yes nor the No forces faced a strong incentive to promote polarization, either within Quebec or between Quebec and ROC.

Another important element in the early campaign was Quebec business. Respected leaders of big business overwhelmingly were staunch federalists, and they waded into the debate to argue that secession would have dire economic consequences. For example,

Marcel Dutil, president of Canam Manac, warned voters that they would be using the "Quebec peso" after sovereignty, and Laurent Beaudoin, president of Bombardier, declared, "It's out of the question that a state reduced to the size of an independent Quebec could adequately support the development of this type of business."[75]

For the Yes side, Mr Parizeau counterattacked, linking his communitarian sovereigntist project with a social-democratic conception of fairness and sharing. Addressing business people in the Beauce region, he declared, "I believe in the equality of chances and I want to build a society based on this principle."[76] More strongly, as Mr Beaudoin and Power Corporation head Paul Desmarais warned of the disruptive dangers of sovereignty, Mr Parizeau not only accused them personally of taking federal grants and moving their assets out of the province, but he decried a neocolonial line of propaganda designed to frighten ordinary voters: "What's this idea of scaring people?" he asked. "This has been going on for what, 25 years now. Saying: 'Don't move. You are never as beautiful as when you are on your knees. And if you ever think of getting up from the ground, we'll leave.' Well, I just don't believe it."[77] Perhaps pressed by his labour supporters, Mr Parizeau continued these attacks, even referring to "billionaires who spit on us" despite Quebecers' loyalty and provincial tax concessions.[78] In a society proud of its economic leaders, however, this line of attack seemed to pay few dividends for the sovereigntists, and it simply testified to the disarray that permeated the Yes camp in the early stages of the official campaign.

Yet another component was injected into the campaign by the Aboriginal peoples. Their negotiations with the PQ government had come to naught, and native leaders were determined not be to caught defenceless by a Yes vote. They aimed to stake out a moral claim to autonomy. Hence the Northern Quebec Inuit (organized as Makavik) decided to hold their own referendum in order to affirm their right to remain in Canada as part of the whole Inuit nation, and the Cree announced similar plans at the same time as they released a lengthy defence of their right to self-determination.[79] "There is nothing you will do without our consent," Grand Chief Matthew Coon-Come firmly stated.[80]

While the Aboriginals' position appeared to present an obstacle to sovereignty, so tending to reduce the Yes vote, it also had the potential to create a backlash against them. It certainly created problems for the Quebec federalists. Mr Johnson felt compelled to say that the Cree referendum concerned "by implication" whether Quebec territory was divisible or not. "My own view," he said, "and that of my party, has always been consistent. The Quebec borders that we have today are Quebec's borders."[81] In the end, the Cree voted No by 96.3 per cent and the Inuit by 95 per cent.[82] While these results were very strong, and the turnouts were reported to be high, there were no international observers present at the polls. Nevertheless, the results did compel the federal minister for Indian affairs to agree that Aboriginals were not "cattle" to be transferred from one jurisdiction to another. They had said "quite clearly that they're staying with Canada," he observed, "and I think they have that right."[83] In the end, though, the Aboriginals' concerns constituted a minor theme in the campaign, and the results of their vote were overshadowed by other events as the day of the Quebec referendum approached.

A striking feature of the campaign was the absence of involvement by political leaders from ROC. The provincial premiers left the battle to Ottawa and Mr Johnson's forces, except for occasional warnings that English Canadians might be embittered by a Yes vote and that the economic status quo would not prevail after "separation." Ontario was a partial exception. Mike Harris, the Progressive Conservative premier elected in June 1995, gave a major speech in Toronto during the campaign. "If Quebec separates," he stated, "Ontario would trade with it on no different a basis than it trades with other foreign countries ... We would have no special obligations tied to history or common national interest ... If Quebec separates, there would be international borders between Ontario and Quebec. And borders do matter."[84] As well, Mr Harris flatly rejected the prospect of negotiations, arguing that a political partnership would not be in Ontario's interest. Finally, he stressed that his government sought a "major rebalancing of responsibilities" in Canada; hence, Ontario would be a "strong ally" of Quebecers seeking change in the federation. Mr Parizeau, however, laughed off any attempt to reform the federation and accused the premier of bluffing about cutting off economic ties.[85] A second partial exception was Bob Rae, former premier of Ontario, who actually went to Quebec to debate and make speeches, and did so increasingly towards the end of the campaign. Fluent in French, he was prepared to deride the sovereigntists' partnership proposal and to show Quebecers how angry English Canadians would be if their beloved country was destroyed.[86]

The Reform Party also sought to be involved in the campaign. Mr Manning was not prepared to accept without question the lead and strategy of the established federalist forces and to allow the No campaign to be defined largely by Quebecers – Mr Chrétien, Mr Johnson, Mr Charest, and their close advisers. In June 1994 he had addressed an open letter to the prime minister, declaring, "We cannot stand by passively and allow Quebec voters to make the decision – separation

– without offering them a vigorous defence of Canada, including a positive federalist alternative to the status quo. And we cannot let them make their decision without disputing the separatist contention that separation will be a relatively uncomplicated and painless process."[87] The letter covered twenty very precise questions about secession.[88] Such questions, Mr Manning wrote, "have been dismissed as 'hypothetical' or answered with the standard line that the best way to convince Quebecers to stay in Canada is to provide them with more of the same."

As the campaign got underway, the Reform Party pressed the government in the House of Commons about these matters and, more generally, about what the government would do in the event of a Yes vote. Mr Manning also predicted publicly that such a result would very likely entail an election, because the prime minister would have forfeited the confidence of the Canadian people.[89] But Reform made little headway either in the House or in the media as the federalist side coalesced around its basic strategy, and when the House rose in September, Mr Manning was deprived of his platform. Still, Reform did attempt to insert itself into the campaign, notably by publishing a twenty-point plan for reforming the federation, which appeared in full-page newspaper advertisements in Quebec at the end of October.[90] This proposed a profound decentralization of powers, including provincial jurisdiction over language, but no special status for Quebec; it probably had very little impact on the referendum results.

With four weeks left in the campaign, Chantal Hébert, a prominent Quebec columnist, declared that the odds were in favour of a "decisive federalist victory," the only obstacles being arrogance on the No side and the possibility of strategic voting for the Yes in order to preserve Quebec's bargaining power within the federation.[91] Jeffrey Simpson, a leading ROC columnist, wrote that the chances of a Yes victory were "exceedingly slim" and were realizable only if the sovereigntists put Mr Bouchard at the head of the campaign, increased appeals to ethnicity, and hinted at a second referendum on the outcome of the partnership negotiations; as well, the No side would have to make egregious mistakes.[92] Not all of these things occurred, but momentum did swing to the sovereigntist side in mid-campaign.

First, Mr Parizeau named five members of the committee that was to oversee negotiations with Canada about the partnership treaty.[93] Much more significantly, he announced that Mr Bouchard would be Quebec's chief negotiator of the partnership treaty. In effect, this passed the Yes leadership into the hands of a trusted politician who could attract moderate nationalists to the sovereigntist side while reasssuring them that the promised partnership was viable.

This move undoubtedly injected new life into the Yes forces on the ground,[94] and the poll results suggest that it was followed by some movement in public opinion. On 14 October, for example, the *Globe and Mail* headline blared, "Yes Side Narrows Gap in Latest Poll," as it reported a Léger & Léger poll which found the No side at 50.8 per cent and the Yes at 49.2 per cent.[95] However, this may have been a matter of perception or the spin put onto the results by the media. From the outset of the campaign there was a considerable difference in the pattern of support registered by different polling firms, an artifact of slight variations in the questions posed and different methods of allocating those who refused to answer or were undecided. In most cases, the gap between the Yes and No support was within the margin of error, and had been so for most polls since the beginning of the campaign.[96]

Nevertheless, many polls showed weaknesses in the federalist message and the rising credibility of Mr Bouchard's partnership. Typical was a very large survey conducted in late September by SOM and Environics. Even though this poll placed the No forces firmly in the lead, it found that 62 per cent of Quebecers believed they would use the Canadian dollar after sovereignty, 45 per cent thought they would retain their Canadian passports, 69 per cent anticipated an economic union, and almost 60 per cent believed there would be an economic and political partnership after a Yes result.[97] Another survey found that one-third of Yes voters were aiming "to give Lucien Bouchard a strong mandate to negotiate a new deal for Quebec within Canada"; the other two-thirds wanted Quebec to become an independent country.[98]

Such results were intensely frustrating for the federalist side. The leaders repeated the message that a Yes meant separation, and they stepped up their attacks on the economic front, warning of trade disruption, heavy job losses, increased government deficits, and a sharp drop in the value of the dollar.[99] In the context of a simmering debate about whether a sovereign Quebec would accede to NAFTA, the federal finance minister Paul Martin warned that admission would not be automatic and therefore, 90 per cent of Quebec exports would be at risk, involving almost one million jobs. While Mr Martin undoubtedly meant only that jobs in these export sectors would have some probability of being subject to protectionist measures, his remarks were scorned by the Yes side as desperate hyperbole. Mr Parizeau had an immediate riposte: "Last week for [Mr] Johnson, it was slightly below 100,000. Next week I suppose we're aiming at ten million ... There are only 3,200,000 jobs in Quebec – and past that point they'll have to import the unemployed."[100] As will be seen, this was a typical counter to the federalists' dire predictions about the economic consequences of a Yes vote.

In fact, the financial markets had been reacting to the sovereignty threat and the referendum campaign, and they moved more in response to the shift in momentum towards the Yes. Even in late 1994, it was apparent that the PQ government's reluctance to confront its budget deficit before the anticipated June referendum was causing some weakness in the Canadian dollar and also a growing interest-rate spread between between Canada and the United States.[101] Quebec debt was duly downgraded by Canadian and American bond-rating agencies, and so were the bonds issued by the federal government (largely because of parallel inaction on the deficit).[102] In July mortgage rates were increased, an event that bank spokespeople attributed to pre-referendum volatility.[103] As the campaign began in earnest, there was downward pressure on the dollar – it lost 1.6 per cent of its value in less than a week – which provoked Bank of Canada intervention and a widening spread between Canadian and U.S. interest rates.[104] Early October was marked by more volatility, driven by polls and rumours.

On 20 October, in the wake of an Angus Reid poll showing the Yes side ahead, the Canadian dollar dropped 72 basis points, and the Toronto stock exchange TSE index slipped 37 points: foreign investors were rumoured to be reducing their Canadian exposure.[105] On 23 October, the TSE plummeted 123 points (or 2.8 per cent), and the dollar dropped another 88 basis points.[106] These movements provided opportunities for some speculators to buy in anticipation of a No, and some did, but the important fact is that the volatility reflected deep underlying uncertainty about the effects of a possible Yes result. Were there to be such an outcome, said an economist at a Canadian brokerage house, we would be "in uncharted territory."[107]

There is some doubt about how markets process data about political events, particularly new public-opinion polls, as was shown by their movement during the Charlottetown referendum, when the markets seem to have absorbed poll information in a relatively straightforward way.[108] During the Quebec referendum campaign, according to an extensive empirical study, the volatility of TSE options held within the normal range until 23 October, when it increased by more than 30 per cent, and it peaked on the day of the referendum at levels almost three times the norm.[109] Uncertainty hit the Canadian dollar slightly earlier, as volatility began to rise on 17 October and broke upward sharply on the twentieth (the day the cover of the *Economist* carried a banner asking, "Will Canada Split?"). Like the TSE options, the volatility of Canadian dollar options peaked on 30 October at over three times normal levels. These results suggest, interestingly, that foreign investors were quicker than domestic ones to take the prospect of a Yes victory seriously. More important, they attest to the very high levels of uncertainty caused by the close referendum race – and they provide a baseline for predicting what stock and dollar values would have been in the event of a Yes result.

Apart from traders in stocks and currency, other foreign actors played a minor role in the Quebec referendum. Foreign governments treated the struggle between federalists and sovereigntists as a domestic matter, for the most part. From the time of its election, of course, the PQ government was concerned to lay the groundwork for eventual international recognition of a sovereign Quebec.[110] In an early trip to Paris, Mr Parizeau received some encouragement from the candidates for the French presidency, but Mr Chirac returned to France's traditional position of "non-indifference but non-interference" after he was elected.[111] Late in the referendum campaign, however, he was reported to have said in an American television interview that his government would recognize Quebec after a Yes vote.[112]

While an early recognition of Quebec sovereignty by France might have some symbolic weight, the Americans held much greater practical influence. Mr Parizeau's first foreign trip was to New York, where he argued that the United States should not become involved in the sovereignty debate.[113] But President Clinton, speaking to the Canadian Parliament in February 1995, "sent an unambiguous signal that the United States would prefer that Canada remain intact."[114] The Americans were careful to provide no guarantees about Quebec's accession to NAFTA; their official position was that "there are numerous and complicated legal issues and we have given no assurances to anyone."[115] During the campaign these thorny issues were highlighted in a new study which showed the difficulties for Quebec of acceding to the GATT, the Auto Pact, and NAFTA. The study emphasized that negotiations would be required in all cases, that Quebec would very likely have to make substantial concessions, and that obstacles would be much reduced if Quebec and Canada had first reached "a close and mutually supportive economic agreement."[116]

As the sovereigntist campaign gained support, the American position became even clearer. Former president George Bush urged unity, and Warren Christopher, the secretary of state, departed significantly from the traditional formulation when he said, "I don't want to intrude on what is rightfully an internal issue in Canada, but at the same time I want to emphasize how much we have benefited, here in the United States, from an opportunity to have the kind of relationship that we do have at the present time with a strong and united

Canada ... I think it is probably useful for me to say that we have very carefully cultivated our ties with Canada, and it has been very responsive in connection with all those ties, and I think we shouldn't take for granted that a different kind of organization would obviously have exactly the same kind of ties."[117] The PQ government responded formally to this blunt statement by writing to Mr Christopher warning him that outside interference by Washington could sour relations with Quebec for decades; more centrally, Mr Bouchard dismissed the American statement as epiphenomenal: "La courtoisie qu'il doit aujourd'hui à la souveraineté canadienne, il la devra demain à la souveraineté québécoise."[118] Meanwhile, as referendum day approached and such arguments appeared to be winning voters' support, the American media began to focus on the contest.[119] Indeed, the referendum in Quebec became a news item around the world.

Towards the end of October, as polls confirmed the decline in No support, near-panic struck the federalist camp. The daily numbers showed the Yes ahead, and as a well-informed Montreal columnist put it on 21 October, "If something doesn't start to happen very soon, probably by the end of this weekend, Canada is one done turkey."[120] Emergency changes were made to the basic No strategy: the prime minister increased his presence in the campaign well beyond his planned three major speeches, organizers desperately threw together a giant pro-Canada rally in Montreal, and there was a major shift in the federalists' constitutional position.

Constitutional movement was pressed by Mr Johnson, who envisaged the Yes forces successfully attracting all those Quebecers who were disaffected with the status quo and were seeking change. So a No-side document promised increased control over provincial jurisdictions.[121] Then, after Mr Chrétien stated in a Quebec City speech that the province formed a "distinct society," Mr Johnson urged all Canadian federalists to "echo our view of what the future holds for Quebec as part of Canada."[122] This was a clear appeal to Ottawa and perhaps the other provincial governments to put some positive constitutional proposals on the table before the referendum, a stance which both responded to public opinion about the campaign and reflected the strong majority opinion in Quebec in favour of constitutionally recognizing the province's distinctiveness.[123] Initially rebuffed by Mr Chrétien, who stated, "There is no desire at this time to debate the constitution," the Quebec federalists were enthusiastically and effectively derided by the Yes forces for believing that Canada could deliver constitutional renewal.[124] Mr Johnson, however, managed to prod the prime minister to issue a joint declaration: "We state unequivocally that Quebec is a distinct society. We remind you that we have both supported the inclusion of this principle in the Canadian Constitution every time Quebec has demanded it."[125]

Pressed hard by the Quebec wing, the No forces went much further than this in promising constitutional change.[126] At a huge federalist rally in Verdun on 24 October, Mr Chrétien embraced the distinct society concept and held out the promise of a Quebec constitutional veto. His government would keep open all the paths for change, he said, "including the administrative and constitutional paths."[127] The next day, in an extraordinary televised address to the whole country, he repeated this position: "We must recognize that Quebec's language, its culture and institutions make it a distinct society. And no constitutional change that affects the powers of Quebec should ever be made without the consent of Quebecers. And that all governments – federal and provincial – must respond to the desire of Canadians – everywhere – for greater decentralization."[128] Of course, these promises were denounced by the sovereigntists as insincere, desperate, and too little – as only "vague allusions" to change.[129] But they represented a major strategic shift by the No forces.

Meanwhile, citizens were mobilized. Unity rallies were held in many Canadian cities, and pro-Quebec resolutions were passed by several municipalities and some provincial legislatures.[130] But organizers concentrated on a massive demonstration in Montreal on the Friday before the referendum. Members of Parliament and many businesses arranged transport to the city, while the two major airlines and the railway offered drastically reduced fares. These preparations provoked scathingly sarcastic attacks from the Yes side, and outrage that they violated the strict regulations on referendum campaign expenditures.[131] But the rally drew well over 100,000 people to Place du Canada in downtown Montreal. There, as well as striking the familiar themes about the uncertainties of a Yes result and the glories of Canada, Mr Chrétien promised to bring about all the changes necessary to maintain unity.[132] And Jean Charest, leader of the Progressive Conservative Party, insisted that he would be a steady force pressing for constitutional renewal. Despite all this, the final published opinion polls were showing the Yes side to be clearly ahead among decided voters.[133]

Given the various polls' margins of error, as well as time lags, it is unclear what stemmed the sovereigntists' momentum (if indeed the Yes was really in the lead). Perhaps it was the No side's shift to embrace change in the federation. Or perhaps the pro-Canada rally weakened commitment to the Yes side, despite the fact that it could be interpreted not only as "an outpouring of abiding love" but also as "a tawdry closing-time seduction."[134] Another possibility was the weather. On the day before the vote, the weather across Quebec was chilly and darkly autumnal, with brooding skies and steady, cold rain. Had this not been a Sunday, and one so much more conducive to sombre reflection than the crisp, sunny, Indian-summer alternative, then the Yes might have carried. Who knows?

The final referendum result was 2,362,648 votes for the No option, and 2,308,360 votes for the Yes. If fewer than 30,000 people had voted differently, the No victory would have been reversed. The turnout was a remarkable 93.52 per cent of eligible voters. But 1.82 per cent of the ballots were rejected as invalid. This was not above the norm in Quebec voting, but there were much higher levels in three Montreal-area districts, and this left a bitter residue among No supporters, especially those who had endured very long waiting periods at some Montreal polling stations.[135]

The general pattern of the results was clear enough. Ridings with large non-francophone populations tended towards the No side, as did voters in the Outaouais region. Throughout the great expanse of rural Quebec and in the Quebec City region, the Yes had a substantial lead, as it did in most of the francophone suburbs of Montreal. The west of the Island of Montreal went strongly No, but, much more surprisingly and perhaps decisively, the sovereigntists could not carry the east end of the island: in these predominantly francophone, working-class neighbourhoods, the No side won overall.[136]

Reaction to the result was calm. There were very few minor disturbances on the streets as the exhausted leaders addressed their supporters. Mr Chrétien saluted the democratic nature of the decision and stated that the page should be turned and that Quebec and Ottawa should work together. He called on all Canadians not to forget their recent appeal to Quebecers, and he declared, "A mes concitoyens et concitoyennes du Québec qui ont appuyé le Oui, je dis qui je comprends votre profonde volonté de changement."[137] For Mr Johnson, it was also time for reconciliation and unity: "Si le camp du Non a manifesté de façon concrète cette réticence à tourner le dos à l'expérience canadienne, il faut maintenant créer la plus grande coalition possible en faveur de changement, avec fierté et espoir, pour les meilleures réalisations que nous pouvons anticiper."[138]

But the sovereigntists, with victory so close, were unyielding. Although Mr Bouchard told his partisans that it was necessary to accept the result, however narrow, and to be proud of the democratic exercise just ended, he cautioned vigilance against Ottawa and rallied his supporters once more: "Les Oui n'ont jamais été aussi nombreux que ce soir et nous sommes encore tous là. Gardons espoir, car la prochaine fois sera la bonne. Et cette prochaine fois, elle pourrait venir plus rapidement qu l'on pense."[139] Mr Parizeau, profoundly disturbed by the narrow loss, also exhorted sovereigntists to prepare for the next encounter, "for which we will not wait fifteen years this time." But, in addition, he attributed blame for the defeat, and in a manner that shocked even his supporters. Pointing out that the Yes had attracted a clear majority of francophone voters, probably 60 per cent, he said, "C'est vrai qu'on a été battus, mais par quoi au fond? Par l'argent et par des votes ethniques."[140]

This remark produced the first big outcome of the 1995 referendum. After uniformly unfavourable comment, and a night's sleep, the premier announced that he would resign. Yet this was only the first manifestation of the changes which the historic 1995 referendum would bring – and which, by its searing campaign and razor-thin result, it had brought already.

CHAPTER TWO

The Logic of the Referendum Campaign

Major campaigns are fought with many tools, but in modern democracies they are fundamentally about language and argument. Given the structure of public opinion in Quebec, it was clear long before the referendum that there would be only a few key dimensions along which the sovereigntist and federalist forces would fight for support. These were Quebecers' sense of national identification (including perceptions of rejection and confidence), their economic expectations, and their views of the Canadian constitutional system.[1] The purpose of this chapter is to analyse the contending arguments that were deployed by the Yes and No sides throughout the course of the referendum campaign, in order to explain why the sovereigntists gained support and came so close to victory.

In some accounts of the campaign, it was national identification that produced the rise in support for the Yes, especially after Mr Bouchard took centre stage when named as chief negotiator. As one commentator wrote, "He, more than the other secessionist leaders, can reach ordinary francophone Quebecers, summoning their *Volksgeist* in a supreme collective act of 'national affirmation' that will, once and for all, enable Quebec to meet the rest of Canada equal to equal, face to face, people to people."[2] Far more cautiously, some political scientists have agreed. Vincent Lemieux, for example, has argued that the replacement of Mr Parizeau by Mr Bouchard heightened the importance of the national-identification dimension and made it far more difficult for voters to maintain a dual Canadian-Quebec sense of identity.[3]

But this explanation encounters two problems. First, it is not evident that support for the Yes side showed a sharp increase coincident with Mr Bouchard's assuming the leadership of the campaign. A straightforward reading of the published polls suggests that support for the No began to decline towards the end of September, well before the Bloc leader was named chief negotiator.[4] On the other hand, Maurice Pinard insists that there was a noticeable "Bouchard effect," with the proportion of voters intending to vote Yes increasing by 4 or 5 per cent after the shift in leadership.[5] This is a moot point: the different polls asked respondents different questions; there is no universally accepted way of allocating the non-respondents (who ranged from 8 per cent to 31 per cent of the samples); some polls were outliers (in each direction); and in many cases the difference between Yes and No support was within the polls' margin of error.[6] But assuming that there was a "Bouchard effect," the important question is why it occurred. Here, the evidence is compelling that the shift of vote intentions towards the Yes took place along the economic dimension rather than being driven by an increase in Quebecers' sense of national identification.

The political scientists Blais, Nadeau and Martin analysed two comparable Léger & Léger polls, one taken in June 1995 and the second in the last week of the campaign.[7] In the first, 52 per cent of francophones were intending to vote Yes; in the second, 62 per cent. Over this period, there was a slight increase in the reported propensity of respondents to think of themselves as "Quebecers only" or "Quebecers first," but this difference was not statistically significant. On the other hand, economic expectations about sovereignty became much more positive (as did expectations about the situation of the French language in Quebec).

In a regression equation that included as variables the respondents' sense of identification, economic and linguistic expectations, age, and domestic situation, it was found that the strongest predictor of voting intentions was the economic variable. A competing explanation might be that the salience of each factor changed in the interval between the two polls, so that national identification, while shifting little in absolute terms, came to have a greater bearing on the voting decision. But this did not occur: there was no significant interaction between the weight of each factor and the different polls. Further experimentation showed that the rise in Québécois identification accounted for a 1 per cent increase in Yes support, as did views about linguistic security. The shift in economic expectations, however, produced an increase of about 6 per cent in the Yes vote. So the rise in sovereignty support took place along the economic dimension.

Substantively, when asked about the short-term economic consequences of sovereignty and the long-term effects, most respondents anticipated only a small short-term deterioration, and the majority envisaged a long-term economic improvement. Thus, it would seem that the sovereigntists' arguments about the smooth transition to sovereignty and the benefits of the partnership were effective in lifting the Yes side to its near victory.

Further evidence about the significance of the economic arguments is provided in a careful analysis of several polls by Guy Lachapelle, who shows that even in April 1995 the option of sovereignty, including an economic association with Canada, would have attracted almost 60 per cent of the electorate (though this was still less popular than the notion of transferring certain powers from Ottawa to Quebec).[8] Between April and October 1995, there was a strong increase in the proportion of voters who felt that sovereignty was feasible (from 40 per cent to over 60 per cent), while the numbers believing that the federal system could be reformed fell from 50 per cent to about 42 per cent.[9] More striking, a massive SOM–Radio-Canada poll done in late September showed that if voters were certain that Canada would negotiate an economic and political partnership, 56 per cent would vote for sovereignty and 34 per cent would vote No. If, however, they were certain that Canada would not negotiate the partnership, only 30 per cent would vote Yes and 57 per cent would vote against sovereignty.[10] Economic expectations certainly could shift votes. Finally, it seems that the credibility of the partnership increased throughout the campaign period. A series of three CROP polls asked voters whether they believed that Canada would indeed agree to negotiate after a Yes vote, and the proportion answering Yes to this question rose from 46 per cent in late September to 51 per cent in late October, while those answering No fell from 39 to 29 per cent.[11]

Yet more evidence is provided by Pinard, who is most concerned with analysing the social and demographic correlates of support for sovereignty, along with underlying attitudinal factors, especially the linguistic, economic, and political grievances of francophones.[12] In explaining the "Bouchard effect," Pinard stresses the leader's charisma and the confidence and trust he inspired, and presents some necessarily fragmentary evidence that some poll respondents had changed their voting intentions after the Bloc leader took centre stage in the Yes campaign.[13] Undoubtedly, Mr Bouchard was a charismatic presence, but which of his messages was effective in shifting votes? In Pinard's analysis, it was the economic partnership. Through the course of the campaign, Quebecers' sensitivity to historical grievances and their sense of insecurity seem not to have budged (although there may have been some increase in pride).[14] What clearly did change was the perception that the partnership was probable. Using some unpublished polls, Pinard shows that the proportion of voters who believed this increased steadily from 43 per cent in the first week of the campaign to 54 per cent in the last week.[15] Thus, Mr Bouchard's impact, as shown in this analysis, was to diminish fears about the economic consequences of sovereignty:

En assumant le rôle de négociateur en chef de ce nouveau partenariat, dont il avait été lui-même l'instigateur lors du virage d'avril 1995, Lucien Bouchard devint pour plusiers, grâce à sa personnalité et à son message, le garant de la réussite de ces négotiations. Il se faisait fort, d'ailleurs, d'insister sur le fait que le reste du Canada ne pourrait refuser de négocier ce partenariat, qu'il était inévitable. C'était important, puisque sans accord préalable sur le partenariat, toute entente future demeurait aléatoire et constituait ainsi un point faible de l'option souverainiste.[16]

This research, like the other studies, shows that the partnership proposal was attractive, that it helped make sovereignty seem realizable, that it weighed substantially on the voting decision, and that it gained credibility during the referendum campaign itself. But this was not the only element of the battle between the federalists and sovereigntists. Indeed, it may not have been the decisive one.

Modern political campaigns are organized around a limited number of dimensions of discourse. On these, the partisan forces adopt positions strategically. The objective is not merely to develop arguments that are persuasive, in the sense that good political rhetoric can draw support, but to structure voters' perceptions of the situation. In the words of William Riker, who coined the term "heresthetic" to describe the structuring of discourse, people can be led strategically to find themselves on one side or the other "without any persuasion at all."[17]

The arguments deployed along these dimensions are crucial, even though they are filtered by the media and even though many voters may put little effort into understanding them. As one experienced strategist has written, "In a close race it comes down to the 3 to 7 per cent available undecided, and you'd better be there with your best at the exact moment they're making up their minds. If you're not, you might as well not even start."[18] Strategic discourse involves choosing dimensions and positions on them according to several considerations. One is winnability. The set of positions must have majority appeal, reaffirming the core supporters' reasons for their choice while also reaching voters who may occupy a rather different position.

Second is constancy: the positions must be consistently maintained over time in order to drive the message home and maintain credibility.[19] As well, the dimensions chosen and the positions taken on them must be logically coherent. This means that contradictory positions cannot be adopted about one theme; more important, taking certain positions on one dimension will preclude the adoption of some contradictory positions on another relevant dimension.[20] Finally, the campaign discourse should be tailored in anticipation of the opponents' positions and arguments. Campaigns are competitive, and counter-arguments must be foreseen, because the requirement of consistency will constrain the responses that can be made to them. If the opponents are making gains, an inability to respond effectively will leave open dangerous areas of vulnerability.

In the Quebec referendum, the critical dimensions were those anticipated by many analysts and actors, and most of the arguments were predictable. The major difference was that the Yes forces did not propose a clear, straightforward question on sovereignty; instead, after Mr Bouchard's *virage*, they fought on the twin proposals of sovereignty and the economic and political partnership. This rendered the argumentative strategy more complex for both sides, because the three main dimensions – national identification, the economic consequences of a Yes, and the existing constitutional system – became tightly interrelated. As well, the sovereigntists opened up a new, unanticipated dimension of discourse – democracy. This one became the crucial underlying element in the campaign. It was because the No side was incapable of taking a position on this dimension that the sovereigntists were able to make such headway with their arguments about the economy and the partnership, and almost to win the referendum.[21]

THE CONSTITUTION

On the constitutional dimension, the No forces stood at zero – the status quo. This was consistent with the position that had helped Prime Minister Chrétien win the 1993 election, when he argued that the economy and jobs were the only matters of real concern to Canadians and Quebecers. After the sovereigntists opened the dimension by calling the referendum, the federalists continued to argue that the existing constitutional framework was adequate and was flexible enough to accommodate, in a cooperative fashion, any genuine demands from Quebec or other regions and groups. As Mr Chrétien put it during the referendum campaign, "The best way for Quebecers to assure positive change is to vote No. A No vote will allow

Quebecers and other Canadians to work together to respond to new challenges."[22] Of course, this position made the Quebec wing of the No side increasingly uncomfortable, but it was maintained until the sudden shift during the final week of the campaign. The federalists argued consistently that the onus was on the sovereigntists to prove why their constitutional option – "separation" – was necessary for Quebecers.

This was not an easy task for the Yes side. On the simple issue of political independence, the sovereigntists could not point to great advantages in having a seat in the United Nations, representation in the Olympics, and so on, and when sovereignty *tout court* was on the table they were often reduced to stating that sovereignty is "normal" for distinct peoples. But the shift to advocating a political and economic partnership brought the Yes side to focus on constitutional relationships with Canada itself. A Yes would bring about a new *rapport de forces* between the partners, as Mr Bouchard so often put it. And sovereigntists like Mario Dumont could argue that "separation" would not actually occur. "Will we be separate?" he asked. "The answer is No." Instead, the system would resemble the European Union. "We look after our affairs without asking permission from others but without being separated; we are united on things where we have a common interest. This is the inverse of separation."[23]

Obviously, the partnership proposal allowed the Yes side to emphasize a range of positions along the constitutional dimension. In fact, as the campaign began, sovereigntists saw some advantages in emphasizing the differences among the Yes leaders, hoping they could convince hesitant voters that Mr Dumont and Mr Bouchard could rein in the harder-line PQ under Mr Parizeau.[24] But the Quebec premier was always clear: "If some people want to vote Yes to change Quebec's bargaining power and join the ranks, all the better. But let it be clear for everyone that by voting Yes they are voting for Quebec sovereignty."[25] Meanwhile, Mr Bouchard also was consistent, especially on the political dimension of the partnership: "I want it clearly understood that the question is on sovereignty and partnership after, but they aren't dependent. There is no hyphen between the two. The first will be achieved for all time, the second will come after as we think it will, but there's no guarantee it will come. There's no link of cause and effect. I have always been extremely clear: sovereignty per se, on its own, as a solution."[26]

The constitutional dimension was associated with two others. First, on the economic dimension, the federalists could and did argue that political separation would necessarily entail a costly long-term reduction in economic integration. On the other side, the Yes position favouring political association had some cost, because it weakened the economic argument that sovereignty would eliminate a lot of waste, overlap, and duplication in the federation. It was logically hard to argue on the economic front that Quebec had *un gouvernement de trop* ("one government too many") when the constitutional position advocated a new set of common institutions. Here the sovereigntists were vulnerable.

Less straightforward was the linkage with the national-identification dimension. One sovereigntist position was that a No vote would hurt Quebecers. As Mr Bouchard declared when the campaign was going poorly, "It's not true that Quebecers are weak, that Quebec will say No to itself. They will say Yes because the consequences of saying No would be too serious."[27] But this line of argument could not be pressed too hard, because it was the sovereigntists themselves who had chosen to hold the referendum, thus creating the very possibility of a damaging No. Yet they did argue that a No would expose Quebecers to Ottawa's centralizing tendencies and to the spending cuts favoured by the Reform Party and several other provincial governments. As Pauline Marois, Treasury Board president, put it, "The Canada we know is disintegrating before our very eyes. The new Canada will be the one of Preston Manning, Ralph Klein, and Mike Harris – and we don't want any part of it."[28]

A much stronger positive effect was achieved by the partnership proposal, which, while allowing for a continued association with Canada, would finally provide for negotiations and policies to be decided on the basis of equality – *égal-à-égal* as it was constantly phrased. This theme had a strong nationalistic appeal, and when Mr Bouchard assumed the leadership of the Yes campaign, he continually stressed it, while emphasizing the solidarity that would result from a collective choice for change: "A Yes vote will lead to unity of all Quebecers. We will all be sovereigntists, so much so that people will no longer refer to us as sovereigntists but simply as Quebecers."[29] Again, typically: "The people of Quebec must take their place in the empty chair facing English Canada to make the changes that we both need ... We will no longer have to ask anyone to recognize us as being specific or as an asymmetrical society or anything else. We don't want labels ... We just want one word – Québécois."[30]

The relationship between the constitutional and national-identification dimensions was problematic for the federalist side. While the No leaders could point to some evidence of flexible federalism, they were not prepared at the outset to promise the symbolic recognition as a "distinct society" that many Quebecers desired. Further, despite strenuous efforts, they could not entirely silence leaders in ROC who argued that all provinces must be constitutionally equal. For example, Clyde Well, the premier of Newfoundland, summarily rejected any notion of a partnership as "totally inconsistent with everything Canadians across the country have been saying for the last ten years."[31] Not only did such observations reinforce the sovereigntists' arguments about the dire effects of a No vote, but outright rejection of Quebecers' constitutional demands could also be portrayed as insulting and demeaning. Hence, Mr Chrétien's preference that federalists in the rest of the country either stay out of the campaign or send messages of affection. As he told a Vancouver audience, "You all have said, 'We want you to stay in Canada.' You didn't provoke them. Some were hoping for that. It's easy to get mad."[32] It was strategically awkward for the No side to formally dismiss the offer of political partnership because this could drive away voters whose sense of community with Canada made them reluctant to vote Yes.[33]

Nevertheless, in his first major campaign speech, Mr Chrétien did make predictions that the partnership could not work: "The proposal for a political partnership flies in the face of the most elementary good sense ... It would be rejected because it would impose another level of government in Canada, with equal representation, even though Canada is three times the size of Quebec, and a right of veto that would totally paralyze both those broken countries."[34] Later, he pointed out some practical difficulties: "Canada with Quebec forms a country. Nobody knows what would remain of Canada without Quebec. Who has a mandate to speak for the so-called rest of Canada?"[35] Similarly, Mr Johnson warned, "Will Canada reach out to seven million Quebecers and say: 'You just broke up our country, but here's your passport?' It's unthinkable."[36] And the prime minister declared at an early campaign rally that a Yes would bring independence, not a new partnership: "In that case, there will be no more Quebecers in the House of Commons, no more Quebecers running the government. Quebecers won't be Canadian citizens or hold Canadian passports."[37] But this theme was muted in the federalist discourse on the constitutional dimension. The No side stuck to the initial, more positive position that the existing constitution was flexible and that whatever the question formally posed in the referendum, the real issue was separation. As Mme Robillard put it at the outset of the campaign, "Why did Mr Parizeau lack the political courage to state very clearly that if we vote Yes, Quebec will be an independent country separated from Canada? That's the real referendum choice that Quebecers will have to make."[38]

NATIONAL IDENTIFICATION

On this dimension, the two sides lavished a great deal of discourse during the campaign, and the empirical studies suggest that the result was a standoff. Here, the federalists simply aimed to hold their ground. They stressed that Canada was a wonderful country, the envy of the world. Within it, Quebecers had a proud and honourable history and a great deal of influence. Separation would end all this. It would bring an end to the country to which many Quebecers felt attached. The No side pressed this theme very hard at the end of the campaign. In his televised address to the nation, Mr Chrétien posed a long series of questions about Canada, concluding with the following: "Have you found one reason, one good reason, to destroy Canada? Do you really think it is worth abandoning the country we have built, and which our ancestors have left us? Do you really think it makes any sense – any sense at all – to break up Canada?"[39] As well, the federalists emphasized that there was no contradiction between being a Canadian and being a Quebecer. In what became a mantra towards the end of the campaign, they repeated that Canada was their country (*pays*) while Quebec was their homeland (*patrie*).[40]

This dimension offered much scope to the sovereigntists, who devoted a lot of emotionally charged discourse to it. The core position was that Quebecers constitute a people, distinct from those in the rest of Canada. So sovereignty would represent a logical stage in Quebec's evolution. In contrast, a No, in Mr. Parizeau's words, "would mean breaking away from what we are and what we have always wanted to become."[41] Part of the Yes position involved reciting the long series of humiliations and oppressions to which the Quebec people had been subjected, beginning with their conquest by the English, emphasizing their conscription in the wars, and peaking with the "imposition" of the 1982 constitution; as well, the failure of the Meech Lake Accord was characterized as a rejection of Quebec by Canada. Always the emphasis was on unity and solidarity, and on the need of Quebecers to put the endless squabblings of Canadian federalism behind them. In a much misquoted remark, Mr Bouchard held out this vision: "A Yes has something magical about it. With a wave of a wand, it transforms the whole situation. It produces within us solidarity and unity."[42] At last, said the sovereigntists, a Yes result would end the historic doubts, the hesitation of Quebecers to declare themselves a people. At the final rally of the campaign, Mr Bouchard beseeched the voters, arguing that now was their best chance: "We have no right to let it pass. God knows when it will present itself again. We have it before us. Seize it and vote Yes. Say Yes to ourselves. Say Yes to the people of Quebec."[43]

The national-identification dimension posed certain problems for the sovereigntists, however. One was that they had been unable to define a common social project for an independent Quebec. Hence, they spoke of unity and solidarity without being very precise about the common goals of the collectivity. As well, the Yes side was officially committed to the position that Quebec constituted a modern and pluralist society. Quebec nationalism might have had its foundations among the *vieille souche* – descendants of the original settlers – but supposedly it was a shared social experience that would impel Quebecers, whatever their ethnic origins, to decide for sovereignty. So stressing too emphatically a common history and ethnicity was logically awkward, and, practically, it would weaken the adherence of genuine pluralists, would further alienate minority-group voters, and would help legitimize the claims for self-determination that were being advanced by the Aboriginal peoples. Nevertheless, the chord was struck often, notably by Mr Parizeau, who declared at the end that the choice was to decide to "no longer be a minority in the country of our anglophone neighbours but a majority in our own country. To affirm, once and for all, our language and our culture as American francophones."[44] But however much the two sides contested on the national-identification dimension, it was not the crucial one.

THE ECONOMY

On this dimension, the sovereigntist position was that secession would entail no economic losses and would in fact be economically advantageous in the long run. The discourse on the latter point was far less intense than on the former, but the Yes side did speak about how sovereignty would end wasteful federal-provincial duplication, allow taxes to be frozen if not reduced, and permit the formation of autonomous policy suited to the Quebec economy. As well, sometimes with rather muddy appeals to endogenous growth theory, the Yes side referred to the advantages enjoyed in the global economy by small, relatively homogeneous, and solidaristic polities.

Yet the critical message concerned the prospect of economic disruption and loss in the transition period. Here, the sovereigntists dismissed every dire prediction as a threat or bluff. It was rational, they argued, for the federalists to make such predictions in the hope of dissuading Quebecers from voting Yes. But after an actual Yes it would be irrational for ROC to retaliate economically, because this would impose losses on its own citizens. Indeed, economic rationality would inevitably lead Canada into a partnership, because of the need to manage the common economic space and avoid losses. In short, rationality was equated with cooperation.

This position meshed well with some traditional stereotypes – that ROC is dominated by business interests (and business would not countenance disruption), and that English Canadians are cold and calculating (and would therefore be willing to cut their losses and support cooperation with Quebec after a Yes). As one anglophone commentator put it, "The separatists portray 'les anglais' as dessicated calculating machines, ready to cut deals the day after the destruction of their country."[45] As well, some aspects of the formal campaign were designed to provide reassurance about items of particular concern to the public; hence the provisions in Bill 1 about use of the Canadian dollar, accession to treaties, and so on. But on the economic dimension it was the logic of threat and bluff that was pushed relentlessly by the Yes side.[46]

Early in the campaign, Mr Bouchard said, "All these stories we are being told that business people in Ontario, for example, will not want to do business with Quebec, we all know ... it doesn't make any sense." After a Yes vote, he went on, the typical Toronto businessman "will go to his office and sit at his desk, and he will examine his sales figures. And he will see that he conducts 25 percent of his business in Quebec. Sure he'll be in a bad mood, but you know what he'll do. He will pick up his phone and call his biggest buyer in Quebec. And you know what he will say to him. He'll say, 'let's not mix politics with business.'"[47] Mr Bouchard was equally dismissive of threats that governments would not cooperate after a Yes, asserting that "English Canada would run after Mr Parizeau to ask him, to beg him, to sit down" and discuss the national debt.[48] Here, the sovereigntists also stressed the international pressure that would be exerted on Canada. As Mr Parizeau put it, "People across the world will want to know what the score is."[49]

Again and again the sovereigntists hammered home their argument about where the self-interest of Canada lay. English Canadians, argued Bernard Landry, "need our help to pay their debt, and they need our market if they want to continue selling us wheat, beef, Western gas, cars and financial services from Ontario ... To put up a border and customs would compromise these jobs, and the first victim would be Ontario."[50] Sensing momentum after mid-October, Mr Parizeau put in a nutshell the logic of the Yes argument about the economy and the partnership: "For heaven's sake, it's perfectly understandable that before the 30th all of these guys in Ottawa will say no, no, no, no. Well, after the 30th, they might say Yes to a few things."[51]

Obviously, this position helped fortify the pride and confidence to which the Yes side appealed on the national-identification dimension. Mr Bouchard's discourse often combined equality and the economy. He said, for example, that sovereignty was "a powerful springboard to go and get a partnership" that would "impose itself after an assessment of each other's interests."[52] Again, towards the end of the campaign: "Those two peoples will talk to each other about their mutual interest and about what they want to deal with in common. The talk will be of commercial exchanges that are to be maintained and increased, of jobs to protect and to create."[53] Mr Parizeau even referred jokingly to the effect a Yes would have. Noting that some provincial legislatures were passing motions favourable to Quebec merely because two polls had found the Yes ahead, he crowed, "Imaginez, avec un Oui, à quel point ces gens vont devenir des partenaires volontaires du Québec!"[54] And summing up at the end of the campaign, Mr Bouchard reflected, "My worries are about the fact that Quebecers have too often been impressed by the attempts to raise a scare in their minds ... But I trust, as we have been seeing in this campaign, that fear has been overcome by confidence. I'm happy to see Quebecers no longer take scare tactics seriously."[55]

For their part, the federalists had little to say about Quebec's long-term economic prospects, except to point out generally that Quebec would be a smaller, more vulnerable economic unit. It would not benefit, for example, from Canada's weight in trade negotiations or membership in the G-7. But on the whole, the No side preferred to couch such matters in more positive terms, referring to the strength and prosperity of a united Canada. In fact, the basic federalist position on this dimension was to make no concrete predictions about the economic effect of a Yes vote. Federalist leaders consistently dismissed the entire issue as purely hypothetical: it would not happen, and there was no point in speculating about it. When pressed, the No forces emphasized the huge risk and uncertainty that "separation" would involve. Rather than say, for example, that Quebecers' geographic mobility would be restricted under sovereignty, they simply insisted that peoples' economic prospects after a Yes vote were entirely unknown. The concrete promises of the sovereigntists certainly were not to be believed, for they could guarantee nothing about the future, which would become radically uncertain after a Yes vote.

It was this uncertainty, with its consequent risk of severe economic disruption and loss, that the federalists believed would dissuade Quebecers from supporting sovereignty. This position was exemplified by the prime minister when he stated, "What is immediately guaranteed after a No vote is that we will still have a sovereign country. A country that guarantees us Canadian citizenship, Canadian passports, and the Canadian dollar ... On the one hand stands separation, which would hurtle us all into the unknown, with all the risks it would involve. It is an invitation to an adventure from which no one, including those who believe in it, would emerge a winner. On the other hand stands an economically and politically strong Quebec, continuing its tremendous development in Canada."[56]

At times the federalists were more explicit. Mr Johnson especially stressed economic issues, arguing, for example, that "voting Yes is a risky adventure that will bring economic upheaval, affect the value of the dollar, mortgage rates, and raise interest rates on other things we buy."[57] He produced a sovereignty budget that showed a very large deficit and consequent tax increases, and he made precise predictions about job losses based on extant studies. But these predictions were derided as blackmail and bluff by the sovereigntists, especially after Mr Martin's comments about one million jobs being at risk. When Mr Johnson stated that a Quebec dollar would be worth sixty-three cents, he had to defend himself against accusations of fearmongering, and he showed the strain of trying to make headway against the Yes side's position: "I am utterly and personally convinced that separation means economic dire consequences for all Quebecers and I certainly am not going to shut up before the referendum date just because I'm being accused of being a fearmonger. I'm a realitymonger. I'm a truthmonger."[58]

The federalist side also pointed out that many economic matters covered by the partnership proposal were strictly within the power of Canada to determine. At their annual meeting, for example, the provincial premiers indicated that interprovincial trade agreements could not be taken for granted by a sovereign Quebec.[59] Federalists also referred to Canada's control of the currency, milk quotas, labour mobility, equalization payments and other transfers, and even the deployment of the military forces and the jobs they created. But consistent with their basic position that a sovereigntist victory would produce enormous uncertainty, they did not state what would actually happen after a Yes. With few exceptions, it was never clearly predicted that labour mobility would end, milk quotas be re-allocated, military bases closed, and so on. The core position was to maintain uncertainty about ROC's behaviour in the expectation that this would induce a No vote by risk-averse Quebecers.

There were strategic weaknesses in each side's position. The sovereigntist argument that a Yes would bring no economic disruption was open to the counterargument that this demonstrated the acceptability of the status quo. What, then, was the purpose of sovereignty? As Mr Johnson said at the outset of the campaign, "I'm still waiting for the government to tell us why we should vote Yes. It's voting Yes to Quebec's departure from Canada with no guarantees – we close all the doors."[60] But the federalists were more vulnerable. Their strategy of sustaining uncertainty led them to make no precise predictions about what a Yes would bring economically, including ROC's response on those matters covered by the partnership proposal, and this left a gap into which the sovereigntists could spin their web of arguments about post-secession cooperation. In the absence of declarations from the No side about what would happen on the economic front, the Yes side advanced with its arguments that ROC would need to negotiate out of its own self-interest, that the secession would be tranquil, and that economic links would not be severed.

There are several reasons why the federalists did not close off this line of argument by spelling out the economic effects of a Yes vote. At the outset of the campaign, the No side was feeling confident, and it probably appeared that stressing uncertainty alone would suffice to deter marginal voters from choosing sovereignty. To have been more definite would also have meant moving towards Reform's position, which was unattractive for partisan reasons. Beyond this, there is no evidence that the federalist leaders and their advisers had spent much time or effort thinking about what a Yes actually would bring, so it would have been difficult, honestly, to make concrete predictions. More important, it was not evident who in the No camp had the legitimacy to lay out the terms of separation on such dossiers as the currency, trade arrangements, agricultural policy, and the division of the debt. Had any federalist leader taken a strong, clear position on these matters, the unity of the No side could have been gravely weakened. Moreover, such positions could have been portrayed by the Yes side as initial bargaining moves rather than a credible bottom line. And if the predictions or positions had been rather harsh towards Quebec's interests, this would have contradicted the No side's position on the national-identification dimension, where the consistent theme was Canada's civility, tolerance, and openness to Quebecers, as well as a long-standing sense of shared citizenship and community. These are all good reasons. But another one has to do with how positions on the economic dimension were associated with those taken on the final dimension of the campaign – democracy.

DEMOCRACY

Democracy was the subject of much less explicit discourse (or commentary) during the referendum campaign, but it was nevertheless the most strategically significant dimension. The sovereigntists opened this debate, and it provided them with an important degree of freedom. William Riker has shown how opening dimensions of discourse is an heresthetic device that can structure debate and produce different outcomes, but he also argued that constraining dimensions, or "fixing dimensionality," can deter counterattacks.[61] In the Quebec referendum campaign, the federalists could not – or did not – shut down the democracy dimension. As a result, the Yes side's position on the economic dimension nearly carried the sovereigntists to victory.

The sovereigntists always insisted on the legitimacy of their *démarche*. They assumed from the outset that Quebecers had the right to determine their collective future, and the process of deciding whether Quebec should become sovereign, they said, was a highly democratic one. It involved a major exercise in public consultation – the regional commission hearings, at which, despite the boycott by the Quebec Liberal Party, tens of thousands of people had appeared. So Mr Chrétien's criticism of the sovereigntist *virage* as deceptive and contemptuous of democracy brought the sharpest possible rebuke from Mr Parizeau on the grounds that the government and the commissions had indeed listened to the concerns of the people.[62] Further, the entire referendum process was valid. The question had been debated in the National Assembly according to the referendum law. That law was itself highly democratic in that it provided a framework for organizing two sides around the issue and imposed strict spending limits on each while providing public funding for the competing organizations. Finally, since Quebec was a highly advanced and democratic society, all those involved would accept the outcome of the public consultation. In a parliamentary system, of course, referendums cannot be binding, but the sovereigntists had accepted the verdict of Quebecers in 1980. Similarly, the 1995 result would be accepted. These themes were fundamental to the whole approach of the Yes side.

On this dimension, the No side simply refused to take a position. A Yes was hypothetical, so there was no point in discussing what its consequences would be. While the federalist leaders condemned the process leading to the referendum as manipulative and attacked the question as ambiguous, they were carefully noncommital about the implications of any result other than a No vote. As one journalist put it, for the federalist side separation was "not so much an evil as a non sequitur."[63] The federalists always refused any engagement to accept a Yes result as valid. Their discourse on this dimension of the debate was minimal – far less than on national identification or the economy or constitution – but their strategic choice here was highly significant. The No position was to insist that separation was an economically uncertain and costly adventure; yet the choice to be noncommital about the legitimacy of a Yes result left the No side vulnerable to the economic counterarguments of the sovereigntists.

The federalist ambiguity on the democracy dimension was shown well before the referendum campaign began. In a year-end interview, Prime Minister Chrétien suggested that Ottawa would not be compelled to negotiate sovereignty after a Yes vote: "It's not in the constitution ... If you want to talk legality and constitutionality, there's nobody who will argue that it is legal and constitutional."[64] Treading lightly, however, an aide to Mr Chrétien said this position should not be regarded as a threat or a refusal to accept a Yes result: "He's just pointing out that the separatists have tried to gloss over a lot of tough questions."[65]

Undoubtedly the federalists' frustration with their heresthetical situation grew when the sovereigntists adopted the partnership proposal and launched the campaign on a question which the federalists regarded as deceptive and ambiguous. But Mr Chrétien still remained noncommital about what a Yes vote would entail, dismissing all speculation about the matter as hypothetical. In his first public comments during the campaign, comments that set the tone for all subsequent remarks, the prime minister refused to say whether he would accept a Yes victory: "You're asking a hypothetical question. We have a referendum and they are proposing separation. We're going to tell Quebecers that, and Quebecers will vote for Canada."[66]

This position was briefly shaken when the same question was put to the federal minister who was formally in charge of the referendum, Mme Robillard. She replied, "We have always said that Quebecers have the right to express themselves about the future of Quebec in Canada, inside or outside Canada. We are in a democratic country, so we'll respect the vote."[67] Pressed immediately on this matter in Quebec, Mr Johnson took a similar line. "The people of Quebec will abide by the results – end of story," he said. "We want a democratic vote – it is. The referendum process is acceptable; the law is clear for everyone – the campaign, financing, timing. It's *vox populi*."[68] But all this was reversed after Mme Robillard consulted with colleagues and advisers to the prime minister. She amended her remarks to the effect that the government would respect "the democratic process" rather than any particular outcome. In a damage-control news conference, Mr Chrétien reaffirmed his noncommital position: "There is a vote and, of course, we'll receive the result of the vote, but you're asking me a hypothetical question. I'm standing here telling you we're going to win."[69] After the matter was the subject of heated questions in the House of Commons, Mr Johnson also reversed field, saying, "How can you break up a country on a judicial recount? It has to be clear either way if you want to go on to other things."[70]

That Commons exchange revealed how steadfast were the federalists in taking no position on the democracy dimension, despite the conflicting pressures on them to do so. First, the Bloc demanded that Mr Chrétien make a commitment to accept the result, and he refused to do so. One reason was that the sovereigntist leaders had indicated they might call yet another referendum if they lost in 1995; hence, the Yes side was refusing to be bound by the results. More important, the question was ambiguous: "I have always said they had the right to have a referendum in Quebec," stated Mr Chrétien. "Quebecers can be consulted and can explain their point of view. However, we on this side of the House are convinced that Quebecers, if they are asked an honest question about the separation of Quebec from Canada, not a trick question, no clever twists and turns but an honest question: Do you want to separate from Canada? If the leader of the Leader of the Opposition, Mr Parizeau, was truly intellectually honest, he would have asked Quebecers: Do you want to separate? And Quebecers would have answered: No, never."[71] Through more than a dozen questions over two days about whether the federal government would recognize a Yes vote, the prime minister remained noncommital, accusing the sovereigntists of posing a deceptively ambiguous question, arguing that Quebecers wanted to put the constitution aside and enjoy economic growth and good government, and predicting that Quebecers would never vote to separate.

But there was also pressure on this dimension from the Reform Party, whose leaders argued that clarity was crucial. Mr Manning asked, "Will the Prime Minister make clear that a yes vote means Quebec is on its way out, that a no vote means Quebec is in the federation for the long haul, and that 50 per cent plus one is the dividing line between those two positions?" Mr Chrétien would not do so. "I have been asking them for a long time in this House of Commons to give us a real question, an honest, clear question on separation. They have clouded the issue talking about divorce and remarriage at the same time. They want me on behalf of all Canadians to say that with a clouded question like that with one vote I will help them to destroy Canada. You might, I will not, Mr Manning."[72]

The following day, answering a question from Mr Bouchard, the prime minister reiterated the point: "Today, we have a confusing and ambiguous question, and I am asked whether we would recognize a vote with a majority of one. As Mr Johnson put it so well yesterday, we are not about to separate from Canada on the basis of a judicial recount."[73] But the Reform Party continued to press, reasoning that if a Yes vote might not actually produce separation, then it would be less risky to cast one. As Mr Manning put it, "They think they can vote for separation and still enjoy the benefits of federalism. That is why we asked the Prime Minister to make clear that yes means separation and only no means federalism. I will again ask the Prime Minister sincerely, as we are not playing games here, why he is so reluctant to make that distinction crystal clear." After repeating that the referendum question was ambiguous, Mr Chrétien responded:

In a country like ours to recognize that at one time a rule of majority plus one could break up the country would be irresponsible on my part. Even in the Reform Party, as a journalist wrote this morning, in order to change its constitution one has to ask for two-thirds of its membership. Therefore I will not break up the country with one vote. It is not real democracy. Real democracy is to convince the people they can express themselves clearly, which is what we are doing. This is why we are telling Quebecers these people want to separate but they will not succeed because it is our collective duty to tell all Quebecers the scheme they have, the virage, the mirage and so on will not work. They will not succeed in fooling the people of Quebec because the people of Quebec will know when they vote 39 days from now that they will not separate. They will stay in Canada because it is their destiny, their future and their desire.[74]

But the issue did not go away. During the campaign, Mr Bouchard continually spoke of the great democratic exercise in which Quebecers were engaged, and in the final days before the referendum the democracy dimension re-emerged strongly. In his reply to the prime minister's televised address to the nation, Mr Bouchard stated, "Quebecers will make a decision on Monday, a decision that they will have carefully reflected upon through a democratic process, the fairness of which does not afford any challenge." He continued: "One supreme and fundamental issue that Quebec and Canada share and cherish is democracy ... With respect to the decision that will be taken by the majority of Quebecers next Monday, I expect this common value of democracy to prevail. I am reassured by the citizens of Canada that I have met who are saying that Quebecers can decide their own future and that such a decision should be accepted by the rest of Canada. The voices of these people have been heard by political leaders, and I call upon all leaders and their sense of democracy to show the same respect for the will of the people of Quebec."[75]

Similarly, Mr Bouchard maintained that the result would be accepted in Quebec, "because we live in a democracy. We sovereigntists proved it in 1980 when we accepted the verdict."[76] On the last day of the campaign, he also predicted that Canadians would peacefully accept a Yes result. "There must be surprise because they have been put to sleep by Mr Chrétien who told them all the time that there was no problem." However, he continued, "I fully expect the rest of Canada, as all Quebecers, whatever happens, to accept the verdict of democracy."[77] Meanwhile, Mr Parizeau, with victory in sight but Ottawa's intentions unclear, insisted not only that the transition would be calm but that all Quebecers would have to show solidarity in accepting the result of the vote, and he singled out his main provincial opponent: "The example comes from the top. Without misgiving, I say that the leader of the Quebec Liberal Party, Mr Daniel Johnson, fought fiercely, but always was a democrat."[78]

Mr Chrétien, however, never said he would accept a Yes result. He was noncommital to the end. In a television interview, while striking the federalist chords of constitutional flexibility, patriotism, and the economic uncertainty that a Yes would bring, he refused to agree that a 51 per cent sovereigntist victory would be decisive: "Non, je n'ai pas reconnu rien. Vous ne savez pas le résultat et moi non plus. Les gens auront exprimé leur point de vue. Les méchanismes, après, c'est très nébuleux."[79]

In the end, these *méchanismes* were never tested. But the federalist decision not to take a position on the democratic dimension had been both risky and costly. The strategy was risky because it precluded a convincing reply to the sovereigntists' position on the economic dimension – that cooperation between ROC and a sovereign Quebec would be inevitable because of each side's self-interest in minimizing economic disruption. Moreover, the partnership idea advanced by the Yes side had a strong appeal: not only was it deeply congruent with the pride and equality that were central to many Quebecers' sense of national identification, but it promised a framework agreement for economic management that would minimize losses in the transition to sovereignty. This is where the sovereigntists made their gains in the summer and autumn of 1995.

To shut down the progress of the Yes side on the economic dimension, the federalists would have had to state clearly that the partnership would never materialize. They would have had to declare that constitutional amendments would excise Quebec from Canada, that economic integration would drop sharply, that there would be border posts around Quebec, that agriculture would contract, that social entitlements and labour mobility would end, and so on. All these outcomes would have been unattractive to the undecided, soft-nationalist voters. The No side did raise questions throughout the campaign about how a Yes vote would affect these substantive matters, but federalists never presented a coherent position about them. Some reasons for this were suggested above – complacency, the difficulty of integrating the No forces, and the unattractive air of harshness that such statements might have conveyed – but a deeper one was the linkage between the economic and democratic dimensions. On the economic dimension, the sovereigntists pressed the vision of a partnership that would protect Quebecers economically, while the federalists mainly predicted only economic uncertainty and risk. For the No side to be more precise about the negative economic implications of a Yes, its leaders would have had to be more than noncommital on the democratic dimension. They would have had to accept in principle that a Yes in the October referendum meant that Quebec would become a sovereign country. Only then could the sovereigntists'

economic arguments – and their sanguine predictions of cooperation and partnership – be countered.

This the federalists did not do. There are undoubtedly many reasons for this decision. Apart from those mentioned are calculations
of possible effects. The No side may have estimated, for instance,
that accepting in principle that sovereignty could occur might make
it appear more legitimate and easier to attain, thus adding to the Yes
total; alternatively, such a position might reinforce the message of
Canada's flexibility and toleration, thus gaining more No votes. Similarly, one cost to the No forces of being ambiguous on the democracy
dimension was that they appeared inconsistent by participating in
an exercise they condemned as deceptive.[80] Accepting that secession
could occur would remove this liability. The No side may have weighed
these various costs and benefits and decided to remain noncommital
about a Yes, but there was also the much larger cost of losing the
battle on the economic dimension as the partnership idea gained
crediblility with voters.

A final reason for not taking a position on the democratic dimension is more speculative. It is that the key strategists on the federalist
side, most of whom had deep roots in Montreal, literally could not
contemplate a Canada without Quebec.[81] The intensity of their discourse on the national-identification dimension is testimony to this
(just as Mr Bouchard's insistence on referring to Quebecers as *nous*
attests to the ethnic nationalism which the cosmopolitan federalists
so abhorred). The federalist leaders commonly spoke of Quebec as
the "heart" or "soul" of Canada, and at the Montreal unity rally Mr
Chrétien shouted, "We say No to those who would strip us of our
Canada."[82] At the final No rally of the campaign, in Hull, the prime
minister expressed his sentiments clearly: "For all of us, Canada without Quebec is unthinkable just as Quebec without Canada is unthinkable."[83] Because of this deep attachment, the key strategists on the
No side were not able to concede, even in principle and even to win
a contest with enormous stakes for all Canadians, that Quebec could
become a sovereign state. As a consequence, they almost lost.

The effects of ambiguity on the democratic dimension were profound. The sovereigntists continued to advance in the polls as the
disincentives to voting Yes diminished because of their winning economic arguments. The No side could not bring itself to move on the
democracy dimension and block those arguments. Since there was a
standoff on the identification dimension, there was only one possible axis along which the federalists could shift. They moved on the
constitution. At the Verdun rally on 24 October and in the televised
speech to the country the next day, Mr Chrétien committed the

federalists to formal constitutional change – recognizing Quebec as a distinct society, decentralizing powers, and restoring Quebec's constitutional veto. This major shift followed profound disagreement in the No campaign and was reported to be very much against the prime minister's own instincts.[84] But it did allow the No forces to portray themselves as agents of the change that most Quebecers wanted within the Canada they enjoyed, and with no risk of economic loss. Given the fundamental refusal to countenance a Yes, this was all the federalists could do, and it may have produced the narrow No victory on 30 October. But there was a cost. This strategic move ensured that the question of Quebec's constitutional status has not been laid to rest.

CHAPTER THREE

Had the Yes Side Won ...

Before moving on from the 1995 referendum to its effects and to the future, it is worth turning to an important and intriguing question: What would have happened had the Yes side won? This, of course, raises a counterfactual proposition, and because the event did not actually occur, no definitive answer can be supplied here or anywhere else. But this is not a radical counterfactual of the sort that interests some historians (such as, What would Europe be like now had the Allies lost World War II?). In this case, the relevant event is not long past, and there are good indications about what pivotal actors would have done within the structural conditions that constrained them. The basic argument here is that the sovereigntists would have worked ferociously to consolidate a narrow Yes victory, but that this effort would have failed because of the transparent breaches of democratic practices that occurred during the counting of the referendum ballots.

INEVITABILISTS AND IMPOSSIBILISTS

From the time the Parti québécois won the September 1994 election, debates across Canada had focused on what the implications of a Yes vote would be. In Quebec these debates became central to the referendum campaign. The issues were hotly contested by politicians, journalists, and editorialists, but they were also joined by academics and members of think tanks. In these discussions, especially as the referendum approached, there was a natural tendency for prediction to slide into prescription, because predictions were deployed as tools by both sides in the campaign – intensely so, as the race sharpened.

The academic studies were categorized by Professor Stéphane Dion, and his analysis provides a useful framework for thinking about what would have happened had the Yes side carried the referendum.[1] Dion divided the studies into two camps. In the first were the authors who predicted the scenario Dion called the "impossible secession." Their argument was that a Yes vote would be of questionable legitimacy, because Quebec has no clear right to self-determination and secession, the question posed can be attacked as ambiguous, and minorities may claim the right to remain in Canada. Hence, a Yes majority would be fiercely contested. Second, a Yes would cause the dollar to plummet and interest rates to rise, which would only deepen the political crisis. Negotiations between ROC and Quebec would not start quickly because of the shock and confusion in ROC and the absence of an interlocutor with a mandate to deal with Quebec. Even if talks did get underway, they would inevitably break down because the agenda would be too crowded, the players too numerous, and the issues too difficult. Then Quebec could be forced into a UDI, which Canada probably would not recognize.

The two sides could then enter a contest for authority over the territory, which would not only cause enormous economic damage but would raise the spectre of "the violence we must fear," as Dion put it.[2] In the view of one "impossibilist," Quebecers in the end would not be able to "endure the kinds of costs and disruptions that secession from Canada would necessarily entail," and as these costs mounted, there would be "little or no likelihood" that Quebec would actually secede from Canada.[3] Most probably, the Quebec government would withdraw the UDI and return to the bargaining table. In Dion's own view, Quebec voters would have discovered before this that the promised smooth transition was not materializing, and support for sovereignty would have waned. This change would be registered through a new referendum or a federal election, in which a sovereigntist defeat would "nullify the referendum victory."[4] So secession would not occur after a majority Yes vote.[5]

In contrast to this prediction is what Dion called the scenario of the "inevitable secession." (Among the analyses he placed in this camp was this book's predecessor.[6]) In this view, intense economic uncertainty would generate strong demands for some positive action to resolve it immediately, and only ROC's acceptance in principle that secession would occur could achieve this. Negotiations would commence quickly, with the federal government taking the lead for ROC. The economic crisis and polarization between Canada and Quebec would help overcome internal divisions in the short run. The substantive issues of the separation would be settled quickly (though the negotiations would be very difficult, and the sovereigntists' partnership would never materialize), and Canadians would turn to their main priority, simultaneously negotiating the reconstitution of Canada as a going concern. In this whole process, some interests would be ignored and some rights infringed, but that would be inescapable; the need to resolve uncertainty would dictate the first steps of the separation, and once the process was underway it would not be halted. As one columnist put it, "Self-interested survivalism would overwhelm any well-meaning attempts to reverse a Yes result."[7]

As Dion points out, the "impossibilists" tend to focus on the effects of political and economic uncertainty for Quebec, while the "inevitabilists" generally do the same for ROC.[8] Predicting what would have happened had the Yes won involves assessing the solidarity of each entity and the effects upon it of the economic and political uncertainty that would have followed such a vote. It also requires estimating what particular leaders would have done under the circumstances and pressures prevailing on 30 October 1995.

Before proceeding to this analysis, it is worth noting how the actual referendum process differed from the one anticipated by most "impossibilist" analysts. First, the question posed was not as straightforward as expected. Second, the sovereigntists' arguments about the implications of secession went beyond predicting that the common economic space would be preserved owing to the mutual self-interest of ROC and Quebec: the sovereigntists introduced the notion of economic and political partnership, arguing that common political institutions could be negotiated on a new basis of equality. Third, the margin of victory would have been exceedingly slim. Last, and most surprising, there were irregularities in the referendum process itself, with an extraordinary number of rejected ballots in three Montreal ridings. Each of these features would have affected the consequences of a Yes vote.

So would the economic situation. It is clear that the deep uncertainties about NAFTA, the currency, savings, pension funds, and so on would have materialized as predicted. More precise estimates about economic variables can also be made. In the days preceding the referendum, there was a strong expectation that a Yes vote would cause the stock market to decline sharply (one analyst anticipated a 25 per cent drop), the dollar to reach record lows, and interest rates to rise by several percentage points.[9] The one systematic retrospective study that has been done used implied volatility indexes and found that the TSE index would have declined by 7–10 per cent right after a Yes victory, while the Canadian dollar would have dropped to between 66 and 68 cents U.S.[10] This study also examined the volatility of stock prices by province and found no significant difference; that is, the referendum result would have affected firms' market valuation wherever in Canada their head offices were located.[11]

With respect to bonds, a survey of Canadian money managers found an almost unanimous expectation that Quebec securities would be downgraded and that interest-rate spreads between Quebec and Canadian government bonds would widen by 100 to 150 basis points.[12] The reaction of foreign investors was even more ominous. Money managers focused their attention on the referendum, and they showed a strong distaste for carrying Quebec debt. Stated one of them, "It's of doubtful value – uncertain government, uncertain direction, not a member of international organizations, it's got a lot of debt, it's arguing about how much to assume of federal government debt. Why would I want to get involved in a credit like that?"[13] But these reactions were not restricted to Quebec. The Canadian money managers expected the spread between Canadian and American government securities to widen by another 100 to 150 basis points and for Ontario bonds to be downgraded. If foreign investors anticipated a long period of uncertainty or thought that Ottawa might have to assume the whole national debt, then federal government bonds would certainly be downgraded, possibly to the point where many investors might be legally unable to hold them. Worse, the uncertainty of "uncharted territory" after a Yes vote could be such that rating agencies might declare it impossible to evaluate the risks of holding Canadian bonds, including corporate bonds, at which point these would not be downgraded but unrated.[14]

All of these effects would lead to enormous uncertainty, not only in Quebec but right across Canada. They would also be very costly, both directly as the value of investments plummeted and the cost of borrowing rose sharply, and indirectly as the markets anticipated decreases in investment and a sharp recession. These events would place enormous pressure on political leaders everywhere to resolve the crisis caused by a Yes result.

It is pretty clear what the sovereigntist leadership would have done after a Yes vote, even a very narrow one. Mr Parizeau's government would have acted swiftly to try to consolidate the victory and make it irreversible. Towards the end of the referendum campaign, the premier began to prepare the public for this, arguing that solidarity among all Quebecers would be essential after the Yes side won. Addressing a business audience, for example, he reassured people that nothing would change immediately in the wake of a Yes. But he also argued that solidarity would be essential to bring Ottawa to the bargaining table, to secure international recognition, and to prevent the growth of sub-secessionist movements among Aboriginal peoples and federalists; in short, to contain uncertainty to tolerable levels.[15]

This resembles the remarkable speech, later made public, that Mr Parizeau had prepared for the event of a Yes victory. He began by declaring that "a simple and strong decision was made today: Quebec will become sovereign,"[16] and he repeatedly emphasized that this affirmation of nationhood had been achieved democratically: "You [Quebecers] have inscribed your name on the face of the world. You have done so in an exemplary fashion, with a democratic, transparent, fair, and enlightened process." Then he reassured the anglophone community, Aboriginals, and immigrants that their rights and privileges would be respected; he emphasized that nothing would change in the short term – "it could take up to a year before the National Assembly makes the proclamation"; and he urged Canadians not to be bitter but to recognize the reasonableness of the partnership: "Our common responsibility is to ensure that our joint economic space is as profitable in the future as it is today." Finally, he noted the "heavy responsibility" of Jean Chrétien – who, he stressed, had stated that Quebecers were making a "definitive" choice of a country – and concluded, "We agree. We can therefore turn the page, respect the democratic verdict and move to a new dialogue which must now begin between Canada and Quebec in the interests of all our citizens and of stability."[17]

The sovereigntists' first priority would be to have as many prominent Quebecers as possible declare that they accepted the result. Among them, no doubt, would be labour leaders, municipal officials, the heads of nationalist associations and other voluntary organizations, and business leaders. A substantial effort had been devoted to securing this acceptance through the organization RESPEQ (le Réseau solidarité pour l'économie du Québec), which had convinced a number of prominent people to sign a letter asking all Quebecers to recognize the democratic decision and to maintain solidarity towards the goal of economic stability and job creation.[18] Lists of these people would probably have appeared in newspapers immediately after the vote. Mr Parizeau also intended to name further members to the negotiating oversight committee very shortly, after consultation with Mr Johnson.[19] In order to consolidate the result, obviously it would be important to get prominent federalists and members of the Quebec Liberal Party to accept it publicly. The position of Mr Johnson on the legitimacy of the result would be absolutely crucial to the sovereigntists' plans for consolidating the win. So would be the attitude of influential Quebec Liberals such as Claude Ryan and Claude

Castonguay, and so would be the views at the grassroots of the party. If the Quebec Liberal Party – or a large portion of it – accepted the Yes result, then the sovereigntists would be well on their way to making it irreversible.

The PQ government had been working on a detailed partnership proposal for some time. This contained specific provisions about all the major dossiers to be negotiated, and their broad lines would be made public immediately.[20] In an atmosphere of grave economic uncertainty, the sovereigntists were hoping that federalists, especially in the business community, would be pressuring Ottawa to respond. Even before then, the Quebec government would be urging its federal counterpart to issue reassuring statements about the debt, which then could be presented as the definitive opening of substantive negotiations.[21] Mr Bouchard, who would return to Ottawa right after the Yes victory, would use the platform provided by the Bloc in Parliament to present the offer and demand that talks begin.[22]

There were other plans. The National Assembly would be called back into session earlier than anticipated, probably within forty-eight hours. There, a motion would be passed accepting the referendum result and proposing that negotiations begin, and then debate on Bill 1 would continue, the measure being passed within weeks if not days.[23]

Meanwhile, the minister of finance and others would depart for the financial capitals of the world to reassure investors and to explain Quebec's plans for the transition to sovereignty. The province had completed its borrowing program early, in anticipation of the referendum, and had no immediate funding needs. Indeed, the Caisse de dépôt et placement, the Quebec government pension fund, had cash in place – billions of dollars – to stabilize the economic situation in the short term.[24]

At the same time, the sovereigntists would attempt to get other countries to take notice of the referendum result. The PQ had worked hard to lay the groundwork for this, especially in France. There, it was anticipated, the National Assembly would pass a resolution of congratulations and support.[25] Recognition would follow later, but the motion would put some pressure on the United States, as well as possibly sparking immediate provisional recognition from some of the lesser states of *La francophonie*. Shortly before the vote, Quebec's minister of international affairs, Bernard Landry, had sent letters to foreign ambassadors in Ottawa asking that their governments be prepared to recognize the result – and also a unilateral declaration of sovereignty, should it later occur.[26]

Letters were also sent by a Bloc member of Parliament to serving members of the Canadian military in Quebec. This letter invited them to prepare to transfer their allegiance in the event of a Yes vote. There is evidence that the sympathies of francophone members of the forces were divided, which would certainly have weakened the army's capacity to enforce federal authority in Quebec, but it is most probable that the command structure would have remained intact.[27]

The sovereigntists were clearly prepared for a UDI. They anticipated that Ottawa would be brought to the bargaining table by financial uncertainty, especially about the debt, and by their early moves to consolidate the Yes vote and make it irreversible. But they also suspected that the federalists might refuse to negotiate quickly. Ottawa might aim to hold a referendum or an election, in which case the sovereigntists hoped that the consensus in favour of accepting the Yes would simply make Quebecers reaffirm the original result as a fait accompli. On the other hand, if Ottawa opted for a federal-provincial conference followed by the offer of a constitutional reform package, the sovereigntists were prepared to depict this as a refusal by ROC to accept Quebecers' democratic decision.

Even before such events, however, some sovereigntists were ready to use the authority conveyed by the Yes vote and Bill 1 to declare a UDI if Ottawa refused to negotiate. While predicting that ROC would indeed be forced to the table, Mr Bouchard made this position quite clear during the campaign: "If Ottawa says it will not negotiate, that it does nothing, then Mr Parizeau will be obligated to draw the conclusions of his mandate which will require him to proclaim sovereignty immediately, which would not be in the federal government's interest."[28] A UDI would have profoundly deepened economic and political uncertainty, and in fact the threat of such a declaration might have served as the final weapon to force Ottawa to the negotiating table. Whether a UDI would have been declared cannot be known for sure. It would have depended on the success of the sovereigntists in generating solidarity and on the conditions prevailing after a Yes victory.[29]

Had there been a Yes vote, the federalists in Ottawa would have confronted a limited set of alternatives. These include calling an election, holding a referendum of one kind or another, and doing nothing. None would be palatable. It seems very likely that Ottawa would have initially resisted a Yes vote. The justification would be as argued during the referendum campaign – that the question was not clear and that the sovereigntists had made duplicitous promises about the partnership to be negotiated with ROC. It was deeply frustrating to the No side that these promises had not been countered successfully and that a substantial percentage of Quebecers believed that after a Yes they would retain Canadian citizenship, send members of

Parliament to Ottawa, use the Canadian dollar, and so forth. The "fact" that voters were misinformed could be used to justify setting aside a Yes referendum result, but the logic here is dubious; and if most Quebecers were convinced that the referendum process had been transparent and fair, then rejecting the result could well create greater solidarity in support of it.[30]

The strategy of refusing to negotiate Quebec's secession could involve assembling a new constitutional offer or holding a referendum in which Quebecers could register their disillusionment with their leaders and their disaffection from a project that was proving very painful economically.[31] Whether the sovereigntists' efforts to consolidate their victory could be countered in this way would depend on several factors. First is the amount of economic damage, and this would have been very substantial as capital (and people) fled from Quebec and as uncertainty raised the economic losses there. But the effects of a declining Canadian dollar and rising interest rates would also be felt right across the country.[32] The second factor is solidarity in Quebec, which would be a function of who would be blamed by the average voter for the economic damage – Ottawa for refusing to negotiate and prolonging the uncertainty or the sovereigntists for leading Quebecers to the Yes result? There was some intense debate about this issue before the referendum, and the answer is not obvious.[33] It would depend largely on the perceived legitimacy of the result.

A crucial factor for Ottawa would be the degree of solidarity in ROC behind the decision not to negotiate. On this, there would be division among political elites. There would certainly be some support for Ottawa's position,[34] but some well-informed and sympathetic observers of Quebec might argue that the Yes should be accepted.[35] The president of the Canadian Labour Congress, for example, was on record as saying that Quebecers' choice had to be respected,[36] and on the right wing of the ideological spectrum some powerful figures, including Conrad Black, were also arguing that a Yes had to be recognized.[37] They would be joined by the Reform Party, which, because of its democratic principles and pragmatic self-interest, was committed to accept a 50-per cent-plus-one referendum result. Reform would oppose any stopgap constitutional offer to Quebec that included distinct society recognition.

Among the public, opinion would also be divided. Well before the vote, polls showed substantial sympathy in ROC for the demands of Aboriginals and others to remain in Canada, a disinclination to accept any Quebec right of secession, and support for a threshold higher than 50 per cent. It was also widely expected that any negotiations about sovereignty would be protracted; and just before referendum day, a poll found that 53 per cent of ROC residents favoured a national referendum before the start of any such negotiations.[38] But other polls gave different results. In the summer of 1995, one poll found that 17 per cent of respondents in ROC thought a Yes should mean that negotiations start, 33 per cent favoured "letting Quebec go," 30 per cent wanted a referendum, and 12 per cent thought Ottawa should refuse to negotiate: so 50 per cent were prepared to allow secession.[39]

These variations in results occur because of differences in the questions posed and the response categories. Moreover, the questions were hypothetical, because until the very end of the campaign, few people in ROC believed that a Yes vote was at all possible.[40] More important, except on basic attitudes confirmed by many surveys, such as people's sense of national or regional identification, poll results are not reliable indicators of what policies citizens would really have supported after a Yes. The respondents are not in the midst of a momentous event, where a deep sense of crisis provides scope for opinions to change. Further, questions in polls do not allow for the trade-offs that would have to be made in such a context. There might be considerable support in the abstract for Aboriginals' desire to remain in Canada, for example, but would this stand up if the value of people's homes and savings were declining sharply?

The answer would depend on the extent of economic damage, and the evidence is that it would be considerable, right across the country. Combined with regional variations in sympathy for Quebec, this means that there would be sharp regional differences in support for a federal government that attempted to hold out against a Yes. It seems highly likely that the overall economic cost would create pressure within the caucus and cabinet to accept the result, and there might be statements to the same effect by one or more provincial premiers. This would make a holdout strategy very difficult to sustain.

The conclusive factor in both ROC and Quebec, however, would be the legitimacy of a Yes result. One element in this is the margin of victory. With a 53 or 52 per cent Yes, the sovereigntists would probably be able to consolidate the result, and opinion in ROC would not countenance a refusal by Ottawa to negotiate. But the logic of accepting a 53 or 52 per cent Yes leads to accepting 50 per cent plus one, and while the sovereigntists would have difficulty rallying Quebecers to accept this, Ottawa would encounter resistance in refusing it.[41]

Legitimacy would also depend on the question. The federalists constantly attacked its ambiguity, while the sovereigntists defended its clarity. There is no doubt that the question could have been clearer and more straightforward. But among Quebec voters, it seems unlikely that the nature of the question could have legitimized a refusal by Ottawa to accept the result. It is true that at the beginning of the campaign, many Quebecers found the question ambiguous,[42] and different people may have been voting with very different expectations about what a Yes would bring, but after a long and intense campaign fought in large part precisely over the implications of a Yes vote, it seems unlikely that objections to the question itself could have rallied public support in Quebec against accepting the result. Most people seemed to feel that they knew what they were voting for. Objections based on the question would be even less persuasive in ROC, where many citizens, unsympathetically, would simply dismiss the Quebec electorate as uninformed. More important, the majority of the attentive public had seen a vigorous campaign by the federalists to the effect that a Yes vote – on this question – meant "separation." In an economic crisis, it is improbable that public opinion in ROC would support a rejection of the result simply on the grounds that the question had been ambiguous.[43]

But legitimacy would also depend on process, and this would have been the Achilles heel of the sovereigntists had the referendum produced a narrow Yes victory. They could not have consolidated the result, because there had been corrupt electoral practices. This is surprising, and to many people shameful, but it would have been decisive.

In the referendum there were 4,757,509 ballots cast, and 86,501 were rejected. This rejection rate of 1.82 per cent was lower than in the 1992 Quebec referendum on the Charlottetown Accord and lower than in the provincial elections of 1989 and 1994. However, the rates were extraordinarily high in three ridings: Chomedey (11.61 per cent), Margeurite-Bourgeoys (5.50 per cent), and Laurier-Dorion (3.60 per cent), and these were antisovereignty ridings, where the No vote (among the valid ballots) amounted to 72.6 per cent in the first two and 62.8 per cent in the third. In some polls within these ridings, the proportion of rejected ballots was astounding. Poll 143 in Chomedey had 12 valid Yes votes, 67 No votes, and 50 rejected ballots for a 38.8 per cent rejection rate; poll 150b had 16 Yes, 45 No, and 77 rejected for a rate of 55.8 per cent.[44]

Such an extraordinary rejection rate suggested that a conspiracy existed within the sovereigntist (government) side to systematically eliminate No ballots. This hypothesis was later rejected by the chief electoral officer after a thorough investigation by his officers and by lawyers, academics, and a respected anglophone judge.[45] As well, a statistical analysis demonstrated that when these three extraordinary ridings were eliminated, there was no significant relationship across the province between the percentage of spoiled ballots and the level of the No vote.[46] Nevertheless, charges of electoral fraud eventually were laid against twenty-eight deputy returning officers, who had allegedly rejected valid ballot papers in a "patently unreasonable manner," and against two official delegates for the Yes national committee in Chomedey and Marguerite-Bourgeoys, who had allegedly urged the officers to do so.[47] When ballot papers were later examined in 289 polling stations, it was determined that in the 89 Chomedey stations studied, between 10.6 and 50 per cent of the ballots had been rejected in a "patently unreasonable" manner; the comparable figures in Marguerite-Bourgeoys were 32.8 per cent to 47 per cent.[48]

It was never revealed whether the rejected ballots were disproportionately No votes, but that is irrelevant to the political implications of the abnormal rejection rate. People could and certainly would have assumed that valid No votes had been unfairly rejected. And they would have assumed this immediately. The official inquiries took a long time to be mounted and to reach their conclusions, but rejection rates were published in newspapers on 31 October, and the abnormalities were quite evident to Quebecers. Similarly, in the wake of the No victory, it took some time for indignation to mount in ROC about this issue and for investigations to be made by the press.[49] Had there been a narrow Yes victory, the questioning would have been immediate. In view of the glaring anomalies, every rejected ballot throughout the province would have been considered a potential No vote, and the legitimacy of the result would have been deeply contested.

It is true that irregularities were also found on the No side, in connection with the funding of the pro-Canada rally in Montreal. But for the average citizen in Quebec or ROC, the fairness of this would be debatable. The rejection of valid ballots would not. Similarly, while neither Quebec federalists nor most citizens in the rest of the country would support a federal government objecting to a Yes vote on the obscure grounds that the question was not clear, there would be outrage were it suspected that the result was manipulated and the Yes vote achieved by deceit. This means that in order for a Yes to have had a chance of being regarded as legitimate, the sovereigntist margin would have had to be at least 50 per cent of the valid votes plus the total number of rejected ballots; that is, 51.85 per cent of the valid ballots. Even then, an odour of fraud would have lingered over the result. What if some of the Yes votes were not really valid?

With such transparent irregularities in the democratic process and widespread suspicion of fraud, the sovereigntists would not have been able to consolidate their victory – unless the margin of victory had been very substantial. Assuming that it was not, one could expect opposition on many fronts. There would be massive protests in the affected ridings and in the anglophone regions of Montreal. The federal government would seize on the voting irregularities to justify refusing to accept a Yes. Prominent Quebecers would hesitate before rallying to the Yes. The Quebec Liberal leadership would not accept a tainted result, and many on the Yes side would have qualms about taking decisive action when manifestly legitimate demands for recounts were mounting. International recognition would be slow in coming, from France or any other country.[50] It would be difficult to pass Bill 1, let alone a UDI, and this could not be done quickly with Quebecers deeply divided. If a UDI was passed, Ottawa could reserve or disallow the act, very probably with solid support in ROC. Even if the costs were very great, Canadians would not be prepared to countenance "letting Quebec go" by electoral fraud.

All of this would allow those interests within Quebec that were opposed to sovereignty – the Aboriginals and the partitionists – to mobilize, and the arguments for their case would fall on fertile moral ground. There would perhaps be time for a reference to the Supreme Court on the legalities of secession, or to mount a federally organized referendum on a different question, or to call an election while the sovereigntists were still in disarray. But it is probable that, long before this, a weakened and divided PQ government facing political protests and an economic crisis would have withdrawn Bill 1, its victory stolen by its own fervent supporters.

In short, the "inevitable secession" would not have come about. That scenario depended on a legitimate result and economic uncertainty forcing rapid acceptance of the principle that Quebec would secede, and on events then moving very quickly towards Quebec's sovereignty and the reconstitution of ROC. Unless the Yes margin had been very substantial indeed, the electoral fraud would have delegitimized it and would have lent support to the leaders who were eager to resist it, despite the mounting economic losses. Canadians – and Quebecers – would have been prepared to pay a high price to oppose a result that could convincingly be portrayed as undemocratic and illegitimate.

CHAPTER FOUR

The Fallout of the Referendum

The purpose of the predecessor of this book, *The Secession of Quebec and the Future of Canada*, was to predict what would happen after a Yes vote in the 1995 Quebec referendum. Its projections were based on analyses of the Canadian economy and society and the political forces at play, as well as comparative studies of the process of secession. One essential contention was that the politics of a secession would be fundamental. Legal arguments might be deployed as weapons by each side, and politicians and publics would also be influenced by economic changes and interests, but the outcomes would be determined by the political events that would follow a Yes.

A second basic argument was that secessions are historic events. This means, first, that they have momentous consequences. It also means that "high politics" are important. In a crisis, decisions taken by a small number of political leaders are critical; more technically, leaders have a great deal of autonomy when decisions must be made quickly and the degree of uncertainty is very large. As well, secessions are historic in that they are path-dependent. At any point, what happens next depends very much on the preceding events, and in the course of secessions there are significant irreversibilities. Big decisions are taken that place events on a particular path, and there can be no going back to revisit options that have been discarded.

Finally, all secessions are different. While there are important commonalities in the developments that bring the issue to the fore, and while the politics of secessions are marked by similar patterns, each case has its distinct features that must be grasped.[1] This last contention applies not only across countries but also within cases, over time. So it is essential to consider what has changed in Canada since the 1995 referendum. In examining the fallout of that episode, it becomes apparent that near-secessions are also historic events. The 1995 referendum capped a tough, searing campaign and produced an outcome that few anticipated. What were the consequences? What changed in Canada and Quebec because of the referendum? Here, evidence suggests that a great deal has changed – players, expectations, opinions, organizations, and strategies. In line with our basic contentions about history, it is clear that the 1995 referendum had big consequences, and that these make it unsound to transfer predictions made about it, in their totality, to any future Yes vote. When thinking about a future Quebec referendum, we cannot avoid taking the recent past into account.

One striking feature is the turnover in political leadership. In Quebec, after Mr Parizeau's resignation, Mr Bouchard became leader of the PQ and consequently premier of the province. The Bloc leadership was assumed by Michel Gauthier and then, after some internal dissension forced him to resign and issued in a hard-fought leadership contest, by Gilles Duceppe, the party's former House leader. In Ottawa, Brian Tobin, a principal organizer of the unity rally in Montreal, left the federal cabinet to assume the Liberal leadership in Newfoundland and become premier, replacing Clyde Wells, a determined opponent of special recognition for Quebec. In British Columbia, Glen Clark took over the NDP leadership and won a narrow election victory: although this was not a direct consequence of the referendum, it has had important repercussions because the BC agenda is primarily a provincial one, just as the Ontario agenda is under Mike Harris, and both involve feuds with Ottawa about national standards and provincial powers. There have also been new premiers in Prince Edward Island, Nova Scotia, and New Brunswick.

After the referendum, Mr Chrétien moved quickly to bolster his Quebec strength. Into the cabinet as minister of intergovernmental affairs he brought Stéphane Dion, an outspoken and provocative opponent of sovereignty, along with Pierre Pettigrew, a cerebral businessman who soon became minister of human resources development, charged with negotiating with the provinces a wide range of sensitive and expensive responsibilities, including employment training and federal transfers for social programs.

Apart from these very considerable changes, there have been shifts in several factors relevant to any future referendum. The credibility of the Chrétien Liberals on constitutional matters was weakened in ROC by the near-victory of the Yes side. They were open to attack for "almost losing the country," as was demonstrated by Preston Manning during the campaign leading to the federal election of 2 June 1997. Reform argued then that the approach of the "old-line", "Quebec-based" parties had failed to resolve the national unity problem and that Canada needed a new constitutional foundation – equality of the provinces and a massive decentralization of powers. As will be shown in the next chapter, this message helped solidify Reform's western support.

Within Quebec the federalists appeared tired and dispirited because of the referendum experience. They had to operate in very close cooperation with their Ottawa counterparts, which restricted their autonomy, and they were frustrated by the slow response of Mr Chrétien on the constitutional front. Mr Johnson easily survived a leadership review, but the Quebec Liberal Party has been left with the task of fashioning a constitutional position within a very limited range of manoeuvre. On the other hand, its main opponent, Mr Bouchard, is now charged with the responsibility of governing under very severe financial constraints, and public disaffection because of unpopular decisions provides hope for the Quebec Liberals about their prospects in a provincial election to be held before the end of 1999.

Then there are the shifts in public opinion. In Quebec, support for sovereignty actually rose after the referendum, and the Yes and No sides continued to be very evenly matched.[2] At the same time, although Quebecers consistently rated the economy and jobs as their principal concerns, substantial majorities continued to be dissatisfied with the operation of the federal system and to favour recognition of Quebec as a distinct society, the decentralization of powers, and a constitutional veto.[3] Throughout 1996, the proportion of Quebecers expecting the province eventually to become sovereign fell by over 21 per cent (to 53 per cent),[4] but the principle of Quebec self-determination continued to be supported by a majority of the population.[5] The prospect of the partnership also remained important; in polls asking how respondents would vote if there were no chance of negotiations with Canada being successful, the number inclined to vote Yes fell substantially.[6] All this suggests that the broad contours of public opinion in Quebec changed relatively little after the October 1995 referendum.

However, one striking change caused by the referendum is the organization and radicalization of interests within Quebec that are opposed to secession. The Aboriginal peoples, especially the Inuit of northern Quebec, have steadfastly maintained their opposition to being included within a seceding Quebec. They assert forcefully that they cannot be separated from Canada without their consent. Their view that Quebec should be partitioned and that their right of self-determination could be exercised has been well propagated and has attracted some support from the federal government.[7] Both their Aboriginal rights under the Canadian constitution and new protections that may emerge from a United Nations working group on indigenous peoples' rights could lay a basis for contesting Quebec's claim to all its territory.[8]

Much more dramatic was the changing mood in the anglophone community in Quebec. The referendum left many non-francophones in bitter despair, frustrated by the narrowness of the Yes defeat, the voting fraud, Mr Parizeau's blaming of "money and ethnic votes," and their continuing economic losses caused by political uncertainty. Within weeks, many new grassroots organizations were forming, and pressures were building for more radical positions within established organizations such as Alliance Québec (which had atttempted to build mutual understanding across the ethnic divide). These new groups included Stability, the Citizens' Committee for a New Province, the October 27 Group, the Quebec Committee for Canada, the Quebec Political Action Committee, and the United Quebec Federalists.[9] Spurred on by the hosts of radio talk-shows, by other journalists, and by more radical political leaders, anglophones mobilized at several impressive demonstrations, including one at the McGill Law School in January 1996 that drew 1,200 people and one in June on Parliament Hill that attracted 7,000.[10]

The anglophone groups had several objectives. First was some guarantee of federal government protection should a future sovereignty referendum carry. As embodied in a petition organized by a councillor for the municipality of Hampstead, for example, the request was for "public assurances that our rights as Canadians will be respected and that we will not be abandoned" after a Yes vote.[11] A second thrust was for partition – that parts of the province where the federalists formed a majority should be excluded from the territory of a sovereign Quebec. Such a partition might involve much of the Ottawa Valley and large portions of Montreal. In the past, this idea had been confined to a tiny minority, but intense pressure to support the principle was exerted on politicians at all levels of government and especially on municipal councils. A coalition of eighteen groups pressed municipalities such as Dollard-des-Ormeaux to pass resolutions calling on "the Government of Canada to ensure that its territory remain part of Canada irrespective of the result of any future province-wide referendum ... in accordance with the legal, moral, political, constitutional, and territorial obligations of our nation."[12]

The partitionist movement received some encouragement from the federal government, though its corrosive effects on Quebec politics led many moderate anglophones to reject it, and commentators outside Quebec declared it unrealistic.[13]

A third thrust was in the sensitive area of language. Anglophone groups pressed for the right to see English signs in stores, concentrating on the west island of Montreal. Several demonstrations were organized, along with boycotts of major retailers, most of whom acceded to their customers' demands.[14] Again, this initiative drew some support from the federal government while provoking harsh criticism from PQ ministers and leading more resources to be allocated to enforcing the language laws.[15] Like the other initiatives of the Quebec anglophones, it placed the Quebec Liberal Party in a difficult position, because electoral success against the sovereigntists could only be achieved with solid support from both the anglophone community and the votes of a large minority of francophones. Upsetting the linguistic peace would make that coalition much harder to assemble.[16]

In ROC, the referendum was accompanied by an upsurge in concern about national unity and a blip in public approval of measures to accommodate Quebec, such as distinct society recognition.[17] This was short-lived. By the end of 1995, there was consistent support in ROC for decentralizing functions to the provinces, but there was very little enthusiasm for any special consideration for Quebec. Fully 58 per cent were against recognizing Quebec in the constitution as a distinct society, and 72 per cent were against a Quebec constitutional veto; only a slim 54 per cent majority favoured making some accommodative response to Quebec in light of the referendum result.[18] Even right after the referendum, 38 per cent of British Columbians said they would rather have Quebec separate than recognize it as a distinct society.[19] Clearly, the majority ROC view rejected special status. At the end of 1995, only 22 per cent of people in ROC regarded Canada as a "pact between two founding groups," while 75 per cent agreed that it is "a relationship between ten equal provinces."[20]

On the one hand, there appears to have developed in ROC a disinterest in the Quebec issue, especially in the western provinces. At the end of 1995, 67 per cent of British Columbians agreed that if Quebecers voted to separate, Canada should "just let them go" rather than "do everything it can to convince them to stay."[21] One year later, with 42 per cent of all Canadians thinking it was likely or very likely that Quebec would separate within ten years, fully 47 per cent of people in ROC favoured letting Quebec go.[22] On the other hand, attitudes towards Quebec hardened after the referendum. Just three months afterwards, as Ottawa was attempting both to accommodate Quebec and to clarify the ground rules of secession, only 17 per cent favoured trying harder to find a compromise, while 46 per cent believed in taking a "tougher stand."[23] A year later, 63 per cent in ROC approved of emphasizing tough secession conditions, and only 13 per cent thought the federal government should "focus on giving Quebec some of the changes it wants."[24] So there was considerable support for an uncompromising approach to the province, both in principle – because of provincial equality – and strategically, from the sense that a harder line about the consequences of secession would deter Quebecers from voting Yes in the future.[25] In any case, there was no sign of change in the strong majorities in ROC against important elements of the sovereigntists' partnership proposals, such as shared citizenship, a common currency, and the free movement of labour.[26]

On the surface, there seems to be little evidence that the referendum produced a shift in Canadians' expectations that Quebecers will vote Yes in the future or that Quebec will separate sooner or later.[27] But poll results about these issues mask a profound change, one that has had – and will have – great effects on how the secession issue unfolds. Simply enough, the very close result in the October 1995 referendum has forced Canadians to think about Quebec secession and what would happen in the case of a Yes vote. Before the referendum, very few Canadians took the prospect seriously or thought much about its consequences. They may have believed, vaguely, that Quebec would or would not separate, but few had firm expectations about the event itself. October 30 changed all that. It made Canadians realize that Quebecers might vote Yes, and it made them think about what this would portend. Millions of Canadians, for the first time, contemplated these questions: What would a Yes vote mean for Canada? How would a Yes vote – and a Quebec secession – affect me? How would my governments react? Even more important, they asked, What *should* my governments do?

This change in expectations has profoundly altered the political landscape of Canada. As Alan Cairns put it, "Outside Quebec, there is a palpable change of mood. It is the ROC version of what happened in Quebec after Meech when, according to Charles Taylor, 'something snapped.' [Well,] 'Something snapped' outside Quebec after the razor-thin victory for the No in the recent referendum."[28] Similarly, David Milne noted "a remarkable change" in Canadians outside Quebec: "Unlike the silence around such questions in the past, the people of ROC now accept that the terms of secession should be spelled out in a tough-minded and hardened spirit; they talk openly of force, of carving up Quebec's territory, and of demanding higher thresholds of consent in any future referendum; on 'track two' they now think about and plan for a Canada without Quebec; they toy with constituent assemblies and other previously radical options on process. Taboos around substance and process all fall before us."[29]

It is debateable whether most citizens in ROC failed to discuss Quebec secession in the past because of "taboos" or because they simply assumed it to be unlikely, but there is no doubt that the referendum had a profound impact on ordinary Canadians. In the wake of the vote, ordinary people as well as newspaper editorialists spoke of "Canada's fate" hanging in the balance, of the country being "in crisis," of watching "our beloved country come perilously close to slipping away," of Canada being at "the abyss," and of the "near-fatal referendum."[30] The polls may show that no greater numbers of Canadians expect Quebec to secede, but the expectations about secession are now embedded in the context of a highly visible game, in which current and future moves are widely understood among the public as being designed to deter it.[31] These moves include measures to accommodate Quebec nationalists and also efforts to make sovereignty appear more difficult or costly to achieve. As a result of the 1995 referendum, the public in ROC has demanded such strategems and follows them closely. Essentially, the referendum has focused attention on three major issues.

The first is the conduct of any future referendum on sovereignty and the process of secession itself. As will be shown, it is here that the federal government has concentrated much of its effort, and the referendum produced strong support for such initiatives. An Angus Reid poll at the end of 1995 found that 74 per cent of Canadians in ROC thought that the rest of the country should develop a "game plan" to deal with a possible Yes in a future referendum.[32] Beyond Ottawa and the public at large, issues of process have occupied business organizations, citizens' groups, and think tanks. A notable example lays out ten rules that should govern secession, given that the 1995 referendum shattered the old "strategy of studied indifference," as Canada suffered "a near-death experience."[33]

Political parties also have debated issues of process. Indeed, whether to prepare for a future Yes and how to respond to it were major issues in the 1997 federal election campaign. Most significantly perhaps, process issues have been taken up by provincial governments; they will expect to be involved in devising pre-referendum strategies, in negotiating with Quebec, and, of course, in designing any reconstitution of Canada. One example is provided by Alberta, where Premier Klein has emphasized that citizens would be involved in determining the province's position in any future constitutional talks.[34]

In Ontario, a legislative committee has recommended that referendums should be held to approve constitutional amendments (as well as tax increases).[35] While some other provinces, notably British Columbia, have such provisions in place, it is clear that this kind of procedural requirement would further reduce the leaders' room to manoeuvre in any future secession crisis.

The referendum immediately focused attention on a second issue – the terms to be negotiated with Quebec. In part this was because the campaign centred on the various elements of the sovereigntists' proposed partnership, but it was also a consequence of the shocking absence of government planning about the matters that secession would involve.[36] After the referendum, issues such as the division of the debt, the army, Quebec's borders, citizenship, Aboriginal and minority rights, international treaties, the currency, and economic arrangements with Quebec all received much more intense discussion in academe, think tanks, the media, business and citizens' groups, and public discourse.[37] One important strand of these debates has concerned Canadians' obligations to Aboriginals and federalists in Quebec, and the legitimacy of partitioning a seceding Quebec. Issues of rights and morality have therefore come to impinge much more significantly upon the question of secession. Again, as some actors take predetermined positions, the fluidity that would have marked a post-Yes situation in 1995 has been reduced. The current premier of Newfoundland, for example, has supported partition of Quebec, stating, "I happen to believe the country is not divisible, any more than Quebec is divisible. But if Bouchard argues that Canada is divisible by a vote, then so is Quebec."[38]

Of course, the terms of secession also involve matters of *realpolitik*. It is hardly surprising that the close referendum result led some provincial governments to assess the consequences of secession. The Ontario Ministry of Finance, for example, was reported to possess eleven documents on the effects of secession. These included studies of agreements between Ontario and Quebec and their business communities, the possible economic consequences of Quebec independence, models for dividing the national debt, relations between Ontario and its creditors in the event of secession, and possible relations between the governments of Canada and Quebec.[39] Such a strategic collection of information and its analysis is essential for contingency planning, and it was virtually absent before the 1995 referendum. Now it is not. In British Columbia, the premier appointed a special adviser on national unity matters. He commissioned studies about the province's options in the event of a Quebec secession, because

"B.C. has no game plan at all. There's nothing that sets out a practical explanation of what the fallout would be, and nothing concerning what B.C.'s position would be. The lack of any studies is alarming."[40]

Obviously, this preparatory work can lead provincial administrations to reach firm conclusions about how the terms of any secession should be tailored to fit their interests. The principle used to divide the national debt, for example, could have strong repercussions for the finances of different provinces, and these have now been understood by all of them. Considering the terms of secession can also lead to public commitments, as when the premier of Newfoundland declared that secession would mean that the contentious Churchill Falls power contract with Quebec would be broken.[41] A retreat from such positions could be very difficult in the event of a future Yes vote.

Finally, the 1995 referendum forced Canadians and their governments to think seriously about the shape of ROC after a future Yes vote and to consider how Canada would be reconstituted. In Atlantic Canada, apprehensions sharpened about the region's geographic isolation and its dependence on federal transfers, and the old issue of Maritime union came back onto the agenda.[42] Ontarians weighed the relative importance of their economic links with Quebec and with western Canada. And in the West, fears of domination by Ontario within a truncated Canada arose. Most notably, the special adviser in British Columbia was contemplating the possibility that his province might also become sovereign in the wake of a Quebec secession: "It's one option. We entered into Canada as a constitutional entity which includes Quebec. Without Quebec, there is no Canada. The Canadian constitution is invalid."[43] While ideas about western separation might be attractive to only a small minority, they have become part of the public debate simply because the 1995 referendum forced Canadians to consider seriously what their constitutional options would be if Quebecers voted Yes in the future.[44]

These changes in perceptions and expectations have profoundly altered the political landscape of ROC. What are their practical implications for the future and for any future Quebec secession? First, they have increased the chances of polarization between ROC and Quebec in the run-up to another referendum, in part because of the estrangement between the two communities – the very sense that they are two communities – which was noted by Alan Cairns in the wake of the 1995 referendum.[45] As well, actors in ROC will not leave a referendum debate to the federal government and Quebec Liberals. They will be more vocal and also more diverse, and some of the positions advanced will have the potential to alienate moderate Quebec nationalists. Moreover, issues such as Aboriginal rights and partition will be part of the debate, encouraged by extremists both within and outside the province, and inevitably infused with the emotion and absolutism intrinsic to debates about rights and morality.

More important, the whole element of surprise has been lost. In the "inevitable secession" scenarios, it was generally posited that a Yes vote in 1995 would suddenly shock a largely unprepared ROC and that the prevailing economic uncertainty would impel leaders to accept secession in principle and move quickly to settle major issues. Although Ottawa's legitimacy would erode gradually, irreversible decisions would have set the secession on its course. There would not be time for opposition – from provinces, citizens' groups, or business – to mobilize effectively. But organization and contingency planning have both taken place now, and political actors will have their demands prepared if another referendum is held. A critical demand will be for participation. After a Yes in the 1995 referendum, in the disarray that would have existed, it was probable that the federal government could have taken a leading role, with decisions being taken at the centre before other actors could demand involvement. This will be far less likely in the future, because citizens, provincial governments, the Aboriginal peoples, and political parties have all assessed their interests and will insist on participating to protect them.

Not only will the negotiating arena be more crowded, but it will be less fluid, because the major actors will bring pre-established positions to the debate. The division of the national debt is a good example. While there are good reasons to settle on population as the principle for its division, a case can also be made for allocating it according to gross domestic product. This would require Quebec to take a slightly smaller share, and some provincial administrations might prefer this – Ontario because it would weaken the Quebec economy less, and the Atlantic provinces because their future implicit obligations would be much lower than under the population principle. But Alberta and British Columbia would be strongly opposed; having assessed their situation and weighed scenarios, they would be most reluctant to accept a principle that would saddle them with a much larger debt share if Canada fragmented and they became sovereign entities. Such pre-established positions are likely to be taken on all the major dossiers to be negotiated with a seceding Quebec. This means that decisions will be much harder to take because of the numerous actors involved. It also transforms the decision-making process from one that was serial and open-ended (with the most critical issues being settled quickly and emerging problems dealt with next) to one that is simultaneous (with all issues on the table at once, subject to complex trade-offs and logrolling). Under these conditions, speedy and efficient agreements would be unlikely.

A final result of these changes renders a quick, clean secession even less likely. This is the linkage of two separate sets of negotiations, those about the terms and conditions of Quebec sovereignty and those about the reconstitution of ROC. In the pre-1995 scenarios of the "inevitable secession," Ottawa and the Government of Quebec would begin to deal with the issues surrounding secession immediately after a Yes vote, with participation widening gradually as the emergency faded. As this occurred, the attention of people in ROC would shift towards the reconstitution of Canada, and it was probable that the result would closely resemble the current constitution. This is because Quebec secession would largely be a *fait accompli*, because the very process of negotiating collectively with Quebec would heighten solidarity in ROC, and because no provincial government would be prepared to plunge the country into uncertainty again by withholding consent to the constitutional amendments necessary to excise Quebec and maintain Canada as a going concern.

Now, however, the secession issues and constitutional issues are linked. It is highly likely that Quebec secession can only be accomplished legally through amendments to the Constitution Acts, which will require the unanimous consent of Ottawa and all provinces, and that this will become widely understood. So every provincial government will be aware before a future referendum that, in theory, it can block secession (and also veto the reconstitution of ROC over matters such as representation in the House of Commons, the make-up of the Senate, and so on); and provincial governments may be more prepared to do so as a consequence of advance analysis and planning.

More gravely, the whole set of Canada-Quebec issues about the terms of secession will be subject to provincial agreement. These substantive matters will be linked to Quebec's exit through a constitutional amendment. Even though many of the issues to be resolved fall squarely within federal jurisdiction, any provincial administration determined to win its way on some substantive matter will be able to threaten to withhold constitutional approval, and this linkage means that the two sets of issues will be on the table simultaneously and that all governments will have to agree to a total package. Quebec's sovereignty, the terms of secession, and the reconstitution of ROC will all be inextricably linked.[46] This was definitely not the case before the 1995 referendum when the almost universal lack of preparedness for the crisis of a Yes vote would have been conducive to a clean, rapid secession and a strong Canada outfitted with a familiar constitution.

One other significant change was wrought by the 1995 referendum. This was the perception of the sovereignty issue held by foreign actors.

In any secession, the attitude of other countries is important, and not only did the referendum campaign heighten worldwide interest in the Quebec case, but the close result appears to have induced other countries (especially the United States) to reappraise their policy on Canadian unity.

Abroad, the run-up to the referendum was accompanied by increased academic interest in Quebec secession,[47] and the campaign itself drew a lot of attention from the international media.[48] This was especially true in the United States, to which Canadian politicians had carried their debate directly, as when Mr Parizeau and Mr Johnson contributed contending articles to the influential journal *Foreign Policy*.[49] The former sought to reassure Americans about Quebec's commitment to democracy, free trade, financial responsibility, and minority rights, while the latter drew American attention to fundamental uncertainties that a Yes vote would bring in such matters as the internal economic union, citizenship, mobility, the currency, and the division of the debt.

As the campaign tightened, the Quebec issue drew more attention in official circles.[50] The Clinton administration revised the traditional mantra of "excellent relations with a strong and united Canada" and non-interference in Canadian affairs to a stance more supportive of unity, with hints that existing arrangements with Quebec would not continue in the event of a secession. This did not generate much domestic attention, but the very close result did. Editorialists across the United States drew from it implications for American policy about multiculturalism, and they stressed that important American interests were at stake in the referendum. A conclusion underlined by most of them was that the close vote had settled nothing and Canada's future remained profoundly uncertain.[51]

After the referendum, the international context of Quebec secession remained important. The prime minister of France visited the province to assure Quebecers "that tomorrow, regardless of the choice of your destiny, France will always be at your side"[52] (and the publication of Mr Parizeau's thoughts about French recognition of Quebec sovereignty stirred up the 1997 federal election campaign).[53] In the United States, there was even more involvement, for Canadian issues were now squarely on the agenda, generating a new round of analysis and planning.

Opinion pieces in the United States profoundly questioned both American indifference towards Canada and the accepted wisdom about national unity.[54] A more important sign of rethinking was a major article published in *Foreign Affairs* by Charles Doran, a leading Canada watcher and international relations specialist.[55] Doran argued that the United States had to contemplate the possibility of Quebec secession because of its great implications for American interests. More provocatively, he argued that Canada might well fragment under the impact of this event, because there would be less incentive for inter-regional redistribution, a jarring geographic discontinuity between the parts of the Canada that were left, and deep suspicion in western Canada about Ontario dominance.

In Doran's view, the "unravelling" of Canada would inevitably mean greater responsibilities for the United States as "peacemaker, adjudicator, rule-maker, and police officer"; hence, "Washington must be prepared for all contingencies."[56] In particular, the United States must design plans for "a form of supranational affiliation with the remnants of Canada."[57] This arrangement would lie midway between accession to American statehood (which would be too disruptive domestically) and simple treaty arrangements (which would be too weak and would leave room for "overseas interests" to become involved). The new "political affiliation" would allow for the free movement of goods, services, capital, and people, with the United States providing foreign security and a military (in which Canadians would serve).[58] Accession to statehood might come eventually but, in the meantime, "North America could look more like the former Soviet Union, with one large state at the centre, the United States, edged by a series of small, isolated, weak entities along its northern border." In any case, Doran called for more imaginative thinking in Washington about "how to manage the aftermath of Quebec separation, which should no longer seem impossible or remote."[59]

This piece drew some sharp responses, but it undoubtedly both reflected and helped crystallize American thinking about Quebec secession.[60] Further evidence of concern in the United States was provided during a brief hearing of a House of Representatives subcommittee in September 1996. Here, the legislators heard about the stakes of secession for the United States. While the strategic and military implications of secession were much reduced as a result of the end of the Cold War, there could be important ramifications for U.S. trade, direct investment in Canada, hydroelectric supplies, transportation on the St Lawrence, holders of Canadian bonds, and the flow of tourists and migrants.[61] Also discussed at some length were the likelihood of secession, how to send signals to Quebecers about what American policy would be in the event of a secession (especially with respect to the difficulties of accession to the NAFTA), and the imperative of advance American planning for a Yes vote in a future referendum.[62] As one expert put it, "I really think that we need to be prepared should Quebec become independent. Not because it is likely, not because it is necessarily inevitable, but because we should never be caught as off guard as we have been in the past."[63]

Some evidence not only of American concern but also of basic rethinking was provided when a senior foreign service officer published an article arguing that "a cool-eyed appraisal of Quebec independence indicates that its dangers have been overstated."[64] The essential thrust of the piece was that Quebecers might well vote for sovereignty if their constitutional grievances were not resolved but that Quebec, as a democratic, rich, peaceful, trading nation, posed no threat to America's essential interests. In consequence, while Canadian unity was definitely to be preferred, the United States "must be intellectually prepared for a sovereign Quebec," and the administration should not provide "open-ended" support for a Canadian government desperate for some dissuasive American interventions in a future referendum campaign.[65] This stance was disavowed by the State Department, of course, but the article attests to the impact that the 1995 referendum had on American calculations about Quebec secession.

Apparently, there has been no comprehensive assessment of the effects that Quebec sovereignty would have on the United States since one was conducted in 1977.[66] There is no agreement now that a firm contingency plan should be prepared, because the situation remains fluid, a vote for sovereignty could still allow time for appropriate strategies to be devised, and public statements could actually increase the chance of a Yes vote.[67] But both in public and in private, American decision makers have confronted the issues of process and substance raised by the prospect of Quebec secession. These include whether to undertake a comprehensive assessment of the issue; whether to enter the Canadian debate by issuing statements about Quebec's succession to treaties and admission to NAFTA, for example; how to react to a UDI by Quebec, especially if Canada rejected it; whether to recognize Quebec's existing boundaries; how to support the Canadian dollar and the Canadian economy in the event of severe economic turmoil; how much to encourage close economic cooperation between Canada and a sovereign Quebec; and whether to promote post-secession unity in Canada or to prepare for a new political structure in North America.[68] These issues have also been plumbed in many conferences involving academics, journalists, and policy makers.[69] And ordinary Americans, in the wake of the referendum, have been exposed to a great deal more information about Canada and the Quebec issue, much of it pointing towards a future secession.[70]

The upshot of all of this is not clear to anyone outside the U.S. administration. No one should expect that some academic conferences and an hour-and-a-half hearing of a minor congressional subcommittee would either galvanize policy makers or accurately reflect their views. Canada remains low on the list of American priorities. It is unlikely that the State Department, the Treasury and the National Security Council have produced some new master strategy about Quebec secession. But Americans' estimate of the probability of secession has certainly been raised, as has their understanding of the substantive issues involved and their appreciation of the enormous stakes for their country's well-being.[71]

In the past, implicitly, Quebec secession was a Canadian domestic issue. It is so no longer. The United States will watch developments with vigilance, and a future referendum campaign would quickly bring Canada right to the fore in Washington. The Americans will no longer accept bland assurances from Ottawa that the situation is in hand, and their government will be ready to protect American interests. It will not countenance the interference of other parties in a future Quebec secession. Nor will it tolerate violence or prolonged economic disruption on its northern border.[72] There is no sign of a fundamental shift in U.S. policy towards favouring annexation of parts of Canada (which would entail tactics conducive to Quebec secession). The status quo is preferable to the disruption, both economic and political, that any secession would involve. Should Quebec secede, the United States would favour a united ROC and a rapid resolution of the crisis – as it would have if the Yes side had won in 1995. But in future the United States will be not only more vigilant but also more prepared to intervene to defend its vital interests.

A central message of the predecessor to this book, *The Secession of Quebec and the Future of Canada*, was that secessions are historic events. This is quite congruent with the basic conclusions to be drawn from the analysis of the impact of the 1995 referendum, because near-secessions are also historic events. The October 1995 referendum in Quebec was a searing emotional experience for millions of Canadians, and the close result was remarked around the world. The event produced profound changes among political actors and citizens in Quebec and across ROC. Now, different expectations prevail about the probability of secession, different and more strongly defined attitudes are held about secession's implications, and new strategies are in place both to promote it and to prevent it. Having contemplated Quebec secession, people are much more prepared to react to it. The course of any future secession is much more difficult to predict than was the case before the 1995 referendum, and a Yes vote might never occur. But if it does, one thing is certain – its consequences will not resemble those that would have occurred in 1995. The 1995 referendum is history.

CHAPTER FIVE

Manoeuvring towards the Next Referendum

Canada's constitutional dilemma was paramount on the political agenda after the 1995 contest about sovereignty. The federal government moved rapidly to implement some of the promises made during the referendum campaign, but these were not fully realized. In anticipation of the next referendum promised by the sovereigntists, the Chrétien Liberals developed a bifurcated ("two-track") strategy. One set of initiatives comprised Plan A, as this strand is commonly called – measures to accommodate Quebec in the constitution and to meet some of the province's traditional demands. The other set of initiatives, Plan B, involved clarifying the process and the implications of Quebec secession, and challenging the sovereigntists' assumptions about these matters. All these initiatives were controversial, as the course and results of the 1997 federal election demonstrated clearly. On both fronts – accommodating Quebecers and confronting the sovereigntists – the federal government moved cautiously and incrementally. So too, in administering Quebec, did the PQ government led by Lucien Bouchard.

THE QUEBEC GOVERNMENT'S STRATEGY

Three weeks after the referendum, Mr Bouchard announced his resignation as leader of the Bloc québécois and his intention to run for the leadership of the PQ.[1] Other potential candidates stood aside, and Lucien Bouchard was sworn in as premier on 29 January 1996. He made it clear from the outset that he was committed to another referendum on sovereignty but that his government would not amend the prevailing legislation that prohibited holding two referendums on similar questions during the life of a legislature.[2] Hence, another sovereignty referendum had to follow a provincial election, which could be held as late as the autumn of 1999. Were the PQ to win that election, another referendum on sovereignty could be held at any time during its mandate. The new premier seemed content to await an opportune time for a referendum. As he put it when declaring his candidacy for the PQ leadership, "Once our partner has drained the last dregs of its inability to recognize our reality as a people, another referendum opportunity will open itself up."[3]

On taking office, Mr Bouchard reconstructed the cabinet and focused his new government on Quebec's economic and social problems.[4] The major target was the provincial deficit, which had been neglected by the Parizeau administration and its predecessors and was increasingly anomalous in view of other provinces' efforts to balance their budgets. The approach taken was to forge a broad consensus among business, labour, and social groups about deficit reduction, government spending priorities, and economic growth. Mr Bouchard's strategy was to emphasize solidarity and mutual responsibility. This reflected the messages delivered during the referendum campaign, of course, but it also forced the various segments of Quebec society to make tradeoffs within the framework established by the government.[5]

The first step was to hold a major conference at which all organizations present accepted a zero-deficit target, proposed strategies to reach it, and established several major working groups.[6] In this, prominent federalist business people and even the Quebec Liberal Party (QLP) felt obliged to participate, because the government's goals were largely congruent with their own. This was followed by a budget that compressed spending, and by a balanced-budget bill setting out deficit levels through to the target of zero in 1999–2000.[7] Then there was a four-day summit meeting on employment and the economy in October 1996. Here, business, labour, and government agreed on a sweeping package of measures aimed at deficit reduction, deregulation, and job creation. Although some groups representing students, the poor, and women left the summit over social-spending cuts, the broad consensus reached gave the impression of progress and provided the government with a mandate for future measures favourable to business while permitting the premier to brandish his social-democratic credentials.[8]

The federalists hoped that the hard decisions necessary in Quebec would diminish the popularity of the PQ and of Mr Bouchard himself.[9]

For the first time in his career, the premier would assume general responsibiliby for governing, and his charismatic aura would become tarnished.[10] In fact, there is some evidence that support for sovereignty declined slightly over this period, along with intentions to vote PQ, but Mr Bouchard retained his personal popularity throughout this difficult time of reorienting the Quebec state.[11]

In part, this may have been due to his commitment to governing the province and also to the deep ambiguity that he brought to many issues which were potentially divisive, especially in the wake of the referendum. The deficit-reduction measures were generally favoured by the public as long as the government maintained its concern about job creation and solidarity with the poor. On language matters and relations with minority communities, the premier attempted to repair the damage caused by Mr Parizeau's remarks on referendum night, notably by calling a televised meeting of prominent English-speaking Montrealers and reassuring them about their rights.[12] At the economic summit, the government tended to ally itself with business by indicating that Montreal could be considered a "bilingual" city.[13] And the PQ eased the enforcement of "francization" in smaller businesses.[14] At the same time, however, it introduced legislation to reinstate the agency that enforced Quebec's language laws, and, in the face of aggressive anglophone agitation and after hearings by a committee of the National Assembly, it tightened the rules about using French in the public service.[15]

The language issue was linked with school-board reform, and this was one of several areas where the PQ government managed some cooperation with Ottawa. Proposals to reorganize school boards along linguistic rather than confessional (Roman Catholic/Protestant) lines were supported by francophones aiming for more certain integration of immigrants into their community and by anglophones who desired to consolidate their resources. But constitutional obstacles prevented rationalization. The PQ government announced, therefore, that it would seek a constitutional amendment, and Ottawa was quick to respond positively.[16] There were some demands by anglophones that their linguistic rights be constitutionalized as their religious rights had been, but Ottawa was not particularly receptive to the idea, even though the federal government promised to act only on a solid Quebec consensus in favour of the change.[17] This was achieved, with a unanimous vote in the National Assembly, and in short order a resolution to amend section 93 of the Constitution Act, 1867, was introduced in Parliament.[18] Its passage was delayed, however, and then stopped by the 1997 federal election. But after the Chrétien Liberals were returned to power, they were eager to introduce a measure that could demonstrate the flexibility of the federation, and the resolution passed a free vote in the House of Commons while surviving a vigorous debate in the Senate.[19] At the signing ceremony, Mr Dion noted with pleasure that this event showed that "the system of Canada works," while Quebec's minister of intergovernmental affairs acknowledged a "certain irony" in the PQ government using the amendment process of a constitution that it refused to accept.[20]

There were various other instances of cooperation. These were in areas where the federal government's desire to keep referendum commitments and to show that flexible federalism could help Quebecers coincided with the sovereigntists' need to demonstrate competent management and generate economic activity. At times, as when Mr Chrétien and Mr Bouchard met in mid-1996 to discuss economic issues, it was as though the two bitter opponents were prepared to make a bet on the effect of economic growth. The prime minister's reasoning was that "a good economy will induce Quebecers to stay in Canada," while the premier argued that "sovereignty will have to be built on a strong Quebec."[21] Mr Bouchard even took part in a Team Canada trade mission to Asia, stating, "I will never hesitate to spend all the time that is needed with a minister, a premier, the entire federal cabinet if I have to, to create jobs in Quebec."[22]

The two governments also agreed on many jointly funded infrastructure projects, and they cooperated with a wide range of organized interests in establishing a new agency, Montreal International, that was to revitalize the city's economy.[23] Most significantly, Ottawa and Quebec City successfully negotiated the transfer of control over employment training programs to the province. This met a traditional demand of Quebec governments and followed a PQ-QLP consensus favouring the transfer, along with a declaration by the new federal minister of human resources development that Ottawa would meet its commitment to withdraw from the delivery of training to the unemployed.[24] The federal offer was made to all the provinces, but it was especially well received in Quebec, and the PQ government came under considerable pressure to negotiate an agreement in good faith.[25] An accord was eventually signed in April 1997, with Mr Chrétien using the pre-election event to declare that he was keeping his promises and that federalism works, while Mr Bouchard argued that the transfer had taken thirty-two years to achieve and was only accomplished after Quebecers had voted strongly for sovereignty.[26]

Of course, there were also many areas of friction between Ottawa and Quebec City. These were most manifest in the area of social policy, where the Bouchard government aimed to innovate unilaterally – as in its $5-per-day child care initiative – rather than join with the other provinces to constrain the federal government. For example, its efforts to set up an extended family-leave program conflicted with Ottawa's expenditure priorities, as did its highly symbolic attempt to establish a provincial blood-bank system.[27] Similarly, it resisted central-government initiatives in funding university research.[28] But these skirmishes were not very much dramatized by the PQ government.

Overall, the PQ under Lucien Bouchard was oriented towards winning the next election rather than fighting a referendum on sovereignty. In fact, the whole sovereignty issue was downplayed. Although the government reacted sharply to the emerging elements of Ottawa's Plan B strategy, no coherent and concerted counterattack was launched against them. In the medium term, it was more important to demonstrate competence in government and to foster economic growth in order to win re-election and lay the groundwork for a Yes in a future referendum. Consequently, few resources were devoted to referendum strategy. Instead, Mr Bouchard's dexterity kept the administration moving forward within its very limited room to manoeuvre. He was also able to keep command of his followers, which is difficult when a mass programmatic party like the PQ actually takes power and is unable to implement all aspects of its platform.[29]

The premier certainly faced dissent within his party. PQ militants objected to the government's fixation on deficit reduction, which to the left wing of the party smacked of neoconservatism and which was strongly criticized by Mr Parizeau in an article published one year after the referendum.[30] Spending cuts threatened traditional party constituencies among women, students, and public-sector workers, and proposals to ease the use of English, especially in Montreal, were explosive. Finally, the premier's insistence on changing the party's program to embrace the post-sovereignty partnership with Canada aroused old suspicions among militants about his dedication to the core goal of the PQ.[31] At the first party convention held since he assumed the leadership, the government encountered grass-roots challenges, especially on language policy. More seriously, only 76.7 per cent of the delegates voted in favour of Mr Bouchard's leadership, a result that caused him to walk out of the convention amidst rumours of a possible resignation. On his return, however, he and his ministers not only managed to swing the members to their position, but Mr Bouchard demanded that the party close ranks, show more discipline, and support the platform – otherwise, clearly, he would resign.[32]

So the premier's position was formidable. This was shown after the economic summit when the government negotiated with the public-service workers, demanding that they accept reductions in the work week and in the overall salary package as the only alternative to large-scale layoffs.[33] With the budget looming, the government was able to force through a compromise involving early retirement, and it met its budget-reduction targets.[34] These struggles, along with the spending cuts in social services, education, and health, certainly cost the PQ government some support among its key allies. Negotiations about cuts in transfers to municipalities were especially difficult, as Quebec City alienated both mayors and municipal workers. Typically, Mr Bouchard isolated the intransigents, accusing them of attempting to escape the government's fiscal framework "au détriment des citoyens."[35] Yet in early 1997, almost 52 per cent of Quebecers were satisfied with the provincial government, and the PQ enjoyed a twelve-point lead over the QLP.[36] Support for sovereignty continued to hover at around 50 per cent.[37]

The success of the sovereigntists on the provincial stage was further demonstrated in the 1997 federal election campaign. This came to be dominated by the national unity issue (or "la question nationale"). Going into the campaign, the Bloc québécois had a relatively inexperienced and weak leader, Gilles Duceppe, and it was still divided by the recent leadership contest. As well, it had lost the support of a major ally, the Quebec Federation of Labour, and the early campaign was so disorganized that the management team was replaced.[38] Further, the whole sovereigntist movement was thrown into disarray by the release of a book by Mr Parizeau in which he seemed to put the lie to commitments made in 1995 about negotiating the partnership with Canada in good faith.

Despite all this, the sovereigntists united throughout the course of the campaign, based on the PQ organization, and in the end the Bloc took forty-four seats (down from fifty-four) and 38 per cent of the popular vote (down from 49.5 per cent). Clearly, the sovereigntists still constituted a potent political movement. Although there was disgruntlement within it and although important divisions remained – especially between the Parizeau hard-liners and the more inclusive nationalists led by the premier – it was dominated more than ever by Lucien Bouchard, whose presence had been vital during the campaign. In spite of the unpopular measures taken by the PQ government, Mr Bouchard had not stumbled. As one experienced observer noted at the outset of the campaign, "There should be no wishful thinking that his government will fail because it can't meet the challenges facing it and that the problem [of national unity] will solve itself."[39] Indeed, the sovereigntist strategy remained intact: govern well, win an election in 1998 or 1999, and then, at a propitious moment, call and win a referendum on sovereignty.

Necessarily, the federalist strategy was much more complex, because in the wake of the 1995 referendum shock, the Chrétien Liberals were faced with strong and conflicting pressures about how to handle national unity, and the QLP was weakened and dispirited. In Ottawa, the government moved incrementally in three ways. First, it aimed to continue its emphasis on good government. Thus, progress towards a balanced budget was continued (along with the substantial cuts in program spending and transfers to the provinces that this entailed), as were limited measures to create employment. Despite the latter and such high-profile initiatives as the Team Canada trade missions, Ottawa maintained its basic economic orientation – creating the conditions for private-sector growth through a shrinking deficit and low and stable interest rates. As Canadians (and Quebecers) continued to be more concerned with the economy than with national unity and as the economy improved, this stance sustained support for the government. In February 1996 the Liberals were the party preferred by 53 per cent of Canadians; by year's end they stood at 46 per cent, and heading into the election they still retained 41 per cent support.[40] On the other hand, Mr Chrétien's personal popularity was slipping over this period, and this no doubt was a major reason for calling the election of June 1997, when the government had served just over three and one-half years of its mandate.[41]

The economic strategy paid dividends. By mid-1997, the deficit stood at $1.5 billion, compared with $31.8 billion in the second quarter of 1995.[42] In June the prime rate on business loans stood at 4.75 per cent, rather than the 8.75 per cent of 1995.[43] The gross domestic product was growing at 4.9 per cent, rather than the 2.3 per cent it had achieved in 1995.[44] Rates for a one-year mortgage had fallen from 8.0 per cent in June 1995 to 5.2 per cent in June 1997.[45] The one soft spot in the economy was job creation; the unemployment rate fell only 0.4 per cent over the period, to 9.1 per cent.[46] Certainly, most Canadians were still no better off than they had been in the late 1980s, and deficit-reduction policies had strained their public services, but as the Chrétien government's economic orientation bore fruit, the situation improved, and by 1997 it was considerably better than at the time of the 1995 referendum. Citizens were more confident about their economic prospects, and Ottawa was not about to deviate from its basic policies.

While maintaining this economic course, the federal government moved on the national unity front in two directions. The first – the Plan A initiatives – involved meeting the commitments made on the

eve of the referendum by recognizing Quebec's distinctiveness, restoring the province's constitutional veto, and decentralizing important functions to the provinces. It also involved other measures to
assist Quebecers, to reaffirm the benevolent presence of the federal
government, and to strengthen the links of identification with Canada.
Plan B initiatives, on the other hand, were to counter the arguments
and tactics used by the sovereigntists in the 1995 referendum and
also to respond to those in ROC who demanded preparedness for
the next referendum and believed that a tough stand on secession
would help deter it. On this front, Ottawa moved more cautiously,
with feints and sorties rather than a full-scale assault, as the government attempted to preserve its room to manoeuvre, to hold the middle
ground in ROC, and to chip away at sovereignty support in Quebec.
Plan B initiatives were timed carefully and were focused only on the
process of secession. While highly provocative on occasion, the federal government trod carefully; it aimed to raise doubts among Quebecers about the ease of secession while avoiding both polarization
and any impression that it regarded separation as probable, let alone
inevitable.

Plan A

In the aftermath of the referendum, there was enormous pressure on
Ottawa for bold action to resolve the national unity issue by responding
to whatever it was that had brought a clear majority of francophones
to vote Yes to sovereignty; that is, to answer their discontent with
accommodative measures. Pressure for Plan A initiatives was maintained by editorialists, academics, and business leaders, who urged
Ottawa to decentralize powers and recognize Quebec's distinctiveness.[47] Some of these proposals called for radical reform; others advocated asymmetrical arrangements for Quebec; still others sought
to broaden the agenda to include the West's demands, Aboriginal
issues, and other matters.[48] Amidst this fervour, Ottawa moved forward quickly on the Plan A agenda, in line with the commitments
made at the close of the referendum campaign.

Immediately after the referendum, the federal government can-
vassed provincial leaders to determine whether there was sufficient
support for constitutional amendments to meet the promises made
to Quebecers. The basic objective was to entrench a distinct society
clause, or at least to have a constitutional resolution passed by six
provinces and Ottawa, so that it would only need passage in Quebec
to come into effect.[49] This would leave the PQ government in an awkward position and would provide a platform for the QLP's campaign

in the next provincial election. But despite a flurry of activity, agreement proved impossible, for the premiers of Alberta, British Columbia, and Ontario were cool to the idea.[50] Each appeared more interested in decentralizing powers to Quebec (and their own administrations) than in a symbolic declaration that would flow against strong currents of opinion among their electorates. Mr Klein, for example, thought that "most people in this province recognize that there is a distinctiveness relative to Quebec," but he added that if "it implies special status, or gives Quebec, through this resolution, any kind of powers that don't exist anywhere else, then the people here would be very mad."[51] Since there was insufficient consensus among the provincial governments, Ottawa decided to move alone, and over three successive days the government introduced into Parliament a resolution about Quebec's distinctiveness, a bill introducing regional constitutional vetoes, and substantial changes to the unemployment insurance and job-training systems. As the prime minister proclaimed, "Less than a month after the referendum, the government is keeping its word and fulfilling its commitments."[52]

The resolution was designed to bind the House of Commons and the executive branch to be guided by the recognition of Quebec as a distinct society.[53] It was attacked by both the BQ and the Reform Party. Because the resolution was nonconstitutional, did not speak to the courts, and narrowly construed "distinct," Mr Bouchard derided it as a "measly proposal" – a "minimalist effort" that "borders on surrealism."[54] The rest of Canada, he said, would never be able to offer a genuine recognition of the Quebec people because that would threaten their view of a single Canadian nation. In any case, Quebecers were past small symbols; they sought a partnership of equality. From the other side, Mr Manning condemned this "narrow backward-looking Quebec package," arguing that Canada had to offer more fundamental change to the federation while also spelling out for Quebecers what would be the terms and conditions of any secession.[55] But the Liberal majority carried the resolution, of course.

The veto proposal fared worse. Bill C-110 was to bind the federal government not to propose a constitutional amendment about some classes of matter unless it had been consented to by regional majorities; hence, Ottawa was "lending" its own veto to Quebec, Ontario, two western provinces with 50 per cent of the regional population, and two Atlantic provinces with 50 per cent of the population. The bill would apply to a limited range of matters, and, intriguingly, it left Ottawa free to define provincial "consent," a latitude that might allow it to undercut an obstructionist PQ government.[56] Of course, the measure was dismissed by the Bloc as hopelessly inadequate, and also by the Reform Party because it did not provide for national referendums and provincial equality. But the real resistance came from the West, where the proposal set off a firestorm of opposition because it treated provinces differently and took a cavalier attitude towards British Columbians' regional aspirations.[57] In short order, the federal government amended the bill to make British Columbia a fifth "region," thereby providing a veto to Alberta as well (by virtue of its percentage of the prairie population). This measure was widely misunderstood.[58] But any positive impact it had in Quebec was far outweighed by the alienation it caused in the West and by the effective criticism from the opposition that Ottawa was conferring a constitutional veto upon the "separatist government of Quebec."[59]

These initiatives had been vetted by a cabinet committee on unity that was assembled immediately after the referendum.[60] Its difficulties may have led the prime minister to strengthen his Quebec team by promptly recruiting Pierre Pettigrew as minister responsible for international cooperation and la francophonie (though he moved to Human Resources Development within a year) and Stéphane Dion as minister of intergovernmental affairs and president of the Privy Council.[61] The latter had proved himself, during the referendum campaign, to be an aggressive and tenacious opponent of the sovereigntists, and his new weight within the cabinet was demonstrated at the swearing-in ceremony, when he issued an unusual written manifesto declaring that Quebec's distinctiveness must be recognized in the constitution. Mr Chrétien agreed that "Mr Dion just said what is the policy of the Liberal Party."[62] The new minister soon embarked on a long and vigorous odyssey to persuade Canadians and their leaders that the constitutional recognition of Quebec was essential for national unity.

The third main element of Plan A – "rebalancing" the roles and responsibilities of the two orders of government – was the highlight of the 1996 Speech from the Throne. The government committed itself to discussions that would lead to "the orderly withdrawal of federal activity in training," to withdrawals from forestry, mining, and recreation, and to new partnerships with the provinces in food inspection, environmental management, social housing, and tourism. Most significantly, Ottawa pledged to restrict its spending power. It would create no new shared-cost programs in areas of provincial jurisdiction without obtaining the "consent of a majority of the provinces."[63] At the same time, however, the government sought provincial cooperation in reducing barriers to mobility and strengthening the social and economic union.[64] Negotiations about all these matters continued, with the major success occurring in job training, where Ottawa prepared to transfer over 2 billion dollars to provincial control.[65]

Other Plan A initiatives followed, notably in the area of "communications," reflecting the prime minister's belief that "there is a lack of knowledge by a lot of people in Quebec."[66] The government took out full-page newspaper advertisements to counter PQ claims that provincial spending cuts were caused by reduced federal transfers, and it distributed to every Quebec household a pamphlet about how Ottawa had met its referendum commitments.[67] Such efforts were to be coordinated by a new federal agency, the Canadian Information Office.[68] Further good publicity was generated when the federal government provided emergency assistance and financial relief after the disastrous floods in the Saguenay region. Even Mr Bouchard was "completely satisfied" with Ottawa's role.[69] As noted above, he took part in the highly publicized Team Canada trade missions. And the federal government continued to provide assistance to Quebec firms, notably in the form of an $87 million loan to Bombardier, the aircraft manufacturer.[70] During the 1997 federal election campaign, Liberal politicians from Quebec could point to many such investments – evident benefits of being part of the federation and voting for the governing party.[71]

Little progress was made on a constitutional package, however. One opening was provided by the obligation, under section 49 of the Constitution Act, 1982, for a first ministers' conference to review the amending formulae within fifteen years; that is, by April 1997. After some confusion, the constitution was put on the agenda of a conference previously scheduled for June 1996 (which Mr Bouchard, unlike his predecessor, agreed to attend). In a bizarre episode, with the premier of Quebec absenting himself in the washroom, the issue was briefly raised and the point made that the Charlottetown Accord negotiations had fulfilled the section 49 requirement. "The obligation," declared Mr Chrétien, "has been discharged."[72] Mr Bouchard took the opportunity to argue that No voters who had hoped for constitutional renewal would be "very disappointed today because there will never again be such an attempt," and indeed Mr Johnson sought to ensure that the manoeuvre had not permanently blocked avenues to constitutional change.[73] In the wake of the conference, Mr Dion continued his efforts to assemble a small package that might be attractive to Quebecers.

At the provincial level, the main interest of many premiers was in decentralization. This, they argued, held at least as much appeal to Quebecers as any symbolic recognition of their distinctiveness. From 1995 on, the provincial governments aimed to reduce overlap and duplication, clarify the responsibilities of the two orders of government, and secure stable program funding, especially in the social-policy fields of health, postsecondary education, social services, and labour market programs.[74] Part of this effort was to replace federal guidelines and rules with pan-Canadian standards set cooperatively. At the 1996 premiers' conference, attended by Mr Bouchard, premiers Klein and Harris advanced strongly decentralist proposals based on the ACCESS models prepared by economist Thomas Courchene.[75] The more radical models of interprovincial control were rejected, mainly because the fiscally weaker governments feared an erosion of the subsidies built into the existing arrangements, but the premiers united to press Ottawa to negotiate new standards jointly.

Part of the rationale for this was to show the federal system's flexibility. As Mr Tobin said, "I think what we're doing here is speaking to Quebec powerfully. We're going to demonstrate over the next seven or eight months that the federation is renewable, that the federal government will be accountable to the provinces."[76] But there were other motives. The Alberta government sought more latitude under the Canada Health Act, and the Harris government, implementing cuts in both taxes and expenditures, was even more stridently demanding than its NDP predecessor had been, arguing that the proportion of federal transfers it received consistently fell short of Ontario's needs, population share, or contributions.[77] Bitterly, the Ontario government maintained that federal-provincial "rebalancing" was preferable to formal constitutional reform, and seemed to suggest that its agreement to the latter was contingent on the former.[78]

Most of Mr Harris's demands were not met, but Ottawa and the provinces did agree on the framework for employment training, on coordinating environmental inspections, and on a new national child benefit, much of this being accomplished by the accommodating Mr Pettigrew.[79] Moreover, in the pre-election period, the federal government introduced a youth employment plan that avoided interfering with areas of provincial jurisdiction, and it spent freely to eliminate several provincial irritants.[80] But Ottawa was not prepared to abandon its defence of the hugely popular Medicare system.[81] Indeed, a powerful current within the Liberal Party and the country as a whole continued to believe that a strong federal presence in social programs was necessary to maintain Canadian unity and preserve Quebecers' attachment to the country, so there was considerable resistance to the decentralizing trend, despite the premiers' persistent pressure.[82] As well, after the 1997 federal election, the Liberals increasingly came to believe that there was little political payoff in Quebec or elsewhere from decentralization and accommodation.[83]

But none of what was accomplished was sufficient for the Quebec Liberal Party and Mr Johnson, who continually stressed that for the federalists the referendum result was "a reprieve rather than a victory."[84] The QLP continued to insist on constitutional change – to recognize Quebec's distinctiveness, provide it with a veto, and limit federal action in areas of provincial jurisdiction. This long-standing position was designed to appeal to the soft-nationalist voters, who had to be integrated with non-francophone federalists if the party was to win an election.[85] Generally, the QLP position was supported by many prominent federalists and their organizations.[86] But it was difficult to sustain in Quebec's polarized environment, where partitionists and disillusioned anglophones wanted to maintain the constitutional status quo while vigorously confronting the sovereigntists, and where Mr Bouchard was successfully building a broad coalition of organizations to confront the province's social and economic problems.[87]

There was also considerable mistrust between the QLP and the federal Liberals, fed by recriminations about the near-defeat in the referendum and by Mr Chrétien's apparent lack of commitment to constitutionalizing distinct society status.[88] As well, Mr Johnson did not welcome the federal government's Plan B sorties on matters such as partition and the legality of secession, asking, typically, "Why is the Prime Minister today worrying about something which isn't about to happen instead of working on the mandate for change that the referendum has given him?"[89] In these circumstances, the QLP leader turned directly to the provincial premiers, hoping that other legislatures would move on the constitution so that his party could campaign in the next provincial election for a mandate to have Quebec finally sign on to a renewed 1982 constitution.[90] While these efforts continued, the party assembled its constitutional position, and Mr Johnson easily survived a leadership review.[91] But there were no challengers to the QLP leader, and the federal Liberals maintained their reserve towards his party. Despite Mr Johnson's hope that the PQ government would become vulnerable as its unpopular measures were implemented, many federalists considered Mr Bouchard unbeatable; hence, if Mr Johnson stayed on, they anticipated finding a new leader for the QLP after the election, one who could win a referendum battle.

Of course, Ottawa had not abandoned hope for constitutional change, especially for the recognition of Quebec. It could ignore neither the official position of the QLP nor the public opinion in Quebec to which it was responsive. Support for sovereignty remained stubbornly high, around 50 per cent, despite solid majorities favouring renewal of the federation and continued adherence to Canada.[92]

Clearly, the early post-referendum initiatives and subsequent changes in federal-provincial program responsibilities had not sufficed to alter the views of many Quebecers.

Mr Dion continued a vigorous crusade in favour of distinct society recognition, making many speeches to groups across the country, especially in the West.[93] But there was not sufficient support among the provincial premiers to proceed formally. This resistance sprang from several sources. No doubt there were genuine ideological barriers to any recognition that would violate the principle of equality of the provinces. Mr Klein, for example, was willing to accept that the National Assembly should "preserve and protect" the French language and culture, but he argued that recognizing a responsibility to "promote" these characteristics would confer unacceptable special powers on the province.[94] Other leaders thought that accommodating Quebec was an inappropriate strategy to deter the sovereigntists. Mr Harris, for example, insisted that concrete changes to the operation of Canadian federalism would be more effective in appealing to Quebecers, and declared that distinct society "is an old-fashioned term for an old-fashioned policy that was a disaster."[95] In the West, this view was bolstered by historic regional grievances and the confidence that if Quebecers voted to secede, the region was strong enough to "survive."[96]

In other quarters, the fear of failure bred reluctance to embark on a new constitutional initiative: if agreement could not be secured, then the raised expectations of Quebecers would be dashed and another referendum would carry. (Failure had become more likely, in fact, because constitutional amendments would be governed by the new system of regional vetoes, which could well be exercised after referendums to be held under provincial legislation in British Columbia, Alberta, and perhaps Ontario.) As well, some premiers were withholding support for distinct society recognition in order to secure concessions from Ottawa on their own priorities. Finally, given public opinion in ROC, especially in the West, any special status for Quebec would be difficult to sell, and partisan and electoral considerations made leaders reluctant to bind themselves to the concept, as was shown during the 1997 Alberta election campaign.[97] All these considerations posed great obstacles to realizing an essential component of Plan A. They were all sharpened during the campaign leading to the June 1997 federal election, when national unity was the dominant issue, hotly debated across the country. Yet when the returns were in, there was an opening for further progress on Plan A, one that was taken by the provincial premiers when they hammered out their Calgary Declaration.

Plan B

The other major prong of the federal government's post- and pre-referendum strategy was Plan B. This comprised a series of initiatives to clarify the process of secession and some of its implications. After the shock of the 1995 referendum, there was a very strong demand for such an approach. Some advocates simply rejected accommodative Plan A initiatives, arguing that sovereignty was now inevitable, that further decentralization would be destructively balkanizing to Canada, or that concessions to Quebec nationalists were counterproductive.[98]

For others, the whole referendum process had been unfair, and if another vote was to be held it was imperative that Ottawa insist on a clear question and an adequate mandate for secession.[99] Another argument was that the federal government had to clarify the issues around secession – such as those involving the rights of Aboriginal peoples – well before another referendum so that Quebecers would better understand the implications of their vote.[100] Finally, there was a widespread view that ROC had to be prepared for a sovereigntist victory, as Ottawa manifestly had not been in October 1995. Out of self-interest, contingency plans had to be developed to maintain the rule of law, minimize economic losses, and ensure that Canada could reconstitute itself as a functioning national entity.[101]

For the federal Liberals, there were other advantages in proceding with Plan B. Its various initiatives helped channel the energies of the aroused minorities in Quebec. It responded to a powerful current of opinion in ROC that blamed the federal government for almost losing the referendum and demanded concrete measures to ward off the sovereigntist threat. Also, it allowed the Liberals to steer between their major political opponents. On the one hand, the Reform Party issued a set of principles to serve as a guide for Ottawa in case of any secession: these were quite detailed with respect to both the process of secession and the terms and conditions that ROC should impose.[102] On the other hand, the Progressive Conservative leader, Mr Charest, condemned any planning about secession as wasteful, counterproductive, and self-fulfilling.[103]

Thus, by focusing on the modalities of secession – the parameters of any future referendum and the legalities of secession – the Liberals could position themselves in the centre. Even then, partly from fear of alienating Quebecers and partly to preserve its room to manoeuvre, the federal government did not take a firm position on many elements of Plan B (such as the precise level of support needed in a future referendum); its stance was one of "studied ambiguity."[104] Nor, since Ottawa aimed to manage the constitutional crisis with a combination of strategies, was it yet prepared to embrace Plan B to the extent of negotiating with the PQ about the process and terms of secession.[105] Instead, its Plan B initiatives were designed to raise doubts among the Quebec electorate about the ease of secession by challenging the sovereigntists and putting them on the defensive. In this, Ottawa moved cautiously and in stages, making intermittent sorties on the Plan B front while taking advantage of any opening for advance left by their opponents.

Immediately after the 1995 referendum, the prime minister hinted that a more robust stance would be taken towards the sovereigntists. Contemplating yet another referendum, he argued, "We've been extremely generous in Canada. We Canadians have done it twice and we cannot carry it on forever."[106] After the early Plan A initiatives, the cabinet was rebuilt in early 1996, and Mr Dion was teamed with Mr Massé and Mr Rock on a special cabinet committee – the G3 – to set strategy about Quebec.[107] Stéphane Dion, the former academic, was not hesitant in adding the weight of his new office to his past observations about the logic of secession.

Mr Dion plunged right into the issue of partition and escalated Plan B enormously by taking the view that, just as it would be undemocratic to hold Quebecers in Canada against their will, so must the will of minorities within Quebec be respected. He stated, "You can't consider Canada divisible but the territory of Quebec sacred. If there are native groups, municipalities or regional municipalities who on an equally democratic basis decided they wanted to stay Canadian, you would have to talk to those people."[108] As he later put it, "The basic rule is if Canada is divisible, Quebec is divisible too. If I give myself a right, I can't stop others from exercising the same right."[109] This position drew a furious response from the sovereigntists, because it cut against their core assumption that Quebecers – all Quebecers – constitute a self-determining people. About to be sworn in as premier, Mr Bouchard fumed, "Canada is divisible because Canada is not a real country. There are two peoples, two nations and two territories. And this one is ours."[110] But the prime minister supported Mr Dion, saying, "if Canada is divisible, Quebec is divisible too. It's the same logic."[111]

This tough new stance triggered heated and divisive debate. Apparently, it was welcomed by Liberal MPs from ROC while those from Quebec found it dismaying.[112] Aboriginal peoples in Quebec demanded stronger affirmation of their right to remain in Canada while casting doubt on similar rights claimed by groups mainly representing anglophones and allophones.[113] Although it was denounced by most sovereigntists, some moderate nationalists were forced to concede the logic of Ottawa's position.[114] And although Mr Dion's principle was embraced by partitionist groups in Quebec, many moderate anglophones disputed both its efficacy as a deterrent to voting Yes and its practicality should the sovereigntists prevail, while the QLP remained staunchly opposed to it.[115] Within the province, it was hard to discern the debate's impact on public opinion.[116]

Outside Quebec, elite opinion was divided. Some opposed the position as counterproductive, unrealistic, and, in its implication that force would be used to secure partitionists' rights, undemocratic.[117] Others insisted that the issue of partition could deter voters from a Yes and that there was a moral imperative to help fellow Canadians.[118] In any case, the issue surfaced intermittently, notably in the summer of 1997 after the premier of New Brunswick apparently encouraged a partitionist group's efforts to have municipalities in Quebec pass resolutions favouring Canadian unity. Mr Bouchard condemned this in a letter as supporting "a fundamentally antidemocratic position that international law and the history of peoples have rejected many times."[119] The fact that this letter was published in a newspaper provided an opportunity for rebuttal, and Mr Dion wrote back crisply, citing precedents and legal opinions about partition, and stating, "Neither you nor I nor anyone else can predict that the borders of an independent Quebec would be those now guaranteed by the Canadian Constitution."[120] Mr Landry replied for the PQ government, condemning Ottawa's "drift towards antidemocracy," but Mr Dion restated his arguments and noted the possibility that "in the difficult circumstances of negotiating secession, an agreement on modifying borders would become the least unfavourable solution."[121]

As usual, the federal government was quick to seize openings left by its sovereigntist opponents, and as with its other Plan B initiatives, Ottawa stuck to general principles, provided no detailed modalities (of how partition might occur), and sought to raise doubts among the voters. Joining the debate, Mr Chrétien insisted, "I don't want partition. I want everyone to stay in Canada and the only way to have absolute insurance that Quebec stays as it is is to stay in Canada."[122] So Ottawa pressed upon the sovereigntists the onus to justify both the legitimacy of their position and their predictions about how secession would occur. It questioned their assumptions – the "myths that have been developed in society," as the prime minister put it – and forced them onto the defensive.[123] But the Plan B strategy also raised the stakes of any future secession, because in the face of resistance by Quebecers or their provincial government, partition would, presumably, have to be accomplished by force.[124]

Some minor elements of Plan B involved prodding the PQ government in sensitive policy areas associated with secession. For example, Ottawa consistently attributed Quebec's low levels of investment and relatively high unemployment rates to the political uncertainty associated with the prospect of another referendum.[125] While the PQ blamed the situation on Ottawa's cuts in transfer payments, Mr Chrétien insisted that the political uncertainty was not created by the federal government. "We try to do what we can do," he said, "but some elements are not under our control."[126] Far more provocatively, Ottawa supported anglophones boycotting stores in Montreal that had unilingual French signs, an explosive issue given the rising polarization between them and PQ militants seeking stiffer controls on English. The prime minister referred with distaste to Quebec's "language police," and declared, "La lutte des minorités francophones, anglophones et amérindiennes n'arrêtera jamais. C'est un des rôles du gouvernement fédéral de s'assurer que les gens ont les moyens de défendre leurs droits en vertu de la constitution canadienne."[127] To the Quebec government, such statements threw "oil on the fire" of the language debate, and it reaffirmed its commitment that official bilingualism would not return to the Montreal region.[128]

These destabilizing thrusts were much less central to Plan B than Ottawa's position about the process of secession, especially about the question to be posed and the level of support necessary for Quebec to become sovereign. As the 1996 Speech from the Throne stated, "As long as the prospect of another Quebec referendum exists, the Government will exercise its responsibility to ensure that the debate is conducted with all the facts on the table, that the rules of the process are fair, that the consequences are clear, and that Canadians, no matter where they live, will have their say in the future of the country."[129] While the federal government now accepted that secession could take place, recognizing the democratic "convention" that people cannot be held in Canada against their will, it insisted that there had to be a "clear mandate" supporting the choice.[130]

This meant, first, that the question put to Quebecers must be straightforward. As the minister of justice put it, "The question will be separation or not – nothing in between; not partnership or any such thing. Separation or not is the clear and honest question that must be asked."[131] Under fire from both sovereigntists and Quebec federalists for appearing to negate the province's right to self-determination, Mr Dion stated that because the decision was momentous and the interests of all Canadians were involved, it was essential that the referendum question be clear. Initially, Ottawa's position had been that since a confusing question would confer no mandate to secede, negotiations simply would not commence.[132] So either the PQ would pose an acceptable question or it would have to proceed towards sovereignty after a Yes through an (illegal) UDI.[133] But the federal government also hinted that it might negotiate with the PQ the wording of a question, and it left open the possibility of holding a referendum on its own question if the ground rules could not be agreed in advance of a Quebec referendum.[134] Of course, the clarity of referendum questions – let alone the plausibility of predictions made during a campaign – is a matter of debate and interpretation. But like other elements of Plan B, questioning the question represented an insistence on the right of ROC to defend its interests and was a challenge to the sovereigntists' assumption that they alone could legitimately establish the modalities of secession; it was designed to force them to defend and justify their procedure.

Soon after the referendum, Ottawa also began to raise the issue of the level of support necessary for a mandate to achieve sovereignty. The prime minister declared that if a "real majority" of Quebecers "want to go, I'm a democrat," but he also argued that the 1995 referendum had only been a plebiscite, and he reiterated that "at a 50.1 per cent vote, I would not let the country break."[135] Similarly, Mr Dion mused that "for a very serious decision, that is hard to revisit, one can consider a qualified majority," and he stated flatly that "the rest of Canada would consider a simple majority unacceptable."[136] These views were hotly contested by the sovereigntists as undemocratic, and like other parts of Plan B they placed Quebec federalists in a difficult position. Mr Johnson said, for example, that trying to stop Quebec from seceding after a Yes vote would be like ordering a man who has jumped off a bridge to "fall back up."[137] In ROC, even some stauch anti-sovereigntists agreed with the Reform Party that the threshold should be 50 per cent of the vote, on grounds of precedent, legitimacy, practicality, and risk avoidance.[138] But the federal Liberals consistently refused to commit to this or any other threshold, notably throughout the course of the 1997 election campaign. Leaving open the necessary level of support was an important part of Plan B, for it raised doubts about Ottawa's response to any referendum result while preserving its room to manoeuvre – and negotiate – in the meantime.

Over time, the main focus of the Plan B strategy became contesting not the legitimacy but the legality of the sovereigntists' plans. Ottawa sought to have the courts declare that a UDI would be illegal. The point of this thrust was to cast into question some cherished assumptions of Quebec nationalists – that Quebecers are a "people," that they have a right of self-determination, and that this right extends to secession. Federal strategists believed that if a unilateral secession were held to be illegal, Quebecers might be less likely to vote Yes in any future referendum. As well, clarifying the legalities of secession would set some ground rules for what should happen after a Yes, and a court decision could also provide some legal armaments with respect to foreign recognition of Quebec. Finally, if a UDI were ruled illegal, Ottawa might gain enough leverage to force the PQ to negotiate the question to be asked and the required level of support. For these reasons, clarifying the legality of secession came to be the linchpin of Plan B.

Ottawa's entry onto this terrain was precipitated by legal cases argued by a maverick Quebec lawyer both before and after the 1995 referendum. Before the campaign, Guy Bertrand, who had once run for the PQ leadership but had become a radical federalist, sought an injunction prohibiting the referendum on the grounds that it promised to violate his fundamental rights as a Canadian. This was contested by the Quebec government as simply beyond the jurisdiction of the courts, and when the court did not dismiss the application, deciding instead to hear arguments, Quebec withdrew. Mr Parizeau declared, "We can't subjugate Quebecers' right to vote to a decision of the courts. That would be contrary to our democratic system. Quebecers want to vote. They have the right to vote. And they will vote."[139] The federalist side, confident at the outset of the campaign and anxious about stirring up the voters, chose not to intervene in a matter that was "political" rather than legal.[140] But a judge of the Quebec Superior Court ruled that Mr Bertrand had a case. While not issuing an injunction against the referendum, he reviewed several matters critical to secessions and to the powers of the National Assembly; he maintained that the Canadian Charter of Rights and Freedoms applies to all government actions; and he held that "the constitutional change proposed by the Government of Quebec would result in a break in continuity in the legal order, which is manifestly contrary to the Constitution of Canada."[141] The sovereigntists' reaction was to dismiss the ruling "because Quebec does not adhere to the 1982 Canadian constitution."[142]

Other cases were also brought before the courts prior to the 1995 referendum,[143] but Mr Bertrand carried on afterwards, aiming to have the issues clarified in advance of any subsequent vote, and to prevent what he called a "constitutional coup d'état," by seeking a ruling from the Quebec Superior Court that the constitutional amendment process must be followed in order to accomplish secession.[144] In the new spirit of Plan B, Ottawa contemplated intervening, but it did so only after the Quebec government stated its arguments, which included a denial that the court had jurisdiction over the matter.[145] It was against this claim, and to have the relevance of both the constitution and the judiciary affirmed, that the federal government acted: "This is a position with which the Attorney General of Canada disagrees. Neither international law nor Canadian constitutional law confer on the National Assembly of Quebec the right to unilateral secession. Disagreement on this important point itself demonstrates that there are substantive *legal* issues in this case that are justiciable in the Superior Court."[146]

The PQ government was outraged. It rejected any denial of Quebecers' "sacred right" to determine their own future; it affirmed that "for us democracy rules over constitutional provisions"; and it considered a snap election on the issue, along with a boycott of federal-provincial meetings.[147] Mr Bouchard attacked a status quo Canada "as a prison from which we cannot escape" and said, "The clear objective is to block the right of Quebecers to accede to sovereignty by affirming that Quebec's neighbours have not only a say – as Mr Chrétien likes to say – but that they have the final word."[148] Yet Ottawa continued to press, with the prime minister insisting "that the laws of Canada must be respected, that there won't be a unilateral declaration of independence and that international law, also, must be respected."[149] Mr Dion emphasized the rule of law "because if we veer out of the law, we will find ourselves in an extremely dangerous situation." He also raised, indirectly, the possibility of force being used in such a situation "against peaceful populations claiming their constitutional rights."[150]

This tougher stance about the process of secession responded to public opinion in ROC and was thought to be strategically effective in shifting Quebec public opinion.[151] At the same time, however, moving to clarify the constitutional ambiguity about secession carried the message that secession could in fact be accomplished. In posing the question of how secession *should* occur, the federalists had to accept that it *could* occur. So Mr Dion agreed that "Quebecers have the right to express themselves clearly on whether they want to remain in Canada or leave," and he declared that "you cannot keep a population against its will."[152] Similarly, the attorney general said that he was not challenging "the right of Quebecers to express democratically" their desire to secede or to say in Canada. "The rule of law is not an obstacle to change," he stated; "rather it provides the framework within which change can occur in an orderly fashion."[153]

The Superior Court denied Quebec's motion to dismiss and allowed the case to proceed. It defined the substantive issues that would have to be decided.[154] But the federal government moved independently, using its reference power to place these issues directly before the Supreme Court. In September 1996 the attorney general posed three questions to the court:

Under the Constitution of Canada, can the National Assembly, legislature or Government of Quebec effect the secession of Quebec from Canada unilaterally?

Second, does international law give the National Assembly, the legislature or the Government of Quebec the right to effect the secession of Quebec from Canada unilaterally? In this regard, is there a right to self-determination under international law that would give the National Assembly, the legislature or the Government of Quebec the right to effect the secession of Quebec from Canada unilaterally?

Third, in the event of a conflict between domestic and international law on the right of the National Assembly, legislature or Government of Quebec to effect the secession of Quebec from Canada unilaterally, which would take precedence in Canada?[155]

The minister argued that it was Ottawa's duty to have these issues clarified, because a UDI would undermine political stability, create enormous uncertainty, divide Quebecers, and damage the province economically and politically. Moreover, he linked the substantive issues to be negotiated with ROC in the event of a secession with the constitutionality of the process. A UDI, he said, "would have been made in the absence of an agreement with the rest of Canada on such fundamental issues as recognition for Quebec internationally, trade and economic arrangements, the rights of citizens to move within the country, the sharing of public debt and assets, the use of currency and scores of other issues." In short, it was a "formula for chaos," and "any government that suggests it would throw Quebec and all of Canada into the confusion of a unilateral declaration of independence is being profoundly irresponsible."[156]

The sovereigntist reaction took several forms. First, the PQ government announced that it would not participate in the proceedings because the fundamental issue was political. Said Mr Bouchard, "There is only one tribunal to settle Quebec's political future and that's the Quebec people."[157] When the Supreme Court announced that an *amicus curiae* would be engaged to present Quebec's position, PQ ministers branded any such person "an imposter and a false spokesperson."[158] (Despite considerable PQ pressure on the Quebec legal community, the court did in fact manage to recruit a credible sovereigntist to advise it.)[159] Second, the sovereigntists argued that the reference showed Ottawa's desperation. Unable to thwart the secessionist impulse by political means, the federal government was reduced to throwing up legal obstacles.[160] Further, they attacked the legitimacy of the court, because its members were all appointed by the federal government. "Like the Tower of Pisa", said the deputy premier, the court "always leans the same way."[161] Finally, the Quebec government maintained that it would ignore any ruling. After a Yes vote – on a question written and adopted by the National Assembly – there would be a period during which Quebec would attempt to negotiate a partnership with Canada, and should this fail, the assembly would unilaterally declare Quebec's independence.[162]

The PQ government's justification for this, apart from the fundamentally political nature of the exercise, was that the 1982 constitution had been imposed on Quebec and had never been accepted by the government or legislature of the province; so its amending formula could hardly be used to keep a province "captive."[163] As well, strong nationalists argued that Ottawa's reference to the court showed how the constitution imposed in 1982 now held Quebecers in an "iron collar."[164] As the hearing approached, the Government of Quebec maintained its position: "No decree, no federal law, no decision from any court whatsoever can call into question or discredit this right of Quebecers to decide their future."[165]

Meanwhile, the legal strategy had become the centrepiece of Plan B. It was seen to have numerous advantages. It could force the sovereigntists to justify some of their core assumptions about self-determination and secession, and if a UDI were declared illegal, law-abiding Quebecers might hesitate to vote Yes.[166] If a Yes vote did occur, the court ruling could be used to hold off recognition of Quebec by foreign governments.[167] Assuming the court held that a constitutional amendment would be required to effect secession, this might possibly deter a UDI after a Yes, thus depriving the sovereigntists of a major threat to ROC. In particular, there could be a linkage between passing an amendment and obtaining satisfactory results in substantive negotiations about the debt, assets, trade arrangements, and so on.[168] Finally, as Plan B unfolded, it appeared that a court ruling against a UDI might provide Ottawa with sufficient leverage to force the Quebec government to negotiate about such matters as the question to be posed and the level of support required to achieve sovereignty. By denying the legality of unilateralism, such a ruling would insert Canada into the secession process and help legitimize its stand on the other elements of Plan B. As Mr Dion put it, "From the instant we know that Mr Bouchard's claim to have a monopoly on control of the procedure, under international law, is false, the federal government receives at that moment, in a way, the duty to propose to the government of Quebec a way to resolve this debate."[169] This could open the path to prenegotiating with the sovereigntists the ground rules of any future referendum.[170]

On the other hand, there were grave risks in this strategy. Most obviously, the Supreme Court could issue a judgment adverse to the federal government's position. While it would be unlikely to deny that the constitution applies to secession, it could hold that a conflict between Canadian and international law has no clear resolution, and this would bolster the PQ's position about a UDI. Second, clarifying the legalities around secession might not deter Quebecers from voting Yes. Persuaded of the unfairness of subjecting Quebec's right of self-determination to the exigencies of Ottawa or any Canadian province, soft-nationalist voters might swing massively to the Yes side in order to avoid being "trapped" in Canada forever.[171] If opinion shifted in this way after a judgment was issued, the legitimacy of the Supreme Court would be gravely undermined. Subsequent decisions – and they could be necessary before a referendum or afterwards, whichever side won – might carry little moral authority in Quebec.

There is also the fact that a court decision will constrain Ottawa's room to manoeuvre. Assuming that the constitution is held to govern secession, then the federal government will be bound to respect this, just as it claims the sovereigntists should. This could mean that Ottawa would have to recognize the right of every province to veto Quebec's secession; or that it would have to give full consideration to the intricate implications of its fiduciary responsibility to Aboriginal peoples in Quebec as well as to other Canadian citizens of the province. The federal government would become bound by a clear legal obligation to enforce the constitution in Quebec. If the modalities of a referendum had not been prenegotiated with the PQ government, this would mean, ultimately, that Ottawa would have to be prepared to deploy force in order to maintain the rule of law – however much federal leaders might try to deny this implication.[172]

All in all, therefore, the legal initiative raised the stakes of any future referendum. If, after a Yes vote, a constitutional secession proves impossible because conditions imposed by Ottawa or the provinces about the process or substance of separation cannot be met, then the sovereigntists may see no choice but to proceed with a UDI, and Ottawa would have little choice but to resist it, with grave consequences. This raising of the stakes is an intrinsic part of the whole Plan B strategy, which is designed in part to reduce the probability of a Yes vote in a future referendum. But, ironically, the measures taken to accomplish this would greatly increase the costs of secession, for both Quebec and ROC, if the strategy failed and a Yes vote occurred.

THE 1997 FEDERAL ELECTION

Plan A, Plan B, and the whole national unity issue dominated the 1997 federal election campaign. This extraordinary development deserves some attention because the interplay of arguments made then may foreshadow how the issue will evolve in the future. Moreover, the results of the election both indicated the state of public opinion in Quebec and ROC and determined for the next several years the strength of the political forces and formations in the federal arena.

The major political parties had quite different core objectives in the election. The Reform Party aimed to hold its western base and also to prove itself a national contender by making a breakthrough in Ontario.[173] For this, it would have to supplant the Progressive Conservatives, whose objective was to regain their position as the major party of the right by returning to strength in Quebec and Ontario and perhaps in the Atlantic provinces, where disaffection with the Liberals could swing votes to their traditional opponents in the region.[174] The New Democratic Party aimed to regain official-party status by concentrating its efforts on a few winnable seats across the country (but not in Quebec). The BQ's goal was to maintain its dominant position in Quebec, preserving the momentum of the sovereigntist movement and securing resources for the next provincial election and referendum. The Liberals, vulnerable on a number of fronts – an unmet promise to scrap the national sales tax, the narrow referendum victory, and high unemployment – sought to hold their strength and win a new mandate to govern.[175]

With these objectives, it was not inevitable that national unity would figure large in the campaign. The Liberals in particular intended to downplay it, insisting that their referendum promises had been met as much as possible and that the initiative on constitutional change now rested with the provincial premiers.[176] Never in recent Canadian history had national unity been a very significant issue in a federal campaign, let alone the dominant one. But the narrow referendum win made the issue salient to voters everywhere, and of course the BQ campaign would be based on it (to the irritation of many in ROC who resented the sovereigntists' status as the official opposition).[177] More important, every party – with the exception of the NDP, which ran on a traditional platform of creating jobs and strengthening the welfare state – had an incentive to focus on national unity, because it was the issue that most clearly differentiated them among critical portions of the electorate.[178] On the major national issues of taxation, unemployment, health care, and social programs, there was substantial overlap between pairs of parties, while other issues (gun control, child poverty, crime, and unemployment insurance) either failed to distinguish the parties or were mainly of regional concern. In the course of the contest, one of these matters might have emerged as the focus of struggle, but instead the major parties each discovered incentives, in the thrust and counterthrust of competition, to keep alive the issue of national unity.

Even before the election was called on 27 April, the Bloc set out to campaign against federalism, headed by its new leader Gilles Duceppe. In this, the PQ organization was fully engaged, and Mr Bouchard was set to play a big role.[179] The Bloc's arguments were familiar – that Quebec's fiscal problems were caused by federal cutbacks, that Quebecers had to maintain a strong voice in Ottawa to defend the province's interests, and that sovereignty must be the goal because the Canadian federation was incapable of change.[180] Mr Bouchard also warned against the Liberal government's Plan B, describing it as a "putsch" designed to eradicate "the dream of Quebec having full responsibility over Quebec's destiny," and arguing that without Bloc victories, there would be "all kinds of deals done on the back of Quebec," as well as more federalists on the ground to fight sovereignty in the next referendum.[181] Apart from fighting the Liberals, the BQ aimed to counter the threatening rise of Mr Charest's popularity in Quebec by identifying him with Mr Chrétien as another overbearing federalist.[182]

In fact, the Progressive Conservative Party was committed to enshrining Quebec's distinct society status in the constitution, and Mr Charest eschewed any contemplation of the elements of Plan B, which he had consistently opposed as counterproductive.[183] Other elements of the Charest platform, however, were initially given the most prominence. For his part, the prime minister was careful to campaign in favour of distinct society, especially in Ontario and the West, and the Liberal platform committed the party to work towards constitutional change, but Mr Chrétien did not emphasize the unity issue.[184] Mr Manning did, however. Reform's platform envisaged radical decentralization of the federation, insisted on the equality of individuals and of provinces, and included explicit principles that should govern a Quebec secession.[185] Seeking a "wedge issue" to distinguish Reform from the "old-line federalist parties," Mr Manning struck early in the campaign by warning bluntly that British Columbia would separate if Ottawa continued to ignore its demands – which were for fair treatment, not special status, he contended. He went on to state, "British Columbians should understand that every Liberal candidate, every Conservative candidate, every NDP candidate standing for the federal election in B.C. is tied by their party leader to the distinct society concept. The federal Reform party is the only federal party committed to the equality of citizens and provinces."[186] This position was designed not only to bloster support in British Columbia but to cut into the Liberals' commanding lead in Ontario by appealing to the large number of uncommitted voters in that province.[187]

In Quebec, the federalist parties were downplaying the unity issue, and the diffuse and disorganized Bloc emitted few messages about sovereignty.[188] But the whole national campaign was brought to focus on secession when parts of Mr Parizeau's memoirs were released and the media reported that the PQ would have moved rapidly to declare sovereignty after a Yes vote in 1995. Leading sovereigntists quickly denied any knowledge of or support for such intentions, but the possibility that the Yes side had lied to Quebecers was a severe blow to the Bloc campaign. The story was quickly used by the Liberals to justify their Plan B initiatives, including the court reference, even in Quebec.[189] They seized the opportunity to insist on Ottawa's "right" to establish a "clear question" in any future referendum.[190]

No doubt their intention was to claim a mandate for future Plan B initiatives from Quebec voters, as well as to attract hard-line support in ROC. But they were joined by Mr Manning, who criticized both his main opponents, deriding the Liberals' unwillingness to thoroughly reform the federation and disparaging the Progressive Conservatives' refusal to prepare for a possible secession.[191] The Reform leader claimed that distinct society status was "not going to happen," but he warned that if Quebecers voted for sovereignty, they would confront no politician from Quebec – since these would be disqualified from negotiating because of "conflict of interest." Instead, Quebecers would find themselves dealing with "some steely-eyed, hard-nosed lawyer from Toronto or Calgary," stated Mr Manning, "and he's going to say to you 'We want money. We want territory. And we want the date nailed down for the revoking of passports.'"[192] All this required a reaction by Mr Charest. He condemned the Reform Party for opposing distinct society, a stance that could lead to Canada's destruction, and he attacked Reform's principles about secession, declaring that "I will never propose to this country any formula to negotiate its breakup."[193] He also stressed, especially during the televised leaders' debates, that the critical requirement for national unity was leadership, and that he was best suited not only to lead the federalist forces in any future referendum but also to reconcile Quebec and ROC. With his strong performance in the debates, it was useful for the Conservative leader to keep the focus on the unity issue.[194] His arguments were persuasive in Quebec, where polls showed that Bloc support continued to slide, with Mr Charest being the principal beneficiary.[195]

This forced the Bloc onto the offensive, and Mr Duceppe began to campaign against Plan B – "the negation of the existence of the Quebec people" – hoping to consolidate the soft-nationalist vote behind his party.[196] The divided sovereigntist camp coalesced once more, Mr Parizeau having persuaded its leaders that his writings had been misinterpreted, and Mr Bouchard having understood that the Bloc faced a major defeat.[197] The new message was that Quebecers must defend their right of self-determination against hard-line federalist leaders who had opposed national reconciliation through the Meech Lake Accord and who would refuse to accept a Yes vote in a future referendum: "Jean Charest and Jean Chrétien will be allies and our adversaries when the time will come to crush Quebec. The Bloc will always be there to guarantee our protection."[198] But the Progressive Conservatives continued to gain in Quebec, despite a very weak organization.[199] Mr Charest also won support from the premier of Alberta and a former premier of Ontario, who endorsed his stance on distinct society and lauded his national vision: the Tory leader continued to insist that he would not countenance Plan B, because "as far as Canada is concerned failure is not an option."[200]

In this fluid situation, Mr Manning saw advantage in keeping his focus on national unity. He insisted on the need for clear rules about secession, including partition, and accused both his principal rivals – from the "traditional parties" that had "made careers out of thirty years of managing this issue" – of avoiding the hard questions.[201] Then he demanded a special debate on the issue, one that would include only himself, Jean Chrétien, and Jean Charest. Explosively, he likened this to the Lincoln-Douglas debates on slavery that took place in 1858.[202] The analogy drove the NDP leader to use words never heard in a national campaign when she said "It's absolutely clear that where Preston Manning's policies would lead us in this country is straight into a civil war."[203]

Undeterred, and seeking to make inroads among Ontario voters, Mr Manning continued to attack the "old-line federalists." They were mistaken in offering distinct society status to Quebec, he maintained, and they had mishandled the 1995 referendum; so they were "as big a threat as separatists."[204] To drive home this point, Reform ran a striking television advertisement showing Mr Chrétien and Mr Charest along with Mr Bouchard and Mr Duceppe, and intoning that the national unity issue required "a voice for all Canadians, not just Quebec politicians." These tactics were condemned by their targets as "desperation" and "extremist," but Reform held its position in order to consolidate its western support and dampen any Conservative momentum in Ontario, where Mr Manning campaigned intensively.[205]

The next thrust was made by the Liberals. In a Quebec television interview, the prime minister insisted on the need for a clear question in any future referendum, and he at last responded to questions about the level of support necessary for secession. "I would find it to be unreasonable," he said, "if the answer was 50 per cent plus one in a third referendum."[206] This widely reported statement was certainly a calculated reply. It could attract voters in Ontario and the West who agreed with a harder line towards Quebec but rejected the logic of Reform's position – that "Yes means Yes," so that even a narrow referendum result would lead to negotiations towards secession.[207] More important, the statement could prove highly polarizing in Quebec, where the federalist vote could be pushed into the Liberal camp, while many soft nationalists would peel away from the Progressive Conservatives and rally to the Bloc.[208] This was the accusation made after the election by Mr Charest and his campaign manager, and late polls did show that Progressive Conservative support had weakened in Quebec.[209]

In any event, the statement provoked a strong counterattack by the Bloc and its allies, who had begun to accent sovereignty more in their campaign and who now tried to associate all major federalist leaders with an anti-Quebec position. For Mr Duceppe, the prime minister's statement was not only "undemocratic," but it showed that Mr Chrétien had lied before the 1995 referendum when he told Quebecers their decision was final: "The rules are good when he wins, but they are not the same rules when he loses."[210] He also claimed that "Jean Chrétien is doing what all federalist parties have done since the beginning of Canadian history, and that is to brag in Canada how they can put Quebec into its place."[211] Mr Bouchard, who sprang back into the campaign, challenged Mr Charest to dissociate himself from the Liberal position and to affirm Quebec's right to self-determination.[212] And at the end of the campaign, the Quebec premier entreated sovereigntists to turn out and vote – to stop Reform from becoming the official opposition, to reject Plan B, and to affirm the existence of Quebecers as a people.[213] Meanwhile, the Liberals continued to campaign in ROC against divisive forces pandering to the "dark side" of voters, while the prime minister urged Canadians to elect a majority Liberal government, one that would have representation from across the country and would be tolerant, compassionate, inclusive, and strong enough to "keep our country together."[214]

In the end, the electorate did so. The Liberals were returned to govern with a narrow majority of 155 seats (down from 177) as their share of the vote dropped only slightly, from 41 per cent to 38 per cent. They took 101 of 103 seats in Ontario, where the electorate appears to have rejected Reform's anti-Quebec message, and they gained 7 seats in Quebec. There, the Bloc vote slipped by over 11 per cent, to 38 per cent, and the party took 44 seats, down 10 from 1993. The Reform Party won 60 seats and became the official opposition. But its support continued to be concentrated in the West, especially in British Columbia and Alberta; it attracted only 19 per cent of the vote in Ontario, the same as its national share, which did not increase over 1993. The Progressive Conservatives also took 19 per cent of the national vote but won only 20 seats, with gains in Atlantic Canada and also – 4 seats – in Quebec. The NDP also regained official-party status, winning 21 seats (on just 11 per cent of the vote), in Nova Scotia, New Brunswick, Manitoba, Saskatchewan, and British Columbia.[215]

Many observers read these results as ominous. They seemed to confirm that the party system was regionally fragmented, and to augur a fractious Parliament in which the Bloc would confront the Reform Party's hard-line position, each seeking to sharpen the polarization between ROC and Quebec.[216] In fact, the electorate was far less regionalized than the seat totals indicated. Only in Alberta did the leading party capture more than 50 per cent of the vote (and even there the Liberals took 24 per cent). Moreover, while regional caucuses in Parliament can focus the attention of party leaders on particular issues, parties with supporters elsewhere and ambitions to expand cannot and do not merely reflect the views of their elected members.

Beyond this, there are forces for moderation in the post-election make-up of the House of Commons. The Reform Party has been weakened by fundamental disagreements about whether it should remain a western party or continue to broaden its geographic appeal, and whether it should continue to operate only at the national level.[217] It is also embroiled in a bitter battle with the Progressive Conservatives about which party can best "unite the right," particularly in Ontario.[218] The Bloc is weaker than before, but its showing was strong enough that it is unlikely to jettison a relatively ineffective leader. The NDP will be in a position to defend Canadian social programs against the other federalist parties, so the Bloc will not be alone in doing so. The Progressive Conservatives had a disappointing result, but their gains were such that Mr Charest will likely stay on as leader: this will help diffuse confrontation. And the Liberals are still in a position to govern – although with greater caution – and to continue their two-track strategy of advancing both Plan A and Plan B.

Despite all this, there is considerable potential for bitter conflict on the national unity issue, for each federal party had perceived advantages in making this the grounds of difference during the election campaign (and undoubtedly Mr Bouchard remains aware of his capacity to polarize opinion). At the federal level, however, on balance the 1997 election produced a structure of representation conducive to flexible debate about national unity among shifting coalitions of political parties. But, of course, the House of Commons was not the only arena in which the politics of another Quebec referendum – or a Quebec secession – would be played out.

THE CALGARY DECLARATION

After the 1997 election clarified public opinion and the party standings, there was an opening for movement on national unity, and enormous pressure was brought to bear on the provincial premiers as they prepared for their annual meeting in August 1997. Former prime ministers Mulroney and Clark urged them to take some initiative, as did leaders such as Claude Castonguay.[219] The business community also pressed for action, and these initiatives received cautious support from Ottawa.[220] Just before the premiers' meeting, the powerful Business Council on National Issues released a draft statement which the provincial leaders might consider supporting. This was carefully crafted to embody the ideals of provincial and individual equality, intergovernmental cooperation, and popular consultation, and it also recognized the "particular responsibility" of Quebec's National Assembly to "preserve and promote the unique character of Quebec's society."[221] This statement was not rejected by Mr Johnson or by the Reform Party, though the PQ government condemned it as "pathetic."[222]

The premiers' conference focused mainly on rebalancing federal-provincial responsibilities, an agenda pursued with determination by the governments of Ontario and Alberta.[223] The goal was greater provincial control over social programs, whose parameters would be set jointly by Ottawa and the provinces.[224] This raised apprehensions among the fiscally weaker provinces that Ottawa's financing of these programs would be reduced. Another obstacle was Mr Bouchard's pledge not to discuss social-policy reform, because this would legitimize a federal presence in areas of provincial jurisdiction;[225] despite considerable pressure to join negotiations with Ottawa, Mr Bouchard maintained this position.[226] The other premiers, however, reached a measure of consensus on rebalancing and on an approach towards the federal government.

They also agreed to proceed on the national unity front (again, despite Mr Bouchard's refusal to participate in the discussion). But there were cautions and conditions. Some premiers, notably Mr Harris, linked any new initiative with progress on rebalancing, which he maintained was far more important in generating support for the federation in Quebec and the West.[227] As well, premiers Klein and Harris insisted on a new approach to national unity, one involving grass-roots processes rather than elite negotiations. Mr Harris publicly condemned any "behind-closed-doors, big-business proposal that is going to be ratified by the premiers" and declared that "any discussions remotely connected to the constitution need to be quite different from the past, need to be from the ground up."[228] What form this "ground-up" process might take was as yet unclear, though Mr Harris had suggested that in Ontario it might involve a legislative committee and public hearings.[229] Ever since the referendum, federalists across the country had been seeking some procedure that would engage ordinary citizens in a mutual accommodation with Quebecers and would allow people in ROC to feel a sense of "ownership" of any proposals for constitutional change – the theory being that the public would then not reject the proposals as having been negotiated by elites, as was believed to have happened with the Charlottetown Accord.[230] In any event, with Ottawa anxiously hoping that the premiers would show some leadership on the issue as well as initiating some "open and transparent" process, and with considerable cynicism on the part of commentators about what public participation might produce, the premiers agreed to meet again shortly to discuss national unity (always without Mr Bouchard).[231] They did so in Calgary in mid-September 1997.

This meeting was preceded by intense consultations. These involved Prime Minister Chrétien, various combinations of the provincial premiers, Mr Dion, Mr Johnson, and even Mr Manning, who was pleased to detect movement towards accepting Reform's principles of equality of citizens and provinces.[232] Gradually, complications became evident. There was some opposition to "appeasing" Quebec with any special recognition.[233] There was insistence by Quebec federalists that the focus be kept on the province's demands, and Mr Johnson was adamant that any proposals had to have concrete implications for Quebec's powers rather than being merely symbolic.[234] And some premiers were clearly hesitant. Mr Clark, for instance, opposed all "arcane constitutional debate" about distinct society, along with elite negotiating processes.[235] Nevertheless, there was substantial pressure to produce some gesture that would appeal to Quebecers and undercut support for sovereignty, and that would provide Mr Johnson with a constitutional plank in the Quebec election that might be held in 1998, while still being positive for all Canadians.[236]

The premiers met for one very long day, mostly without advisers present, and produced the Calgary Declaration. This was accompanied by a set of guidelines about the consultative process that would be undertaken within each province and territory (the process was to be open to the general citizenry, with separate mechanisms but a coordinated time frame, and with governments acting as "catalysts" for consultation). The premiers also agreed to meet again in early 1998 and to press Ottawa for action on Aboriginal issues, which had been excluded from the agenda.[237] The declaration itself consisted of seven principles:

1 All Canadians are equal and have rights protected by law.
2 All provinces, while diverse in their characteristics, have equality of status.
3 Canada is graced by a diversity, tolerance, compassion and an equality of opportunity that is without rival in the world.
4 Canada's gift of diversity includes aboriginal peoples and cultures, the vitality of the English and French languages and a multicultural citizenry drawn from all parts of the world.
5 In Canada's federal system, where respect for diversity and equality underlines unity, the unique character of Quebec society, including its French-speaking majority, its culture and its tradition of civil law, is fundamental to the well-being of Canada. Consequently, the legislature and government of Quebec have a role to protect and develop the unique character of Quebec society within Canada.
6 If any future constitutional amendment confers powers on one province, these powers must be available to all provinces.
7 Canada is a federal system where federal, provincial and territorial governments work in partnership while respecting each other's jurisdictions. Canadians want their governments to work co-operatively and with flexibility to ensure the efficiency and effectiveness of the federation. Canadians want their governments to work together particularly in the delivery of their social programs. Provinces and territories renew their commitment to work in partnership with the government of Canada to best serve the needs of Canadians.

This short declaration attempted to square several circles drawn by public opinion, governmental interests, and partisanship. It was greeted positively by the federal government and Mr Charest, and the Reform Party leadership did not condemn it. Indeed, Mr Manning claimed credit for having shifted the ground of debate towards the positions Reform had enunciated during the federal election campaign.[238] Mr Johnson also welcomed the declaration, regarding it as a basis for negotiations to entrench some recognition of Quebec in the constitution and as an advantage to federalists in a Quebec election campaign.[239]

Commentators, however, were quick to note that the declaration conceded far less to Quebec than had been offered in the past, notably in the Meech Lake Accord, and that the premiers had made no firm commitment to inscribing their principles formally in the constitution.[240] The sovereigntists, of course, derided the premiers' work as "pseudo-recognition," as "another plunge into nothingness and insignificance," and after some reflection, Mr Bouchard roundly condemned the declaration.[241] Recognition of Quebec as "unique" was "insipid and banal," he scoffed. "What a great discovery. Quebecers are unique ... 'unique' like the SkyDome, Cape Breton, Labatt Blue or Wayne Gretzky. This expression would render us both socially unique and a political eunuch."[242] The premier insisted that no such description as "unique" or "distinct" was adequate: "We want to be recognized as a people able to assume our destiny and development."[243]

After Calgary, the provincial and territorial governments proceeded with their public consultations. The objective was to complete these by the end of the year and then to pass legislative resolutions – nonconstitutional ones – by the spring of 1998. An important component of the accommodative Plan A strategy, this would demonstrate the willingness of ROC to recognize symbolically Quebecers' special place within Canada. In fact, there was considerable substance to this, as the initial polls showed that in every region at least 70 per cent of respondents agreed that the premiers' unity initiative was "a positive step in the right direction."[244] Strong majorities in ROC accepted the "unique society" formulation and agreed that the constitution should recognize this, as long as all powers received by Quebec were available to the other provinces.[245] In Quebec, the early indications were that the Calgary Declaration had an effect favourable to the federalist cause. Some 62 per cent of Quebecers agreed with the initiative, Yes voters were evenly split on it, and some Yes voters said they would shift to the No side if all the provinces passed resolutions about the unique character of Quebec society.[246]

Meanwhile, the provincial consultative processes were getting under way. These were diverse, though all were focused on the items in the Calgary Declaration. Manitoba set up a special task force to receive submissions. In Newfoundland, legislators convened meetings in their constituencies, and the government set up a toll-free telephone line to receive citizens' views. Households in Ontario received a pamphlet and questionnaire, and voters could also register their opinions by telephone, fax, or through a web site. In Alberta, an important province with volatile opinion, the process started quickly, as newspaper advertisements informed citizens about the declaration and how to express their opinions about it. Each MLA held meetings in the constituencies, and every household received a pamphlet containing a six-item questionnaire.[247] The exercise, which was supported by all major political parties, drew three to four hundred submissions per constituency, while over 44,000 questionnaires were received.[248] The opinions expressed were generally favourable, though there was some obvious unease with the provision about the "unique character" of Quebec society.[249] Afterwards, the legislature was recalled for a special three-day debate, at the end of which a motion approving the "Calgary framework" was passed unanimously.[250]

Yet as the consultative processes unfolded across the country, the Calgary Declaration proved somewhat fragile. The leaders of Aboriginal groups sought substantial amendments and managed to extract promises from the premiers that changes would be made or a companion document issued.[251] Mr Manning wanted the declaration bolstered by a commitment to reform the Senate.[252] And the federal government wrestled with the problem of whether, how, and when to consult Quebecers about the accord.[253] But the process continued, and this despite considerable federal-provincial friction. This was caused in part by disagreements over issues such as the B.C. fishery and Ottawa's unilateral commitment to large reductions in greenhouse-gas emissions.

A more serious and sustained area of contention was social policy, where the premiers continued their efforts to establish mechanisms that would constrain Ottawa's spending power and allow them a role in setting national standards. Indeed, during their Calgary meeting, they had extracted a promise from Mr Chrétien to hold a first ministers' conference on the issue, and this took place in December 1997.[254] Here, there was sharp disagreement, not least because the Liberal strategists in Ottawa were concerned about further decentralization, an orientation evident in the autumn Throne Speech, when the Chrétien government announced several new initiatives in health and education.[255] Nevertheless, it was announced that negotiations towards a framework agreement for social policy would continue.[256] Once more, though, Mr Bouchard was isolated. The Government of Quebec would not participate in discussions that would ultimately license Ottawa's intervention in areas of provincial jurisdiction, and this stance was generally supported by commentators in Quebec.[257]

CONCLUSION

By the end of 1997, the federal government had recovered from its post-referendum disarray on the unity issue. It had moved beyond the early, ill-conceived attempts to meet its referendum promises and had offered concrete demonstrations of the federation's flexibility and of Ottawa's solid management of the economy. The Plan A strategy had helped the Liberals win the 1997 election, after which it came to include promises of constitutional change built around the Calgary Declaration. Ottawa had also moved steadily forward with Plan B, challenging the sovereigntists' assumptions and tactics, most notably through the Supreme Court reference about the process and legalities of secession. In Quebec City, meanwhile, Mr Bouchard remained solidly entrenched. His fight against the provincial deficit was on track, and although this had cost his government some support, its popularity remained high.

In 1998 or 1999, a Quebec election will be held. Then Plans A and B will converge for Quebec voters, forming much of the terrain over which the federalists and sovereigntists will fight. If the PQ wins that contest, then the initiative on the national question, which rested largely with ROC after October 1995, will shift back to the Quebec government as it begins to plan for another referendum on Quebec sovereignty.

CHAPTER SIX

What Would Happen after a Yes in a Future Referendum?

The purpose of this chapter is to set out predictions about what would happen after a sovereigntist victory in a future referendum. It should be clear from the outset, however, that this chapter's central question is hypothetical in the extreme. There may not be another referendum on Quebec sovereignty at all. The current PQ government might lose a provincial election, and any future referendum on sovereignty would then take place under vastly different circumstances. Or the PQ might win an election but not hold a referendum, for a variety of reasons. Finally, the sovereigntists might lose a future referendum, so rendering the question moot.

Predicting an outcome in the event of a Yes is very difficult – much harder than it was before the 1995 referendum. The approach taken here is to lay out a number of possible scenarios and to describe the preconditions and events that could bring each of them about. This is less satisfying than making a single prediction, but in the current circumstances it is the best that can be done.

YES OR NOT?

Politics is fraught with vagaries, and a number of developments could obviate a referendum. One is the resignation of Lucien Bouchard. Like all provincial governments in Canada, the PQ in Quebec City has a momentum that is generated by a handful of individuals, and a huge responsibility rests with the premier. If Mr Bouchard were to tire of his role, become involved in some scandal, or have his health fail, there would be a leadership void that would be debilitating to the sovereigntists. No one else within the movement currently has the experience, charisma, and determination necessary to carry it forward into a referendum with any chance of winning. Of course, a new leader with such qualities might emerge, but in the medium term the absence of Mr Bouchard would derail any referendum planning.

Second, the PQ could lose the next election. One must be held before the end of 1999, and as matters stand, another referendum on sovereignty will take place only after a PQ victory in that contest. The Quebec government has had to take some very unpopular decisions, especially in cutting spending to meet its commitment to a zero deficit by the year 2000. While the PQ has consistently led the QLP in the polls, disaffection among its core supporters in the peripheral regions, in the broader public service, and in the trade union movement could lead to abstention or a shift in support to the ADQ of Mario Dumont or even to the Quebec Liberals. A credible and appealing Plan A initiative could help this shift, as could the effects of Plan B in undercutting some basic sovereigntist arguments. If the QLP took power, a referendum would probably be deferred for several years at least.[1]

Alternatively, the PQ might win an election in 1998 or 1999 but hesitate to hold a referendum on sovereignty. There are three periods of battle, after all – the provincial election, another referendum campaign, and (assuming the PQ wins the election), the whole period before the referendum. A new Bouchard government would hesitate to hold a referendum that it could not win, and several factors might keep Quebecers' support for sovereignty at insuffient levels to risk a vote. Continued economic growth might restore some voters' faith in the federal system while sharpening the economic arguments against secession, because more citizens would have more to lose in the uncertainty it would bring. Or Plan A might achieve a rebalancing of the federation and a symbolic recognition of Quebec that was attractive enough to depress support for sovereignty so much that the PQ would not risk a referendum. Finally, the elements of Ottawa's Plan B might peel away some Quebecers from the Yes side. Federal politicians at least seem persuaded that Plan B is working. Reflecting on the 1997 election results, Mr Chrétien noted the 10 per cent decline in Bloc support since 1993, declaring, "This is, for me, a big story. People don't believe that the solution is separation – people are afraid of it."[2] Of course, all three factors working together could substantially dampen the Yes support and deter the sovereigntists from holding a third referendum.

There is also the possibility that Mr Bouchard could make an historic compromise by signing on to an agreement renewing the federation within the 1982 constitutional framework. Whatever the terms of an accord, this inevitably would split the sovereignty movement, but Mr Bouchard and his followers could rely on the opposition parties to carry it with the public and through the National Assembly. Such a huge partisan realignment seems improbable, but it is suggested by some analysts who point hopefully to the Quebec premier's apparently erratic career as a federalist Liberal, protosovereigntist, Progressive Conservative, Bloc founder, and PQ leader, and also to precedents when francophone (and anglophone) leaders broke sharply from their established positions to make constitutional compromises and resolve costly deadlocks.[3]

There certainly is some suspicion among long-standing members of the PQ that Mr Bouchard's commitment to sovereignty is not absolute, because of his insistence on a partnership with Canada.[4] Mr Bouchard explicitly denied this when announcing his candidacy for the PQ leadership, stating that he would accept no arrangement in which Quebec would remain within the federation. "No, it's not possible," he insisted, "I'm a sovereigntist."[5] But there have been some indications to the contrary from both the premier and the moderate wing of the PQ. After the referendum, for example, the party's house leader said that his government would examine "serious" and "substantial" proposals for change from Ottawa and the other provinces.[6] Later, the deputy premier indicated that more detailed Quebec proposals on the partnership were being developed and that a new "Canadian union" might conceivably be negotiated before another referendum. The "core of the matter," he said, "is dialogue between two equal nations. And from that cornerstone we can go very far."[7] Similarly, Mr Bouchard reacted to the federal government's post-referendum initiatives by saying, "I will not waste any time reading constitutional proposals made by the Prime Minister if they look anything like this."[8] The qualifying clause here suggests that he might be ready to consider other, more satisfactory proposals. Finally, at the 1997 premiers' conference, to the apparent surprise of his advisers, Mr Bouchard was almost prepared to participate in an interprovincial initiative to set national standards in social policy and to constrain – not eliminate – the federal spending power in this domain, one in which Quebec has traditionally rejected any federal presence.[9] As Stéphane Dion put it soon after taking office, "He will not hold a referendum if he thinks he cannot win it. Therefore, if it will not be sovereignty, it could be something else. So we must hold out our hand and ask him: 'Mr Bouchard, how far are you willing to go in Canada?'"[10]

Despite all this, it is highly unlikely that a constitutional compromise can be reached between ROC and a PQ government before another referendum. From his record as a minister during the Meech Lake period and later as Bloc leader and PQ premier, Mr Bouchard's bottom line has always been that Quebecers must be recognized as a "people" rather than as a province like the others – "one of the good little chicks around the federal hen."[11] Only as representing a people could the Quebec government negotiate as an equal with Canada, and only then could it assure Quebec's future development (albeit within the constraints, self-imposed, of a partnership with Canada). In Lucien Bouchard's view, Quebecers must give themselves this status of a people by voting for sovereignty, because English Canada will never concede it.

Perhaps this fundamental position might change under the pressure of an economic crisis or a crippling constitutional impasse, but it is not obvious that the change would be in the direction of compromise. Conceivably, ROC might offer both this recognition and a very radical decentralization of powers, but given the contours of public opinion in ROC and their reflection in the 1997 federal election results, this is most improbable, and so is the prospect of some grand federal coalition negotiating a new partnership directly with Quebec political parties. So Mr Bouchard is correct. Without a Yes vote in a referendum, Quebecers will not achieve the status and powers that he and the sovereignty movement seek. Of course – and this cannot be emphasized too much – a Yes vote would not necessarily produce this result. After a Yes, there are several possibilities, one of which is that Mr Bouchard and the PQ would accept far less, constitutionally, than their stated objectives. Others involve ROC negotiating radically different arrangements with Quebec. But in any case, it seems unrealistic to expect the sovereigntists or ROC to make such compromises without another referendum being held.

If there is another referendum, the Yes side could lose. One cannot be certain about who the principal actors would be in another campaign or what specific issues would animate it. Nor are the parameters of the campaign established. Quebec could pass new legislation about referendums, and the question would certainly be different. It is also possible that a PQ government and Ottawa might agree in advance about the question to be posed and the level of support necessary to achieve sovereignty, and this would alter the nature of the campaign. This sort of prenegotiation was not on the horizon in 1995. But in a future campaign many arguments would be familiar, and the federalist side might carry the day by showing that Canada can accommodate Quebec constitutionally, that secession is illegal and risky, that separation would entail uncertainty and economic loss, and that there would be no cooperation from ROC. Against these arguments, the sovereigntists might make little headway, with the result that there would be another No victory. Even if they were leading at the outset, the Yes forces could falter, just as the federalists slipped in 1995.

On the other hand, the Yes side might win. Several factors could prove conducive to a federalist defeat. One is the way the economy evolves. Continued growth could reinforce adherence to a Canada that works; alternatively, as Stéphane Dion once argued, rising economic confidence could be conducive to support for sovereignty.[12] A sharp economic downturn might also help the Yes side. Although it would make some voters more risk-averse and less likely to take a chance by voting for sovereignty, an economic depression could lead others to act on the assumption that "things can't get worse" and to vote against the status quo. While it was not widespread during the 1995 campaign, the latter sentiment was heard in Quebec.[13] A recession could cause the number of hopelessly disenchanted voters to outweigh those who become more cautious.

Another factor is how Plan A develops. ROC's initiatives on this front may raise Quebecers' expectations that powers will be decentralized and their distinct status entrenched in the constitution. The principles of the Calgary Declaration are perhaps just minimally acceptable to Quebec federalists, and if efforts to constitutionalize even these cannot succeed, it could be interpreted in Quebec as a terrible rebuff, with support for sovereignty rising to the level reached after the failure of the Meech Lake Accord. A PQ government could seize this occasion to call and win a referendum.

Similarly, the development of Plan B could provide an opening for a Yes victory. The critical element here is the Supreme Court decision in the reference case on Quebec's right to secede unilaterally. No doubt this will be a carefully written and nuanced judgment, but it will very likely state that secession is illegal under domestic law unless accomplished through an amendment of the Canadian constitution. However supple the judges may be about the legitimacy of a vote triggering and justifying the amendment process, the sovereigntists could argue that the decision is a final denial of Quebecers' status as a self-determining people, one that renders their future subject to the whims not only of the federal government but of all the other provinces too. How the public would receive these arguments is difficult to estimate, but the decision clearly will offer an opening for persuasive sovereigntist rhetoric.[14]

Another factor conducive to a Yes vote would be any perceived threat to the linguistic security of Quebecers. None is currently apparent. Indeed, calm has prevailed, despite the provocative tactics of

the "anglo-rights" movement in Quebec. This is a consequence mainly
of Mr Bouchard's insistence that the PQ not reopen the language
dossier (despite pressure to do so from constituency groups in
Montreal). But a threat could be manufactured. And here lies another
potential route to a Yes vote. Since taking office, Mr Bouchard has
generally counselled calm and moderation in relations with Quebec
anglophones and with English Canadians generally. Perhaps because
he has believed that a Quebec-Canada partnership can in fact be realized after a Yes vote in an atmosphere of rationality and mutual
respect, the Quebec premier has eschewed aggression and provocation.[15] But this could change. Towards the end of finally achieving
sovereignty, Mr Bouchard and the PQ might adopt a strategy of polarization, even though this could raise secession's costs to Quebecers both during the transition period and in the long term.[16] So far,
the sovereigntists have been restrained – notably, in the government's
refraining from a sustained counterattack to Ottawa's Plan B initiatives – but there is no doubt that Mr Bouchard is aware of his potential to inflame anti-Quebec sentiment, and this could become powerful
enough to make francophone Quebecers coalesce behind the sovereignty option.[17] Events could conspire to persuade him to mount an
apocalyptic campaign, one of whose themes – an idea already bruited
publicly – might be that the PQ would vow that the next referendum
would be the last and that Quebecers would never again have the
chance to vote for sovereignty.[18] This strategy would involve putting
"the knife at the throat" of one's own potential supporters, but it
might be effective. In any event, this is one way that a Yes vote could
occur. Given the factors sketched here, there are others.

POST-YES SCENARIOS

In the summer and autumn of 1994, with the PQ forming a government and Mr Parizeau driving towards an early referendum, it was
relatively straightforward to make predictions about the campaign
and what would happen if the Yes side won. Of course, those predictions were contestable – and were indeed contested – but one could
discern a single path along which the politics of a secession would
probably move. In the spring of 1998, this is not feasible. One reason
is that the politics of secession have become much more complex.
The issue is now high on the public and partisan agendas, it is intensely debated and analysed, and it is also the focus of many political initiatives that will create turbulence in the future. These include
the Supreme Court's decision about the legality of a UDI, some coherent and vigorous response by the sovereigntists to Ottawa's Plan
B, the outcome of the consultative processes launched by the premiers

at Calgary, continuing changes in federal-provincial program responsibilities, and policy initiatives by Ottawa and Quebec City as falling deficits provide more room for innovation. As well, there inevitably will be external shocks – a stock-market correction, a recession, foreign wars, American intransigence in fisheries or trade disputes, and so on. All of these predictable developments will affect public opinion in Quebec and ROC in ways that cannot now be foreseen, as will the strategies adopted by the protagonists of sovereignty and unity.

Prediction is also harder because the time horizon is more extended. There may well be a provincial election in Quebec in 1998, but it could take place in 1999. Another referendum, therefore, could be called as late as 2004. If a week is a long time in politics, six years is an eternity. There is time for underlying economic and social conditions to evolve, the main political actors to change, strategies to be reworked, and unpredictable events to intervene. All that can be known for sure is that some significant aspects of the drama will be different. So it is not reasonable to try to trace a single path that events would follow after a Yes vote. Instead, we must contemplate a set of possible scenarios – six in all – representing the broad outcomes that a Yes could produce. Nor is it realistic to describe in detail how these outcomes would transpire. At best, it is feasible to work backwards in time to deduce the preconditions of each scenario and some of the steps that would produce (or avoid) it.

Although political developments over the next few years are uncertain, some features of any Quebec secession remain constant. If it is to be triggered by a referendum, then the question posed, the support level achieved, and the tone and content of the campaign will all help shape the consequences. The essential issues to be resolved during a secession will still be its terms and conditions (covering the armed forces, the debt, assets, borders, citizenship, First Nations, minority rights, monetary policy, and economic and commercial relations) and also the reconstitution of ROC (and Quebec). There remains a wide menu of economic and political configurations that can possibly result from a secession, both within and between Canada and Quebec: no structural forces or constraints make any one inevitable. The transition itself will be crucial, and although economic considerations and legal rights will be important in shaping what happens after a Yes vote, it is in the political arena that the outcome will be determined.

If these elements are constant, some of the changes wrought by the 1995 referendum and subsequent events should be underscored. In ROC, expectations and attitudes have evolved so that there will be much more public pressure against accepting that a Yes result will necessarily entail secession. Paradoxically, though, because of constitutional fatigue, hostility towards Quebec nationalists, and more awareness of the cost of uncertainty, there will also be more pressure to accept a Yes and settle the matter. Consequently, it will be harder for any government to act quickly and coherently. Second, there will be a strong demand in ROC for broad participation in any negotiations with Quebec, and the actors involved – provincial governments, Aboriginal leaders, and minorities in Quebec, to name only the most obvious – are now prepared for a Yes vote and are aware of the interests they will aim to protect. Because of this, and the critical linkage now established between the substantive issues of secession and the constitutional changes needed to achieve it, there is a much lower probability of rapid agreement on either the terms of Quebec sovereignty or the reconstitution of ROC. In Quebec, polarization and pre-commitment have much increased the likelihood that a secession will be resisted with civil disobedience and violence, and Ottawa may have taken on obligations to partitionists in the province. Finally, external actors – particularly the United States – will be much more vigilant about the whole process and more prepared to safeguard their interests in the wake of a Yes vote.

Despite the perennial aspects of secession, then, all these developments and those that will occur before another referendum open up a wide range of possible outcomes. The first bears the closest resemblance to that depicted before the 1995 referendum in the predecessor to this book.

Clean Split

In this scenario, there is a Yes vote for sovereignty, and ROC accepts the result. Matters develop much as predicted by the "inevitabilists" before the 1995 referendum. There are immediate negotiations between ROC and Quebec about the crucial issues of the secession – the debt, the army, currency, borders, and so on – and Canada reconstitutes itself quickly, excising Quebec from the Constitution Acts while making only minimal and essential changes to its fundamental law. The secession involves a very sharp shock, but a relatively brief one, and it produces two functional and stable sovereign entities.

How could such a result occur, given what has changed since 1995? One possibility is that there would be a very high Yes vote – on the order of 70 or 75 per cent. This could occur if the federalists in Quebec collapse, perhaps after some great shock comparable to the failure of the Meech Lake Accord, or if for some other reason there develops a strong polarization between ROC and Quebec. In this case, the polls would show well before the vote that a Yes was inevitable.

Each side would have time to prepare for the result. The financial markets would anticipate the event, and mounting costs could induce preparations for secession, such as the formation in ROC of a government of national unity. Measures like this taken in anticipation of a Yes vote, of course, would help make it materialize. But in any case, Canada could not resist a Yes of this magnitude, and ROC would have to negotiate the secession.

Another possibility conducive to a clean split is that those issues most likely to cause uncertainty and turmoil in the wake of a Yes would be prenegotiated by the two sides. Ottawa would concede in principle that secession can occur, which the ruling Liberals and all other parties have now accepted. Beyond this, if the governments of Canada and Quebec agreed on the question posed and the level of support necessary for secession, then even a narrow Yes victory would be enough to trigger negotiations. As well, there would probably have to be joint supervision of the campaign and the ballot counting, or perhaps there would be external observers. There might also be some agreement within ROC about its constitutional make-up should Quebec secede, perhaps in the form of a commitment to maintain the status quo as far as possible through a transition period of several years.[19] If all this occurred, even a narrow Yes could produce a clean split.

Nevertheless, some other modifications of previous "inevitabilist" scenarios would have to occur in order to make a clean split possible. One involves the Aboriginal peoples, who have received strong indications from Ottawa about their right to remain in Canada and who may receive stronger guarantees from the Supreme Court. The Quebec government might simply concede their right of secession in order to prevent delay and severe civil unrest caused by well-organized (and well-armed) native groups and their allies, even though this would potentially cause a substantial loss of territory in the north and several large enclaves in the rest of the province. Alternatively, Canada and Quebec could agree not only that all existing Aboriginal rights continue to apply to native peoples in Quebec – including Canadian citizenship rights – but also that Quebec's native people would enjoy rights identical to those that evolve in Canada in the future.

A clean split would also require circumventing other minorities and staunch federalists organized in the partitionist movement. Firmly entrenching rights in the new Quebec constitution would be essential, but this does not solve the issue of borders. There are two alternatives here. Either some process for partition could be prenegotiated, or the existing borders could be accepted in advance of the vote by both sides. Each solution could be accompanied by the commitment to provide relocation assistance and transitional aid, along with a clear position on such people's right to retain Canadian citizenship. These are very awkward requirements, and having them in place beforehand might affect the referendum results significantly, but given the level of mobilization of minorities and hardline federalists within Quebec, it would be impossible to achieve a rapid, nonviolent secession without installing some such arrangements. Only these ones could both dampen unrest to manageable levels and legitimize joint action to contain it.

Two further observations should be made about the clean split. First, it depends on solidarity being maintained in ROC. This would be more likely if the Yes vote followed polarization rather than prenegotiation. The former route to an irresistible secession would heighten in ROC a sense of estrangement from Quebecers and a collective determination, so that the loyalty to Ottawa that was predicted to underpin its negotiating power after a 1995 referendum would do the same after a future Yes. Prenegotiation would be much more contentious in ROC, and differences about any agreements with the PQ would make it harder after a Yes to form a coherent negotiating body or a government of national unity.

Second, after a clean split, any economic and political arrangements negotiated between ROC and Quebec would fall far short of the level of integration inscribed in the PQ's partnership proposals. Elaborate new institutions would not arise after polarization produced a clean split, nor would they be prenegotiated. Even after a Yes vote that was accepted by both sides as legitimately leading to secession, there would be no more reason for ROC to contemplate joint institutions than there was in 1995.[20]

Renewed Federalism

This scenario, broadly speaking, resembles that depicted by the "impossibilists" before the 1995 referendum. Here, the sovereigntists win a referendum vote – but not overwhelmingly. In ROC there are no outstanding commitments about a Yes leading inevitably to secession or about the terms and conditions that would accompany it, and time is taken to broaden the central government or to empower it to deal with the crisis through an election or a referendum. Negotiations then commence with Quebec. The provincial governments participate fully in these, perhaps through representation on a special negotiating authority. Meanwhile, the legitimacy of the Quebec government and the sovereignty project begins to erode. Most of the

Quebec federalists refuse to rally behind sovereignty, while opinion in the province about fundamental options remains deeply divided. Civil unrest is destabilizing. The economic costs of uncertainty mount, and the citizenry comes to blame Quebec City for its persistence more than Ottawa for its delay. The negotiations bog down because of the number of interests involved and the difficult issues addressed, and their focus shifts from sovereignty and the partnership towards reforming the existing constitution. As a result of all this, the sovereignty movement splits. Most of the PQ leadership agrees to an historic compromise, as do the ROC leaders, and agreement is reached on a set of amendments to the Constitution Acts. These achieve popular ratification, though they contain some dualistic or asymmetric elements. Sovereignty is avoided, and Canada stays intact.

While the "impossibilists" thought this scenario likely in 1995 (placing more or less stress on constitutional change), getting to renewed federalism in the future could be even more difficult than it would have been then. First, the Yes might attain a majority so overwhelming as to sustain a drive straight to sovereignty. As well, there was no prospect in 1995 that Ottawa and a PQ government might prenegotiate (if only indirectly) issues about the question and support level, so that a Yes would legitimately trigger secession, but this is now possible. Hence, renewed federalism could be bypassed by a clean split.

Nevertheless, it should be recognized that renewed federalism would still be possible even if there had been some prenegotiation. In a future referendum, although the legal requirements for secession will be clearer and although the rules of the game may be accepted by both sides, the precise terms and conditions of a secession cannot be specified or agreed in advance of any vote. In negotiating these terms, ROC would retain considerable room to manoeuvre – scope for justified delay and resistance that eventually could result in a constitutional compromise. Also, ROC might be profoundly divided about these substantive matters and unable to negotiate coherently for some time.

If there were no joint agreement about the referendum rules, negotiations would be slower to start and more protracted, for the governments of ROC (and especially Ottawa) would face the same range of alternatives to accepting a Yes as in 1995 – doing nothing, calling an election, or holding a referendum (in ROC or Quebec or both).[21] All of these could slow the sovereigntists' momentum and foster divisions among Quebecers. There is also the possibility that Ottawa would move to exert its continued authority in Quebec. In these circumstances, the Quebec government might proceed towards a UDI. Then several things could happen. The threat of a UDI, the damage it would cause, and the countermeasures it could require might well bring ROC to the bargaining table with attractive constitutional offers. Or a UDI might be passed, but with provision for a period of negotiations, which might then commence, bog down, and result in renewed federalism. Alternatively, a straightforward UDI might be passed after a Yes vote rejected by ROC and many Quebecers – in which case, this scenario ends and one of the remaining four occurs.

However it is reached, renewed federalism would depend on some essential preconditions. One is that foreign powers are generally supportive. Another is that the economic damage, while painful (especially in Quebec), is manageable enough that governments are not stampeded into quick action but have the time to conclude complex negotiations successfully. A joint agreement, right after a Yes, that there will be an economic standstill might help bring this about. Most important is the degree of solidarity within each side. In ROC, there must be enough so that coherent negotiating positions can be credibly advanced, if only after some delay. More difficult, renewed federalism requires in the end an agreement on how to reconstitute Canada – an agreement that must be widely acceptable in ROC yet still be attractive enough to Quebecers that some sovereigntist leaders will sign on to the amendments. This could be hard to achieve if the sovereigntist bottom line is recognition of Quebecers as a "people."

In Quebec, there must be continuing division and very little solidarity after a Yes if renewed federalism is to be achieved. But as was pointed out by Stéphane Dion, the "impossibilist" analysts (who were primarily Quebecers) tended to assume that this would be the case.[22] Sensitive to the deep cleavages within Quebec about the advisability and morality of secession, they foresaw that political confusion and economic loss would erode support for the sovereignty adventure. This remains integral to the renewed-federalism scenario: there is no massive rallying to sovereignty in the wake of a Yes. Obviously, the Aboriginal peoples and most minority groups will be even less likely to rally in the future than they were in 1995, but the scenario depends critically on francophone opinion remaining divided and fluid, open to no persuasive arguments that attribute economic losses to ROC's intransigence, and remaining prepared to countenance new constitutional proposals.

The precise outcome of renewed federalism would depend on the circumstances of the campaign, the level of Yes support, and the extent and distribution of economic damage. Essentially, this scenario posits a Yes that causes enough of a shock in ROC to generate constitutional movement, which would appeal to Quebecers as the sovereigntist project loses momentum. The most doubtful element here may be the capacity of ROC to extend constitutional proposals that would be attractive enough to split the sovereigntists. This would appear to require a substantial Yes vote, along with considerable economic damage in ROC and much coherence in its position. A significant alteration in any of these factors would tilt the precarious path leading to renewed federalism towards some other scenario.

Another possibility is that ROC might be tempted simply to wait out a narrow Yes result, undertaking no negotiations and making no offers of constitutional change, in the expectation that a divided Quebec would eventually crumble and accept the status quo. This outcome is improbable because mounting losses in Quebec could credibly be blamed on ROC's inaction, and Quebecers might be moved to support a UDI. As well, most Quebec federalists are still committed to constitutional renewal, and if there were no such prospect even after a Yes, many of them would rally to the sovereigntist side. The QLP would split. After this, even if economic losses ultimately led to the nationalists and the PQ making a humiliating retreat and accepting the constitutional status quo, there would certainly be left in the province a sovereigntist movement ready to rise again, along with a disorganized and disillusioned rump of Quebec federalists.

The renewed-federalism scenario would probably play out over a longer period than the clean split. Economic loss and the tension of negotiations would make it difficult to meet the complex preconditions for this result. If ROC held, however, and Quebec did not, then this certainly is one conceivable outcome of a Yes vote.

ROC Caves

This scenario, essentially, is the obverse of renewed federalism. Here, one possibility is that the Yes vote is accepted as legitimate by ROC and negotiations begin. But these drag on because of confusion and disagreement in ROC – among both the federal parties and the provincial governments – about the terms and conditions of secession. Coalitions of provinces block agreements about the terms because of their power to stop the constitutional amendments that are necessary for Quebec to secede.[23] The Quebec government then issues a UDI.

Alternatively, the Yes vote is not accepted in ROC, and negotiations are delayed as politicians debate how to react. Despite the mounting economic losses, it may prove essential to hold an election or a referendum, but whether opinion in ROC is expressed through such a popular consultation or not, it remains seriously divided. In Quebec, meanwhile, the Yes result is widely accepted, so if there is a popular consultation, either the Bloc receives massive support or the original referendum vote is decisively reaffirmed. Alternatively, Quebecers simply rally behind the government as their economic losses are blamed on ROC's inaction or opposition. A UDI is declared.

Faced with a UDI, the citizens and leaders of ROC face a terrible choice. Should they attempt to enforce the federal government's authority over Quebec territory or not? Should they respond to the pleas for assistance of Aboriginals and partitionists, based on their rights as Canadians? About these matters there is profound disagreement, both ideological and interregional, which is sharpened as interest rates rise, trade is disrupted, investment dries up, and unemployment increases across the country. As well, foreign countries begin to deal with Quebec, so the UDI threatens to become a *fait accompli*. Under these conditions, there is insufficient support in ROC to resist the UDI. In this scenario, ROC caves and ultimately accepts that Quebec will secede. Canada then comes to the bargaining table. The terms and conditions of secession are negotiated successfully, and the constitutional changes necessary to excise Quebec from Canada are passed. Despite its internal discord, ROC remains united. Although embittered and divided, the governments and citizens of ROC nevertheless agree to maintain Canada as a going concern.

For this scenario to occur, several preconditions have to be met. First, Quebecers must rally behind the Yes vote (however narrow it may have been), whether they do so immediately or as they gradually come to attribute disruption and economic costs to ineffectiveness or malevolence on the part of Ottawa and ROC as a whole. This scenario also requires that divisions within ROC remain substantial – that there is insufficient polarization between ROC and Quebec to overcome them. These divisions would concern whether to negotiate with Quebec and what ROC's positions and priorities should be. After a future Yes, for example, many more British Columbians than Ontarians might favour "letting Quebec go." Similarly, there would be sharp interprovincial differences about how to settle such matters as the national debt and the extent of Canada's trade relationships with Quebec. There would also be nongeographic cleavages about the stance to take on citizenship issues and the extent of Canada's obligations to Quebec's minorities and Aboriginal peoples. In the ROC-caves scenario, all these divisions lead to negotiations failing, and also to ROC's inability to resist Quebec's UDI.

This scenario's outcome also requires that the Quebec government is able to assert its authority over the territory it claims. This means that the Canadian Armed Forces remain intact on their bases and that the provincial security forces – the municipal police and the Sûreté du Quebec – are united and reliable. It also implies that unrest among those Quebecers opposed to secession is relatively limited and that civil disobedience is geographically confined. Aboriginal peoples, for example, might either exclude Quebec authorities from their territories after a Yes or move more aggressively to blockade autoroutes and airports; in this scenario, they limit themselves to defensive tactics. That Quebec can maintain order is a critical requirement of ROC caves. If violence mounts or if ROC concretely contests Quebec's authority, this scenario could quickly shift onto another path.

Two other factors are ROC's solidarity and the stance of foreign governments. Here, the effect of other countries on the process is mixed. On the one hand, they do not impede Quebec's progress towards sovereignty and may even encourage it. On the other hand, they may promote continued unity in Canada, as well as a reasonable final settlement between Canada and Quebec. The latter benign stance may be essential in this scenario, which depends on there being insufficient collective determination in ROC to oppose the UDI, but enough unity that Canada can continue as a sovereign state. Once again, these conflicting requirements imply that the path towards this scenario would be a narrow and tricky one.

Further, the ROC-caves scenario could develop at various tempos. One can envisage an extended process in which opinion in Quebec consolidates slowly, elections or referendums are held in Canada, negotiations gradually bog down and break down, and so on. But the basic scenario could also develop very quickly. All that is required, essentially, is that division within ROC prevents a consensus on how to deal with Quebec after a Yes, and that solidarity within Quebec behind a UDI far outweighs that within ROC against the UDI.

Finally, this scenario would entail over the long term a low level of economic and political integration between Canada and a sovereign Quebec. This is because "losing" the contest with the sovereigntists would leave a bitter residue among Canadians, and because the same discord in ROC that made negotiations fail and the UDI succeed would also prevail about the arrangements to govern the relations between the two states. Apart from particular agreements made with individual provinces, Quebec-Canada economic integration would fall to the NAFTA floor – and Quebec would be exposed to NAFTA provisions that discipline sovereign states but not provinces.

Meltdown

This scenario is a dismal combination of the two preceding ones. Here, a Yes vote may be seen as legitimate or not in ROC, but it is definitely regarded as valid by most Quebecers, who rally towards sovereignty. However, the result is contested aggressively by the Aboriginal peoples, minorities, and the partitionists. To produce meltdown, ROC must maintain its coherence. It might refuse to negotiate with Quebec, after which it would confront a UDI (which in turn would fuel the resistance within Quebec by the anti-sovereigntist hard core of perhaps 25 per cent of the population). Or, if the Yes is accepted conditionally and negotiations begin, they break down. This occurs because of differences of interest between ROC and Quebec about economic matters such as the division of the debt, agriculture, and trade relations, along with more serious conflicts about matters of principle and symbolic issues such as citizenship and the rights of Aboriginals and minorities. As well, the borders are not agreed; they are contested on the ground by native peoples and partitionists. In the face of demonstrations, civil disobedience, and sporadic violence, the Quebec government breaks off negotiations and issues a UDI.

As relations between ROC and Quebec become thoroughly polarized, a contest ensues to exert control over the territory. This could begin with the deployment of forces to protect federal installations and citizens, but it rapidly escalates into violence and disorder. Of course, the economic damage caused by the meltdown is enormous, but this only increases the determination of each side to prevail. Civil disorder is ended by foreign intervention, led by the United States, perhaps under United Nations' auspices. The two sides are forced into negotiations. Since the bitterness of the struggle makes any other result impossible, secession takes place. But Quebec cedes some territory, and very strained relations make economic cooperation difficult. Political relationships are hostile.

Before the 1995 referendum, the meltdown scenario, while having a certain abstract logic, fitted the Quebec-ROC case so poorly that it could be quickly dismissed.[24] This is no longer true, because of the new radicalism among some federalist Quebecers, the Plan B commitments made by Ottawa, and the insistence on rights in ROC. One cannot attach probabilities to the likelihood of meltdown or to any of the other scenarios, but it clearly now is a possible outcome.

Of course, certain requirements would have to be in place for it to be realized. One is that the Yes result and subsequent events increase solidarity within both ROC and Quebec (in contrast to the two preceding scenarios). This is possible because a Yes result could provide an incentive for politicians on each side to adopt increasingly radical positions, pulling moderates with them. In an intensely monitored situation with heavy media coverage, provocation – or, in the extreme, atrocities – by tiny minorities from either side could quickly move public opinion in the other side to support positions that shortly before were unthinkably extreme.[25] Even the antagonism generated through negotiations about intractable matters of principle could induce solidarity in each side and polarization between them if the positions taken by one's negotiators were widely regarded as legitimate but were summarily rejected. As well as feeling that one's fundamental rights were being threatened, heavy economic damage also could be blamed on one's opponents as solidarity and polarization strengthened further.

The meltdown scenario involves a level of disorder and violence that contradicts the normal view of Canada and Quebec as stable, tolerant societies. But unrest can escalate rapidly, and there are few agents of control. The operational ground forces of the Canadian military that are available to maintain order in this country could not fill Montreal's Olympic Stadium. Also the military might fragment, given the substantial number of Yes voters among the armed forces in 1995. The municipal police forces also might be divided, especially in Montreal, and the loyalties of the Sûreté du Québec are unclear, so there is an obvious possibility that order could not be maintained if there were large-scale protests, civil unrest, and vigilante activity. Radicals from ROC might well come to the aid of partitionists, and Aboriginal people from all over North America might lend support to Quebec's native peoples. On the other side, small groups of radical sovereigntists undoubtedly would be prepared for violent confrontations; indeed, threats have been made to this effect.[26] So the severe disorder envisaged in the meltdown scenario cannot be denied, despite Canadian traditions of civility and peacefulness.

The resolution of the crisis depends on foreign intervention. This may appear to be an unlikely conclusion, one depending on a *deus ex machina*, but this view is quite erroneous. First, mediation or intervention could be requested by one side or the other. This could occur if the rule of law broke down and existing institutions such as the courts and security forces became totally ineffective or discredited. Foreign powers would be hard put to deny such requests, but they also could decide to intervene in the crisis because of their own self-interest. All too often, Canadian analysts treat secession as a domestic matter and assume that ROC and Quebec will have sufficient latitude to reach whatever outcome they may jointly determine. But this is wrong. Foreign powers have an interest in stability. Despite the end of the Cold War, defence considerations remain important to Canada's allies. Much more centrally, they have an enormous stake in the integrated North American economy. Americans, in particular, have billions of dollars invested in Canada and millions of jobs dependent on trade with this country. The United States simply will not tolerate prolonged and heavy losses throughout the process of secession. As has been shown, Washington will pay much more attention to a future referendum, and it certainly will be better prepared to defend its interests. Should matters ever lurch into meltdown after a Yes vote, the United States will use its enormous economic leverage and deploy its military if necessary in order to force a negotiated end to the disorder and conflict. The American government, in fact, might well be the agent that prevents meltdown, because its determination to have a settlement reached would not permit any extended stand-off between ROC and Quebec. Indeed, the United States would be a significant actor in every scenario, aiming not to generate any particular outcome but to ensure that some equilibrium is quickly restored.

Regardless of all of this, meltdown remains a possible scenario, even if all participants agree at the outset that it is unlikely, disturbing, and to be avoided at all costs. The preconditions for other outcomes involve delicate balances of factors, and events could swing out of control to produce meltdown.

Reconfederation

This outcome is qualitatively different from the preceding four. In all of them, a Yes vote results either in alterations to the existing constitution or in two sovereign states, with ROC having a constitution similar to today's and with Canada and Quebec cooperating only minimally at the political level. In reconfederation, ROC fragments into several sovereign states, and together with Quebec these enter into a new confederation along the lines of the European Union, with certain powers delegated to a new central authority.

In this scenario, a Yes vote triggers negotiations that quickly founder. Ottawa's legitimacy and power are gravely weakened and the provinces take the lead, but fundamental differences among them emerge. As discord becomes evident and costs mount, one provincial government bolts, announcing that it too will contemplate sovereignty (probably by holding a referendum on the issue). British Columbia or Alberta are the obvious candidates here. Alternatively, one or more provincial governments could declare their intention to enter into a new set of arrangements with Quebec, ones that would mean renouncing the existing constitutional structure. Here, given its substantial economic linkages with Quebec, the foremost possibility is Ontario.[27] In reconfederation, then, ROC does not cave: it fragments and reunites.

This might also occur after a UDI by Quebec. Intense disagreement on whether to resist it could greatly erode Ottawa's power, which also would be reduced if the UDI appeared to be succeeding. One or more provincial governments might then aim to bolt from a collapsing federation or to create new institutions to maintain a union with Quebec. The prospect of meltdown also could produce a movement towards reconfederation.

At the most abstract level, reconfederation is one way to reconcile Quebec sovereignty with the continuation of Canada (or a "Canadian union"). Apart from renewed federalism, the other scenarios result in ROC becoming Canada, with few or no institutions integrating Quebec with Canada. In reconfederation, however, a central government continues, though its functions are reduced dramatically.[28] It would have far less capacity to engineer positive economic integration, and there would be much less interregional redistribution, if any.[29] The central institutions would shrink in size and power, but along with a bureaucracy they could include a legislature. Because of the number of units involved, the problem of parity that would bedevil any dualistic ROC-Quebec political arrangements would be resolved in favour of proportionality. So Quebec would be formally sovereign, but there would be no equal-to-equal partnership in this scenario. Instead, Quebec would be one of a dozen sovereign entities in a confederation where, it has been suggested, it might play a rather limited role, "similar to Britain's position in Europe."[30]

Reconfederation has several preconditions. One is that the Yes vote is not massive enough to lead inevitably to a clean split, though it must be large and solid enough to produce negotiations, and perhaps to sustain a UDI. Moreover, the sovereigntists must be able to remain united and retain public support in the face of the offers for renewed federalism that would likely precede any definite movement towards reconfederation. Given the extent of unrest that would be generated by hard-core Quebec federalists, this balance would be very difficult to achieve.

As well, reconfederation depends on divisions within ROC that would cause power to flow to the provinces. Ottawa would have to be gravely weakened. But this could occur, first, through its very failure to win the referendum and, second, if it proved impossible to form a government of national unity because of basic disagreements about the strategy necessary to deal with the crisis. Next, the negotiations would reveal profound disagreements among the provinces. But governments do not readily go out of business. At least one provincial government would have to cross the Rubicon – to declare that its primordial responsibility to the interests of its citizens could not be met through ROC's collective action. This would be an enormous step to take. But such assertions have become more likely because of the contingency planning that has taken place since the 1995 referendum. In British Columbia, according to a close commentator, secession is now recognized as an option: it is "on the public's radar screen."[31] In Atlantic Canada, contemplation of a future without Quebec has forced thinking about Maritime union and new relationships with the United States, and recent Ontario governments have stridently expressed dissatisfaction with the existing federal arrangements. After the shock of a future Yes, it is not inconceivable that some provincial administration would make a radical departure if Ottawa faltered gravely. It would only take one such move to throw the course of events onto a new path.

Finally, reconfederation requires that the provincial governments (and a weakened Ottawa) prove capable of negotiating a complex set of new institutions quickly and efficiently. This would be hard if the referendum campaign and the Yes result left a heavy residue of acrimony, one supplemented by bitterness and disorder within Quebec.[32] Bargaining over financial arrangements would be especially difficult. Presumably, the central institutions would retain responsibility for Canada's debt, and this would require either ironclad guarantees about transfers to it from the new entities or, more credibly, the maintenance of some taxation powers by Ottawa. The issue of foreign relations would also be thorny. If the confederal authorities were to retain control of tariffs and the customs union, they would need to be delegated considerable authority over trade negotiations. All of these difficulties would be harder to resolve without the encouragement of foreign powers, and a severe economic collapse could make the successful negotiation of re-confederation even less likely. Nevertheless, an outcome that allows for Quebec to become sovereign while preserving the Canadian union – however weakly at the centre – certainly is conceivable.

Fragmentation

If the centre did not hold and one or more provinces left the federation, fragmentation could occur – the last logically possible scenario. Here, Quebec's UDI succeeds, or negotiations break down, and in a rapidly deteriorating economic situation the components of ROC adopt a *sauve qui peut* strategy, scrambling to secure their bilateral links with the United States. The outcome would be rather like that sketched by Doran, with a band of impoverished mini-states straggling along the Americans' northern border, joined to Washington and each other only through NAFTA (perhaps) and through separately negotiated bilateral arrangements. This scenario would require some minimal cooperation among the remnants of Canada about debt repayment. It presupposes both severe economic loss and the absence among Canadians of a sense of national identification strong enough to underpin even a mere confederation. But after a future Yes, these are genuine possibilities, and so is fragmentation.

CONCLUSION

This chapter concludes the sequel to *The Secession of Quebec and the Future of Canada*. That effort was driven by the need to anticipate a Yes vote in a 1995 referendum and to think through its consequences, a task that required basic analysis of the long-term structural possibilities for Canada and Quebec, of the previous research on Quebec secession, and of the comparative politics of how secessions have occurred. Upon this foundation were constructed detailed predictions about what a Yes vote would produce, the terms and conditions of a Quebec secession, and how ROC would reconstitute itself. Now, times have changed, but the struggle for Quebec continues.

Here, three chapters have dealt with the 1995 referendum, while two have analysed subsequent developments – the impacts of the 1995 result, and the various strategies deployed since then by the sovereigntist and federalist sides. As was noted at the beginning of this chapter, prediction is much harder now than it was before. The political situation is more complex and contested, and the time horizon is more distant, so a range of possible scenarios has been put forward here. The six suggested above seem exhaustive, but creative readers may imagine other variations.

In any case, the consequences for Quebecers of a Yes are not encouraging. In no scenario does the result resemble the political and economic partnership espoused by the PQ and its allies. The closest to this is the clean split, where acrimony is avoided and economic integration remains relatively high; but joint political institutions still would not emerge, because the disproportionate sizes of Canada and Quebec would make parity unacceptable as an operative decision rule (as opposed to the *de jure* equality that sovereignty would bring). So Quebec would adapt to the economic policies of Canada rather than helping formulate them in any significant way. As for the reconfederation scenario, political institutions and economic cooperation would result after a Yes, but here Quebec's influence would be proportional to its economic weight – undoubtedly less than it currently is – and pan-Canadian economic integration would be much weaker and more fragile than at present. Even so, some Quebecers might find sovereignty a fair compensation for these costly defects. The other scenarios are much less attractive. Some forms of renewed federalism might represent what the average Quebecer genuinely desires, but they would be achieved only after heavy economic losses had caused a crippling reversal of support for sovereignty. In the ROC-caves scenario, Quebec would be left with a bitter and uncooperative interlocutor; and meltdown and fragmentation would entail huge costs. These possibilities should give pause to any rational voter.

For ROC, most post-Yes outcomes are at least as disquieting. A clean split would leave Canada in operation as a going concern, but it certainly would not be costless in the short or long term; nor is it without risks. Renewed federalism might appeal to those English Canadians who resent Quebecers and are eager to "call their bluff," but it would either entail major constitutional concessions or leave Canada poisoned from within by Quebecers' resentment. The scenario in which ROC caves would exact enormous economic and psychological costs, meltdown even more, and in the fragmentation scenario Canada would be lost, not only as we know it but altogether. Reconfederation would preserve only the shell of a country as provincialism triumphs, but this outcome probably would be only temporary because confederations are notoriously unstable. All of these possibilities should sober those Canadians who believe that their country, as it stands, can readily cope with a Yes from Quebecers.

No scenario has been assigned any particular probability of occurrence. There are two reasons for this. First, each depends on a particular combination of the relevant underlying political factors – the size of a Yes vote, its perceived legitimacy, the degree of solidarity in Quebec and ROC and the extent of polarization between them, the negotiating strategies and objectives of political leaders, and the position of foreign countries. To the various combinations that these factors would take after a future referendum, no probabilities can at present be assigned. Second, as events unfold, each of the possible outcomes could shift towards one or more of the other results. ROC caves, for example, could easily slide into fragmentation; renewed federalism could deteriorate into meltdown, and so on. Given the delicate interplay of factors necessary to reach any outcome, none can be assured, even if political leaders on all sides were to seek to achieve it.

So the future after a Yes in another referendum is radically uncertain. Many of the possibilities can have no appeal for reasonable citizens, wherever they live and whatever their position on the political spectrum. Yet Canadians may move and be moved ineluctably towards another referendum, and the Yes may then prevail. What exactly would happen after that, no one can now foresee.

Postscript

Many events have transpired since this book was finished. Because most are routine – for instance, changes in the economic outlook, federal-provincial discord, and new policy initiatives in Ottawa and Quebec City – they are not worth adding to the record of post-referendum events laid out in chapters 4 and 5. Nor are they significant enough to be taken into account in the forecasting that is the core of chapter 6. However, there are three developments that merit discussion. The first is the resignation of Daniel Johnson as leader of the Quebec Liberal Party on 2 March 1998. Mr Johnson was in a difficult position. As the PQ was threatening a spring election, the QLP stood at only 42 per cent in the polls while Mr Bouchard's party stood at 49 per cent.[1] The QLP's relations with Ottawa were difficult, not least because the leader had criticized the Supreme Court reference and because the radicalized anglophone community was disaffected from the QLP's traditional constitutional position.[2] Even so, Mr Johnson's resignation was a typically selfless act. It was timed to allow the QLP to renew itself, and because of political traditions in Quebec, it eliminated the genuine possibility of a PQ electoral victory in the spring of 1998.[3]

Mr Johnson was replaced by Jean Charest after immense pressure had been exerted on the Progressive Conservative leader by the QLP, the federal Liberals, members of his own party, and political elites from across the country. Despite his reluctance, there could ultimately be no resistance when the polls showed that the QLP under his leadership would take 53 per cent of the votes while the PQ would slip to 39 percent.[4] On 26 March, Mr Charest finally announced that he would run for the leadership, giving a major speech that defended Quebec, attacked the PQ, and advanced no constitutional demands whatsoever.[5] His assumption of the leadership clearly threw the PQ into some strategic disarray.

This was a striking event, but it does not require a change in the predictions about how another referendum on sovereignty might unfold or what might follow a Yes vote. Mr Charest's presence on the provincial scene may deter the PQ from holding an early election, and it may increase the chances that the federalists would win an election, thus rendering a referendum unlikely for years, but these are marginal rather than substantive changes. Indeed, Mr Charest's impact may be evanescent. He faces a difficult task in uniting the fractious QLP, and he and his party are still in the awkward structural position of having to support the federal Liberals, for the most part, while appealing to the soft nationalist francophone voters (and holding onto anglophone support at the same time). Also, Mr Charest's popularity may fade. Lucien Bouchard's personal support still registered high in the polls even as Mr Charest announced he would run for the leadership.[6] Moreover, polls in August 1998 indicated some slippage in QLP support.[7] For these reasons, the change in QLP leadership deserves to be noted, but it does not alter the parameters of the predictions laid out in chapter 6.

The second noteworthy development concerns the Supreme Court reference case. This was heard in February 1998, and as the hearing date approached, controversy grew. Splits deepened among the Quebec federalists as both Daniel Johnson and former QLP leader Claude Ryan argued that the issue was fundamentally political and should not have been placed before the court.[8] Mr Charest also made clear his misgivings about Ottawa's approach.[9] Meanwhile, the sovereigntist rhetoric escalated, and opinion polls suggested that a large majority of Quebecers felt they had the right to choose secession democratically rather than have the Supreme Court define the rules of separation.[10] Under these conditions, the prospect of an early election loomed, but this was eliminated when Mr Johnson resigned just ten days after the hearings concluded.

The Supreme Court's judgment was pronounced on 20 August 1998.[11] It was a unanimous decision and a masterful one. After first dispensing with the argument that they had no jurisdiction to decide the reference, the justices embarked on a long disquisition about some of the fundamental principles underpinning the Canadian constitution – federalism, democracy, constitutionalism and the rule of law, and respect for minorities. They then examined how these should operate "in the secession context," and managed in the core of the decision (paragraphs 84-97) to eliminate two "absolutist propositions": that after a Yes vote, ROC must accede to secession, whatever the terms Quebec may dictate; and that even a clear Yes vote on a clear question would impose no obligation on ROC to negotiate. The court's reasoning was that since both of these extreme positions would ignore important underlying constitutional principles, they were unsustainable. Hence, if a clear majority of Quebecers were to vote Yes on a clear question, there would be an obligation for Canada to enter into negotiations that could lead to secession. Similarly, the Quebec government would be constrained by the need to respect the existing constitution, the rule of law, and minority rights; a unilateral declaration of independence would not meet this test. Having laid out this position, the court then exercised restraint, refusing to specify what amending formula would be necessary to achieve secession, to define "clear majority" and "clear question", to delineate Aboriginal and other minority rights, or to discuss the content of any Quebec-ROC negotiations; these questions lay, at least for the moment, in the political arena. In the final part of the judgment, the court rejected the argument that Quebecers have a right in international law to self-determination extending to secession, and also the contention that the prospect of taking effective control of Quebec's territory could legitimize, in advance, a UDI.

Although arising from a very controversial initiative, this decision had several interesting effects. First and possibly most important, it preserved the legitimacy of the Supreme Court itself. There was nothing in it that could be used to provoke a sense of humiliation or rejection in Quebec that could be directed against the court's authority.[12] Indeed, the sovereigntists were quick to use parts of the decision to support their position. Mr Brassard, minister of intergovernmental affairs, claimed that the court had "recognized the democratic legitimacy of both the option and the process leading up to the realization of the sovereignty project."[13] Meanwhile, Mr Parizeau argued that the decision would force the kind of negotiations that the PQ had always sought.[14] Mr Bouchard saw the judgment as legitimizing the sovereigntist project because the "obligation to negotiate has a constitutional status."[15] One commentator predicted that "no one should be surprised to see the Supreme Court of Canada quoted in future campaign literature and on the posters of the Parti Québécois."[16] Such reliance on aspects of the court ruling to buttress a political stance would of course make it more difficult to dismiss other elements of the ruling in future, and it would also be hard for the sovereigntists to disregard rulings that might be delivered in the course of a secession contest. So because the moderates on both sides accepted the decision, extremists were pressed towards the fringes of the political arena. This was most obvious in Quebec, where attempts by some sovereigntists to assail the whole exercise as "taking away our right to decide our future" attracted little support.[17] In ROC, there was no major assault on the decision from any quarter; instead, the reaction from those most confrontational towards Quebec was that the federal government should proceed quickly to set down a position about the question and about the level of Yes support necessary to trigger negotiations – actions justified by the decision itself.[18]

Finally, while excluding the more extreme arguments from the discussion, the court preserved a large political arena for debate. Hence, the federalists focused on certain elements of the decision, arguing that in a secession attempt, Quebec would have to take ROC's interests into account, along with minority rights; that the principles of the constitution would have to be respected throughout negotiations; that there was no right to a UDI; and so on.[19] Mr Bouchard in turn could argue that the judgment had destroyed several "federalist myths," because the court had "demonstrated that Ottawa's arguments do not stand up to analysis," and that it had "struck at the very heart of the traditional federalist discourse."[20] Further, the judicial reserve had left room for debate about matters that were already contentious: What is a clear question? What majority is clearly sufficient that negotiations must start? In the absence of a court dictate, Mr Chrétien could speculate about supermajorities, and Mr Dion could contend both that the federal government should be involved in setting the question and that Quebec's borders certainly are not inviolable.[21] So while the Supreme Court had encouraged moderation in the debate about secession, the decision had shifted its substance very little. All the major issues involved in a referendum on sovereignty remained deeply contested. Moreover, in the heat of a future campaign or in the uncertainty that would probably follow a Yes result, the judicial bulwarks erected in 1998 against extremism could still prove terribly fragile. In the end, therefore, this important decision has little bearing on the scenarios laid out in chapter 6.

A third significant development is Quebec's decision to participate fully in the federal-provincial talks on social policy. As outlined in chapter 5, part of Ottawa's post-referendum strategy has been to show that the federation is flexible and accommodating to provincial needs. This involves negotiating new guidelines for delivering social programs, and throughout 1996 and 1997 the provincial governments moved beyond a limited agenda (child poverty and the disabled) to aim for a broad framework agreement on the "social union." At the first ministers' meeting in December 1997, all governments –

except Quebec's – agreed to work towards such a framework, which would involve basic principles about social policy (such as mobility and monitoring), "collaborative approaches" to the use of the federal spending power, mechanisms to settle disputes between governments, rules for intergovernmental cooperation, and clearer roles and responsibilities for the two orders of government.[22] Standing aside from the consensus, Mr Bouchard rejected the collaborative approach, and reaffirmed his government's "will to exercise fully its control over the development, planning and management of social policies in its territory, in full accordance with its exclusive jurisdiction in this field."[23] This position was forcefully re-emphasized by Quebec's minister of intergovernmental affairs (who attended the talks only as an observer) in April 1998: he stated that in line with its historic stance, his government would join in the talks only if the social-union agreement provided for full compensation for any province that chose not to participate in any new federal spending program in a field of provincial jurisdiction.[24]

The central government's response to the social union proposals continued to be tepid, and there were signs that Ottawa would not abandon or allow to have constrained its presence in health care and other high visibility fields.[25] But there were also signs of federal flexibility as the annual premiers' conference approached.[26] Much more striking was the movement by the Quebec government. At the conference, Mr Bouchard announced that Quebec would participate fully in the social union negotiations. Even more important, he dropped Quebec's traditional demand for full compensation for federal initiatives. Instead, Quebec would accept that compensation would be required, "provided that the province/territory carries on a program or initiative that addresses the priority areas of the Canada wide program."[27] In other words, Quebec would accept that Ottawa's spending plans could, to some extent, dictate provincial social policy priorities. Other premiers recognized this as a major concession and incorporated it as an "essential dimension" of their bargaining position. Mr Bouchard argued that it was "very important because it's a move that Quebec has never made."[28]

This historic change of position fitted the PQ government's purposes very well. First, it showed that Mr Bouchard was willing to try and cooperate with Ottawa and other governments, something that accorded with the wishes of the citizenry and could therefore be electorally useful. Second, if the talks collapsed without a new agreement, the PQ could argue that the federation was unreformable – that Mr Bouchard had tried one last time, in concert with the other provinces, and that Ottawa was too instransigent. This would help the Yes side in a future referendum. So would a third possibility – that Quebec would end up isolated. At least some of the other provincial governments were clearly willing to proceed towards the social union whether Quebec joined the talks or remained on the sidelines, and it was equally evident that Quebec's position on compensation was not a non-negotiable, bottom-line item for all of the other participants.[29] With no further room to manoeuvre on compensation, therefore, Mr Bouchard might be unable to sign on to an agreement that did not accord with his government's position, and Quebec would be isolated again, as in 1982. This would be used to reinforce the PQ's arguments that Quebecers must leave a federation in which no suitable place can be found for them. A last possibility is that the talks would proceed to an agreement and that the government of Quebec would be party to it. This would be difficult to push through the PQ cabinet, but it might be possible. In a later referendum campaign, Mr Bouchard presumably would argue, not that the substance of the social union agreement was appropriate but rather that it was a step towards the kind of partnership that a sovereign Quebec would negotiate with ROC. All in all, then, it seems that the social union process and its probable outcomes do not change the basic position of Quebec or of ROC; nor do they alter the set of scenarios about what might happen after a Yes vote in the future. The struggle for Quebec continues.

London, Ontario
September, 1998

Notes

INTRODUCTION

1 Young, *The Secession of Quebec*, 3.
2 ROC, I argued, an acronym as irritating as it is common, should be used because the alternatives – Canada without Quebec, English Canada – are hardly less irritating and are more cumbersome.
3 Ibid., 125.
4 Ibid., chapter 11. See also Young, *The Breakup of Czechoslovakia*.
5 See Young, "How Do Peaceful Secessions Happen?"
6 Young, *The Secession of Quebec*, 293.
7 Ibid., 184–91.
8 Young, *The Secession of Quebec*, 208–44.
9 Ibid., 245–66.
10 Ibid., 306.
11 Coleman, *The Independence Movement in Quebec*; McRoberts, *Quebec: Social Change and Political Crisis*.
12 The best general account is Russell, *Constitutional Odyssey*.
13 Monahan, *Meech Lake*.
14 Pinard, "The Secessionist Option"; Pinard, "The Dramatic Reemergence of the Quebec Independence Movement"; Québec, Commission sur l'avenir politique et constitutionnel du Québec, *Report*.
15 McRoberts and Monahan, *The Charlottetown Accord*.
16 For a general account of this history, see McRoberts, *Misconceiving Canada*.
17 Cloutier, Guay, and Latouche, *Le Virage*.
18 Johnston, et al., "The People and the Charlottetown Accord," 35.
19 Cloutier, Guay, and Latouche, *Le Virage*, 169.

20 Stéphane Dion, "Why Is Secession Rare?" 12.
21 Pinard, "The Dramatic Reemergence," 487–8; Nemni, *Canada in Crisis*, 15–18.
22 Pinard, "The Secessionist Option," 2; Pinard, "The Dramatic Reemergence," table 2.
23 Pinard, "The Secessionist Option," 2. See also Cloutier, Guay, and Latouche, *Le Virage*, 45.
24 Johnston et al., "The People and the Charlottetown Accord," 42–3, n20.
25 Pinard, "The Secessionist Option," 4.
26 Blais and Nadeau, "To Be or Not to Be Sovereignist," 96.
27 Blais, "Quebec: Raising the Stakes," 10–12.
28 Archer and Ellis, "Opinion Structure of Party Activists," 297.
29 *Globe and Mail*, 19 October 1994.

CHAPTER ONE

1 On 8 December 1994, Finance Minister Jean Campeau announced that the deficit would be $5.7 billion, rather than the $4.4 billion projected by the former Liberal government and the $5.5 billion estimated in November. Canadian Bond Rating Service reduced its rating on Quebec government and Hydro-Québec debt from single-A-plus to single-A (*Globe and Mail*, 17 December 1994).

2 David Cliche drove to reach agreements, and almost succeeded with the Atikamekw and Montagnais peoples (*Globe and Mail*, 15 and 16 December 1994).

3 The issues were too complex and mistrust too high, and provincial and national organizations condemned the initiative. The First Nations were concerned about losing sovereign title through these agreements, and they also did not want to countenance the notion that Quebec's borders were inviolable, a concept rejected in October by the Assembly of First Nations of Quebec and Labrador. The position of the national Assembly of First Nations was that Quebec could not become sovereign without Aboriginal consent. As Matthew Coon-Come, grand chief of the Quebec Crees, put it, "My people are extremely wary of exchanging our place in a federal system, with all of the inherent checks and balances that we have been able to use to advance our status, for a precarious relationship with a unitary state" (*Globe and Mail*, 24 November 1994). He also said in Toronto on 13 March 1995, "There will be no annexation of ourselves or our territory to an independent Quebec without our consent" (*Globe and Mail*, 30 March 1995). The comprehensive self-government negotiations with Quebec were abandoned soon afterwards (*Le Devoir*, 19 March 1995).

4 *Globe and Mail*, 24 November 1994.

5 *Globe and Mail*, 19 January 1995; *La Presse*, 28 February 1995.

6 *Globe and Mail*, 27 January 1995.

7 *Globe and Mail*, 13 December 1994. Quebec was also the first province to table legislation to implement NAFTA (*Globe and Mail*, 20 December 1994).

8 *Globe and Mail*, 23 November 1994. Mr Parizeau was certainly aware of the potential for polarization. In an interview with the *Los Angeles Times*, he was optimistic about getting a majority Yes vote: "Give me a half-dozen Ontarians who put their feet to the Quebec flag, and I've got it" (Don MacPherson, "Parizeau Proves His Tongue Is Too Loose," *London Free Press*, 15 December 1994).

9 These propositions were disputed, of course, by ROC leaders. One of the more outspoken premiers was Bob Rae, who warned about the emotions that a Yes vote would unleash: "To try to reduce it [the country] to some sort of an economic calculus, or some sad, miserable calculation about economics, is a huge, huge mistake" (*Globe and Mail*, 23 November 1994).

10 See the statements by the premier's chief strategic adviser, Jean-François Lisée, *London Free Press*, 25 November 1994.

11 See Lise Bissonnette, "Continuer," editorial, *Le Devoir*, 3–4 December 1994: "Soutenue ou non par la foi, une prière l'entourait dont on aime penser qu'elle peut l'avoir touché, avoir rencontré sa volonté." ("Rooted in faith or not, a prayer encompassed him, and one likes to think it could have touched him, meeting with his will"). See also Gilles Lesage, "La passion selon Lucien," *Le Devoir*, 3-4 December 1994. (All translations are by the author.)

12 "Let us keep going. Thank you."

13 *Globe and Mail*, 7 November 1994. In ROC, this early blurring of the PQ commitment to secession drew quick criticism, of a kind that later became more common and more heated: see Jeffrey Simpson, "Why the Separatist Argument Has Become Intellectually Cloudy," *Globe and Mail*, 9 November 1994.

14 *London Free Press*, 17 December 1994, quoting Deputy Premier Bernard Landry.

15 Québec, Assemblée nationale, Avant-projet de loi, *Loi sur la souveraineté du Québec*.

16 See the strategy paper reported in the *Globe and Mail*, 21 January 1995.

17 *Globe and Mail*, 19 January 1995.

18 Montreal *Gazette*, 8 December 1994.

19 Ibid.

20 Montreal *Gazette*, 7 December 1994.

21 *Le Devoir*, 8 December 1994 ("If I don't answer you, it's because I don't want to answer you, and if I don't want to answer you, it's because right now that's not the question").

22 *Globe and Mail*, 10 December 1994; *London Free Press*, 20 December 1994.

23 Montreal *Gazette*, 8 December 1994.

24 *Globe and Mail*, 10 and 16 December, 1994.

25 *Globe and Mail*, 9 January 1995.

26 *Globe and Mail*, 31 January 1995.

27 *Globe and Mail*, 25 March 1995; *Le Devoir*, 4–5 March 1995.

28 *Globe and Mail*, 8 April 1995.

29 *Globe and Mail*, 16 January and 4 February 1995. There were sixteen regional commissions, as well as one for youth and one for the elderly. They were to hold 304 sessions in 223 communities.

30 Lysiane Gagnon, "L'avenir avec un petit 'a'," *La Presse*, 18 February 1995.

31 *La Presse*, 16 March 1995 ("The Commission believes that it has discerned the greatest source of apprehension about the sovereignty project: bread and butter after such a major political change"). See also *Globe and Mail*, 17 March 1995.

32 *La Presse*, 10 March 1995.

33 *Le Devoir*, 12 March 1995, on the Société Saint-Jean-Baptiste de Montréal; *La Presse*, 18 February 1995, on the Confédération des syndicats nationaux.

34 *La Presse*, 18 February and 9 March 1995.

35 *Globe and Mail*, 20 February 1995. In his re-entry to politics, through an interview on the Quebec current affairs program *Le Point*, Mr Bouchard strongly stated the need for a Yes in order to avoid a dominating federal government. If the sovereigntists were unsuccessful, he said, the Bloc would not return to Ottawa to "manger des claques de Jean Chrétien" ("eat the slaps of Jean Chrétien").

36 *Globe and Mail*, 10 and 27 March 1995.

37 For a frank exposition, see Daniel Latouche, "Trois scénarios, quatre variantes: Faites vos choix," *Le Devoir*, 4–5 March 1995.

38 *La Presse* and *Le Devoir*, 10 March 1995.

39 *Globe and Mail*, 28 March 1995.

40 *London Free Press*, 6 April 1995.

41 Canada, House of Commons, Office of the Leader of the Opposition, "Discours de l'honorable Lucien Bouchard," 18 ("First and foremost, sovereignty is a matter of confidence").

42 Ibid., 10–13.

43 Ibid., 8 ("They don't want to say NO to sovereignty in a referendum that sweeps aside their anxieties and fails to answer their questions. They are ready to say YES to an inclusive approach. The sovereignty project must rapidly make a sharp turn that brings it closer to Quebecers and that responds to their legitimate concerns by opening a credible avenue towards new Quebec-Canada relations").

44   Michel C. Auger, "Un peu de démocratie dirigée ..." *Le Journal de Montréal*, 10 April 1995.
45   *Le Devoir*, 10 April 1995. A Bloc policy adviser, Professor Turp had already written a draft treaty providing for common institutions, in his submission to the Bélanger-Campeau Committee; see Turp, "Réponses aux questions." Compare Bloc québécois, *Proposition pour un Partenariat*.
46   Alain Dubuc, "Le lâcheur," editorial, *La Presse*, 15 April 1995.
47   *Le Devoir*, 15–16 April 1995.
48   *Le Devoir*, 11 April 1995.
49   *Globe and Mail*, 20 April 1995. Mr Parizeau stated, "The national commission report gives us a strong hand in establishing the gradual progression between the unavoidable economic association, the desirable political association and the association that is conceivable. At first hand, it appears to me that this approach offers the possibility of a common agreement between all forces of change in Quebec." See Québec, Conseil exécutif, Commission nationale sur l'avenir, *Rapport*, esp. 15, 34–6, 64–5.
50   This gibe was made in a speech at a conference organized by the Institute for Research on Public Policy, Montreal, 9 April 1995.
51   *Le Devoir*, 16 April 1995.
52   The agreement is found as the schedule to Québec, National Assembly, *Bill 1, An Act respecting the Future of Québec*. It arose from the Bloc committee headed by Daniel Turp and from an ADQ position paper; see Rocher, "Les aléas de la stratégie," 36–9.
53   *Globe and Mail*, 13 June 1995.
54   Ibid.
55   *Globe and Mail*, 12 July 1995; *Maclean's*, 24 July 1995.
56   See Québec, Directeur Général, *Referendum Act*, and, for the composition of the Yes and No committees, Québec, Directeur Général, *Rapport des résultats*, 679–725. In September, Mr Parizeau and Mr Johnson were named head of the Yes and No committees, respectively. The internal rules of these committees differed considerably. For example, the executive committee of the No campaign included the president (Mr Johnson), five members of the National Assembly chosen from the QLP ranks, six QLP members chosen by the leader, five members of the Liberal Party of Canada, one member from the Progressive Conservative Party of Canada, and three members chosen by the others. The Yes campaign had an executive committee (named by Mr Parizeau) and also a consultative committee on the referendum, which included Mr Parizeau, the leaders of the BQ and the ADQ, four PQ members of the assembly and four Bloc deputies, a representative of the Conseil de la souveraineté, the officers of the committee and members of the

executive committee, and people working in different *milieux* of Quebec society (named by Mr Parizeau). Spending was fixed at $1 per elector, or (when the lists closed on 9 October) at $5,086,980 for each committee (of which one-half was supplied by the state). On the organization of the campaigns, see *Le Devoir*, 26–7 August 1995.

57 *Globe and Mail*, 25 August 1995.

58 Ibid.; *Globe and Mail*, 16 August 1995.

59 *Globe and Mail*, 26 August 1995.

60 *Globe and Mail*, 8 August 1995.

61 For an analysis incorporating these assumptions, see J.-H. Guay et al., "For Mr. Parizeau: The Courage to Say 'Another Time'," *Globe and Mail*, 29 August 1995. See also Lysiane Gagnon, "The Ghosts Who Haunt Our Nights: The Undecideds," *Globe and Mail*, 7 October 1995. For a gripping account of the federalist campaign, see Greenspon and Wilson-Smith, *Double Vision*, 305–32.

62 Montreal *Gazette*, 7 June 1995; *Globe and Mail*, 4 July 1995.

63 "Acceptez-vous que le Québec devienne souverain, après avoir offert formellement au Canada un nouveau partenariat économique et politique, dans le cadre du projet de loi sur l'avenir du Québec et de l'entente signée le 12 juin 1995? OUI ou NON?"

64 *Globe and Mail*, 12 September 1995.

65 *Globe and Mail*, 2 September 1995.

66 *Globe and Mail*, 9, 11, 16, 26, and 30 September 1995; *Le Devoir*, 23–4 September 1995.

67 *Globe and Mail*, 26 September 1995. The official campaign did not begin until the writ was issued on 1 October; until then the vote could have been delayed.

68 *Globe and Mail*, 17 and 19 May, 2 June, and 1, 19, and 30 September 1995.

69 *Globe and Mail*, 4 May 1995.

70 *Globe and Mail*, 5 May 1995.

71 See, for example, the remarks of Jean-Pierre Charbonneau, MNA, *Globe and Mail*, 26 September 1995.

72 One notable exception occurred when the BQ obstructed back-to-work legislation to end a national rail strike. The *Toronto Sun* showed the potential for polarization when it ran a full-page, front-cover photograph of Mr Bouchard under the headline "Late for Work? Blame This Man" (21 March 1995).

73 A midsummer poll revealed that 76% of Quebecers had visited at least one other province, and 82% of these said they had been "very well" or "generally well" received there (*Globe and Mail*, 15 July 1995).

74 *Maclean's*, 9 October 1995, 18.

75 *London Free Press*, 25 September 1995.

76 *Globe and Mail*, 3 October 1995.

77 *Globe and Mail*, 4 October 1995.

78 *Globe and Mail*, 6 October 1995.

79 *Globe and Mail*, 22 August and 13 October 1995. Grand Council of the Crees, *Sovereign Injustice*.

80 *Globe and Mail*, 13 October 1995. See also Chief Coon-Come's longer statement on the issue, in *Globe and Mail*, 26 September 1995.

81 *Globe and Mail*, 13 October 1995.

82 The votes were on 24 and 26 October, respectively. The Cree question was "Do you agree as a people that the Quebec government will separate the James Bay Cree and the traditional Cree territory from Canada in the event of a Yes vote in the Quebec referendum?" The Inuit question was "Do you agree that Quebec should become sovereign?" (*La Presse*, 26 October 1995; Montreal *Gazette*, 27 October 1995). The Montagnais also organized a referendum, in which 99% voted No to associating themselves and their territory with a sovereign Quebec (Montreal *Gazette*, 28 October 1995; *Le Devoir*, 28–9 October 1995).

83 Montreal *Gazette*, 28 October 1995.

84 Ontario, Office of the Premier, "Notes for an Address."

85 *Globe and Mail*, 13 October 1995.

86 Mr Rae's brother, John Rae, was the federal Liberals' main representative in the No campaign's Montreal headquarters.

87 E. Preston Manning, "Open Letter to the Prime Minister," 8 June 1994, reprinted in the *Globe and Mail*, 9 June 1994.

88 For example, "What principles and procedures would the Government of Canada apply to securing ratification by the other provinces of the terms and conditions of any settlement between itself and a province that was seceding from the federation?" "What principles would guide the Government of Canada in determining any division of the federal debt and in seeking compensation for federal assets located on the territory of a seceding province?" "How would the Government of Canada respond to a formal request from a seceding province to enter into an economic union, free trade agreement, or any other 'special association' with Canada?"

89 *Globe and Mail*, 15 September 1995.

90 See, for instance, *Le Journal de Montréal*, 28 October 1995.

91 Chantal Hébert, "No Side's Early Success Could Come Back to Haunt It," *London Free Press*, 5 October 1995.

92 Jeffrey Simpson, "How the Strategists View the Battle for Quebec's Hearts and Minds," *Globe and Mail*, 4 October 1995.

93 *Globe and Mail*, 7 October 1995. They were Jean Allaire, former Liberal and founder of the ADQ, Jacynthe Simard, head of the Union of Regional Municipalities and Counties, Denise Venault, president of a shipyard firm, Serge Racine, president of a furniture company, and

Arthur Tremblay, a former Progressive Conservative senator and constitutional adviser.

94 *Globe and Mail*, 12 October 1995.

95 See also *Globe and Mail*, 18 October 1995, reporting a SOM poll that placed the two sides almost even among decided voters.

96 For a comprehensive chart of poll results through the campaign, see the Montreal *Gazette*, 28 October 1995. See also Maurice Pinard, "Le cheminement de l'opinion."

97 *Globe and Mail*, 3 October 1995; *London Free Press*, 2 October 1995.

98 Montreal *Gazette*, 20 October 1995.

99 *Globe and Mail*, 11 October 1995; Montreal *Gazette*, 20 October 1995.

100 *Globe and Mail*, 18 October 1995. See also *Globe and Mail*, 19 October 1995.

101 *Globe and Mail*, 10 December 1994.

102 *Globe and Mail*, 17 December 1994, 16 June and 13 April 1995.

103 *Globe and Mail*, 29 July 1995.

104 *Globe and Mail*, 14 and 15 September 1995.

105 Montreal *Gazette*, 21 October 1995.

106 *Globe and Mail*, 24 October 1995.

107 Montreal *Gazette*, 21 October 1995.

108 Shum, "Stock Market Response to Political Uncertainty."

109 Poole and Westerterp, "Financial Markets and Instability," 11–14, 17–18. This paper uses an implied volatility index derived from the Black-Scholes pricing formula for options.

110 For background, see *Globe and Mail*, 5 November 1994.

111 *Globe and Mail*, 27 January and 17 June 1995.

112 *Globe and Mail*, 26 October 1995.

113 *Globe and Mail*, 13 December 1994.

114 Douglas Jehl, "Clinton, in Talk to Canadians, Opposes Quebec Separation," *New York Times*, 24 February 1995.

115 *Globe and Mail*, 9 September 1995.

116 Roh, *The Implications for U.S. Trade Policy of an Independent Quebec*, 19. See also *Globe and Mail*, 17 October 1995.

117 *Globe and Mail*, 19 October 1995, and, for Bush, *Globe and Mail*, 10 October 1995.

118 *La Presse*, 27 October 1995 ("The respect that he owes today to Canadian sovereignty will be owed tomorrow to Quebec's sovereignty"). This did not end American commentary, however. Five days before the vote, President Clinton extolled the virtues of Canada, which, he said, "has been a great model for the rest of the world and a great partner for the United States and I hope that can continue" (*Globe and Mail*, 26 October 1995).

119 See, for example, William C. Symonds, "Would Quebec Survive Sovereignty?" *Business Week*, 30 October 1995, 54–5. This magazine

had intended to make the referendum its next cover story if the Yes side won.

120 Norman Webster, "C'mon Canada, It's Time to Do Something. NOW," Montreal *Gazette*, 21 October 1995.

121 *Globe and Mail*, 18 October 1995.

122 Montreal *Gazette*, 20 October 1995; *Globe and Mail*, 23 October 1995.

123 For poll data, see *Globe and Mail*, 19 and 20 October 1995.

124 *Globe and Mail*, 23 October 1995.

125 Ibid.

126 *Globe and Mail*, 24 October 1995.

127 *Globe and Mail*, 25 October 1995.

128 *Globe and Mail*, 26 October 1995.

129 Ibid.

130 *Globe and Mail*, 26 and 27 October 1995. An Ontario resolution, for example, passed unanimously in the legislature, recognized Quebec's "distinctive character" and stated, "The status quo is not acceptable. Ontario will be a strong ally for change within the Canadian federation. We agree that we need a more functional harmonious country and a more flexible and decentralized federation."

131 *La Presse*, 27 and 28 October 1995.

132 Ibid.

133 *Le Journal de Montréal*, 28 October 1995. Following their techniques for dividing the undecided voters and those who refused to answer, the pollsters put the two sides at 50% each, which was what the lurid cover of this newspaper blazoned.

134 André Picard, "A Nation United by a Seat Sale," *Globe and Mail*, 26 October 1995. For a debate among pollsters about the rally's effect on public opinion, see *Globe and Mail*, 11 and 15 November 1995.

135 Montreal *Gazette*, 31 October 1995.

136 See *La Presse* and Montreal *Gazette*, 31 October 1995, for the preliminary results and useful maps.

137 *Le Journal de Montréal*, 31 October 1995 ("To my fellow citizens of Quebec who supported the Yes, I say that I understand your profound desire for change").

138 Ibid. ("Although the No side has shown concretely the reluctance to turn our back on the Canadian experience, it is now necessary to assemble the largest possible coalition for change, with pride and hope, to get the best results that we can").

139 Ibid. ("The Yes supporters have never been so numerous as tonight, and we are all still here. Keep up your hopes, because the next time will be the right one. And this next time could well come more quickly than expected").

140 Ibid. ("It's true that we have been beaten, but by what in the end? By money and ethnic votes").

CHAPTER TWO

1 See Young, *The Secession of Quebec*, 178-84.
2 Jeffrey Simpson, "Bouchard Electrifies Yes Voters, Fulfilling an Old and Powerful Dream," *Globe and Mail*, 12 October 1995.
3 Lemieux, "Le référendum de 1995." The issue is more nuanced, of course. For a detailed analysis of the undecided francophone voters and how they might have responded during the campaign, see Lemieux and Bernier, "L'électorat flottant," esp. 245.
4 Montreal *Gazette*, 28 October 1995.
5 Pinard, "Le cheminement de l'opinion."
6 See ibid. Pinard divides non-respondents proportionally. He also uses rolling averages of Yes support that incorporate the results of three preceding polls, and he excludes for some purposes the polls by Léger & Léger that showed no sharp increase in Yes support (rather than eliminating the SOM and CRÉATEC polls of 3 and 5 October that found very low proportions of Yes voters). In any case, with the Léger & Léger polls included, Pinard's own best-fitting polynomial function shows a fairly smooth, steady increase in Yes support between mid-September and the end of October: see fig. A.
7 Blais, Nadeau, and Martin, "Pourquoi le Oui a-t-il fait des gains?"
8 Lachapelle, "La souveraineté partenariat."
9 Ibid., 60, fig. 1.
10 Ibid., 52, table 5.
11 Ibid., 58, table 8.
12 Pinard, "Le contexte politique" and "Les déterminants psychosociaux."
13 Pinard, "Le contexte politique," 287-8.
14 Ibid., tables 9.3 and 9.4.
15 Ibid., table 9.2.
16 Ibid., 288–9 ("In assuming the role of the chief negotiator of this new partnership, of which he had been the instigator through the virage of April 1995, Lucien Bouchard became for many, thanks to his personality and message, the guarantor that the negotiations would be successful. He brought himself, moreover, to insist on the fact that the rest of Canada could not refuse to negotiate this partnership, that it was inevitable. This was important, because without a preliminary agreement on the partnership, any future accords remained uncertain and this constituted a weakness in the sovereigntist option").
17 Riker, *The Art of Political Manipulation*, ix. Riker's analysis of heresthetic – of "structuring the world so you can win" – is the classic work in this field. While many of his cases concern normal agenda control, several show how support can be amalgamated or the opposition split by opening up new dimensions of argument, by

strategically linking dimensions, and by closing off potentially threatening ones. Riker's brilliant analysis of Abraham Lincoln shows how he linked the dimension of agrarian/commercial expansion with the slavery/antislavery dimension by posing the question of whether American citizens in new territories could exclude slavery. This split the Democratic Party and produced Lincoln's 1860 victory. See Young, "Secession, Games and Strategic Discourse."

18 James Carville, in Matalin and Carville, *All's Fair*, 19.

19 See Page, *Choices and Echoes in Presidential Elections*, 108–51.

20 As James Carville put it, "In politics you are on the record, and often the things you can say are limited by the things you've already said" (Matalin and Carville, *All's Fair*, 134).

21 See Young, "'Maybe Yes, Maybe No.'"

22 *Globe and Mail*, 19 October 1995.

23 *London Free Press*, 5 October 1995.

24 Rhéal Séguin, "Parizeau Remains Firm on Secession," *Globe and Mail*, 8 September 1995.

25 *Globe and Mail*, 13 October 1995.

26 Montreal *Gazette*, 20 October 1995.

27 *Globe and Mail*, 25 September 1995.

28 *Globe and Mail*, 9 October 1995. On this general line of argument, see Gagnon and Lachapelle, "Québec Confronts Canada."

29 Ibid.

30 *Globe and Mail*, 11 October 1995. See also Jeffrey Simpson, "The Most Powerful Voice for Secession Utters an Appealing Message," *Globe and Mail*, 13 October 1995.

31 *Globe and Mail*, 14 October 1995.

32 *London Free Press*, 11 October 1995. This dilemma had bedevilled the federalist side since Mr Bouchard's *virage*; see Anthony Wilson-Smith, "A New Can of Worms," *Maclean's*, 24 April 1995, 18–19. See also the report on an internal Privy Council Office strategy document released by Mr Parizeau, which showed that one important federal objective was "to keep the focus on the issue of separation and to create doubts about the idea of an association, without provoking a feeling of being rejected" (*Globe and Mail*, 27 July 1995).

There was some resistance to this general position, primarily from the Reform Party, and it found some echoes among westerners who felt excluded from the debate. When Mr Charest adhered to the No side's strategy, for example, a popular Vancouver columnist wrote that he had joined "a political separatist-fighting blob. The blob makes no distinction for regions. B.C. is part of the mass out there that is everywhere-in-the-country-that-is-not-Quebec" (Barbara Yaffe, "West Has Little Use for Eastern Politicians," *London Free Press*, 10 October 1995).

33 There was considerable attachment, even among those intending to vote Yes. See the poll results discussed in Jean Paré, "Noui au Canada, Non à Ottawa," *L'Actualité*, 15 March 1995, 51–8.
34 *Globe and Mail*, 7 October 1995.
35 *London Free Press*, 19 October 1995.
36 *Globe and Mail*, 13 September 1995.
37 *London Free Press*, 7 October 1995.
38 *Globe and Mail*, 8 September 1995.
39 *Globe and Mail*, 26 October 1995.
40 Montreal *Gazette*, 30 October 1995, reporting on the final No rally in Hull, Quebec.
41 *Globe and Mail*, 12 September 1995.
42 *Globe and Mail*, 19 October 1995. The federalists derided this as implying that the "magic wand" would solve all of Quebec's problems, not just that of internal division.
43 Montreal *Gazette*, 30 October 1995.
44 *Le Devoir*, 28–9 October 1995 ("de ne plus être une minorité dans le pays de nos voisins anglophones mais une majorité dans notre propre pays. Affirmer, une fois pour toutes, notre langue et notre culture francophone d'Amérique"). According to the premier, the 1995 referendum might be the "last collective rendez-vous" of Québécois. If the No won, he said it would be possible that "our only difference will be to speak English with a French accent" (*Globe and Mail*, 2 October 1995).
45 Norman Webster, "C'mon Canada, It's Time to Do Something. NOW," Montreal *Gazette*, 21 October 1995.
46 This was predictable; see Young, "The Political Economy of Secession."
47 *Globe and Mail*, 28 August 1995.
48 *Maclean's*, 9 October 1995, 19.
49 *Globe and Mail*, 7 October 1995.
50 *London Free Press*, 18 October 1995.
51 Montreal *Gazette*, 21 October 1995.
52 *Globe and Mail*, 20 October 1995.
53 *Globe and Mail*, 26 October 1995.
54 *La Presse*, 28 October 1995 ("Imagine, after a Yes, the extent to which these people will become voluntary partners with Quebec!").
55 Montreal *Gazette*, 27 October 1995.
56 Montreal *Gazette*, 20 October 1995.
57 *London Free Press*, 11 September 1995.
58 Montreal *Gazette*, 20 October 1995.
59 This was dismissed by Mr Parizeau as evidence of a conspiracy to frighten Quebecers; see *Globe and Mail*, 24 and 26 August 1995.
60 *London Free Press*, 11 September 1995.
61 Riker, *The Art of Political Manipulation*, 66–77.

62 *Globe and Mail*, 5 May 1995.
63 Wells, "Be Vewy, Vewy Quiet," 17.
64 *London Free Press*, 20 December 1994.
65 Ibid.
66 *Globe and Mail*, 12 September 1995.
67 *Globe and Mail*, 13 September 1995.
68 Ibid.; *London Free Press*, 13 September 1995. Earlier, Mr Johnson had stressed the need to make Quebecers' choice clear by emphasizing that a Yes would give the PQ government the power to declare Quebec sovereign, whether the negotiations with Canada produced a partnership or not (*Globe and Mail*, 3 August 1995).
69 Ibid.
70 *Globe and Mail*, 20 September 1995.
71 Canada, House of Commons, *Debates*, 18 September, 1995, 14528.
72 Ibid., 14530.
73 Canada, House of Commons, *Debates*, 19 September 1995; 14608.
74 Ibid., 14610.
75 *Globe and Mail*, 26 October 1995.
76 Montreal *Gazette*, 27 October 1995.
77 *Globe and Mail*, 30 October 1995.
78 *Globe and Mail*, 25 October 1995.
79 La Presse, 27 October 1995 ("No, I haven't recognized anything. You don't know the result and neither do I. People would have expressed their point of view. After that, the mechanics are very nebulous"). See also *Le Devoir* and the *Globe and Mail*, 27 October 1995.
80 For an analysis of this weakness in the No side's position, see Lysiane Gagnon, "It's Too Late for Chrétien to Change the Rules," *Globe and Mail*, 23 September 1995.
81 See Guy Laforest, "L'establishment du nationalisme canadien," *Le Devoir*, 5 May 1995, and Jane Taber, "Ministers Come and Go, but Kitchen Cabinet Stays," *Ottawa Citizen*, 28 January 1996.
82 Montreal *Gazette*, 28 October 1995.
83 Montreal *Gazette*, 30 October 1995.
84 *Globe and Mail*, 23 October 1995.

CHAPTER THREE

1 Dion, "The Dynamic of Secessions." (For later works not treated by Dion, see Valaskakis and Fournier, *Le piège de l'indépendance*; McRoberts, ed., *Beyond Quebec*; and the publications throughout 1995 in the "Referendum Papers" of the C.D. Howe Institute's *Commentary* series and in *Choix* [Série Québec-Canada], published by the Institute for Research on Public Policy.) See also Brown, "Thinking the 'Unthinkable.'"
2 Dion, "The Dynamic of Secessions," 537.

3 Monahan, *"Cooler Heads Shall Prevail,"* 5.
4 Dion, "The Dynamic of Secessions," 551.
5 Apart from Monahan, the other analyses in the "impossible secession" school were Côté, *Le rêve de la terre promise*, and Derriennic, *Nationalisme et démocratie*.
6 Others were Gibson, *Plan B*, and Freeman and Grady, *Dividing the House*.
7 Richard Gwyn, "Robillard's 'Slip' Was, in Fact, a Warning to Quebec," *Toronto Star*, 17 September 1995.
8 Dion, "The Dynamic of Secessions," 546.
9 *Globe and Mail*, 30 October 1995.
10 Poole and Westerterp, "Financial Markets and Instability," 19–23.
11 Ibid., 27–36.
12 *Globe and Mail*, 25 October 1995.
13 *Globe and Mail*, 26 October, 1995.
14 Montreal *Gazette*, 21 October 1995.
15 *Globe and Mail*, 25 October 1995.
16 *Globe and Mail*, 23 February 1996.
17 Ibid. In his televised speech to the country, Mr Chrétien had in fact said that the voters' decision was "serious and irreversible," and he had warned those thinking of voting Yes in order to bring change to Canada to beware: "Listen to the leaders of the separatist side. They are very clear. The country they want is not a better Canada, it is a separate Quebec. Don't be fooled" (*Globe and Mail*, 26 October 1995).
18 Philip Authier, "The Yes Plan," *Ottawa Citizen*, 3 March 1996.
19 *Globe and Mail*, 23 February 1996.
20 *Globe and Mail*, 13 September 1995.
21 *Globe and Mail*, 9 November 1995.
22 *Globe and Mail*, 19 October 1995.
23 *Globe and Mail*, 9 November 1995; *La Presse*, 28 October 1995.
24 *Globe and Mail*, 9 November 1995. Just before the referendum, the Caisse and Hydro-Québec were reported to be heavy buyers of Canadian currency and bonds (*Globe and Mail*, 25 October 1995). Mr Parizeau later claimed that his finance minister had $17 billion in liquidities at his disposal (Parizeau, *Pour un Québec souverain*, 45). See also *Globe and Mail*, 3 and 18 November 1995.
25 *Globe and Mail*, 9 November 1995.
26 *Ottawa Citizen*, 3 March 1996, *Globe and Mail*, 9 November 1995.
27 Four major bases in Quebec are at Bagotville, Saint-Hubert, Valcartier, and Saint-Jean. Voting results are available for the first three. Taking only those polls located within the base perimeters, the Yes vote was 41.8%, 45.2%, and 45.0%. These figures must be interpreted with caution because not all voters in the polls were military personnel, some military personnel lived off-base, and those posted outside

Quebec could vote by mail. (The information on the precise polls located on bases was provided by the office of Quebec's director general of elections.)

28 *Globe and Mail*, 19 October 1995.

29 See Parizeau, *Pour un Québec souverain*, 49, 283–8. These pages demonstrate the premier's preoccupation with international recognition and explain his "Grand Game" – getting a quick recognition from France in order to pressure the United States to accept the inevitability of Quebec sovereignty. This would require, within a week or ten days after the Yes, "qu'un geste solennel soit accompli par le Québec pour proclaimer sa souveraineté" ("that Quebec make a solemn act to proclaim its sovereignty"). During the 1997 election campaign, when Mr Parizeau's book was released, these passages became a major issue because they were taken to imply that the PQ government would have issued a UDI soon after a Yes vote. There is no doubt that under certain conditions this would have been contemplated and even attempted – for instance, if Canada refused to negotiate and if opinion in Quebec, and in the Quebec Liberal Party, regarded the Yes as legitimate. But Mr Parizeau also writes (286) that the declaration could be suspended for six months or a year in order to pursue negotiations towards a partnership treaty and that it would still have the same effect on international recognition. If he believed this, then the existing language of Bill 1 might have sufficed as a "solemn declaration" when it was passed. Alternatively, his government might have amended the bill so that it declared sovereignty right away. This would not be uncharacteristic of a premier whose commitment to sovereignty was primarily intellectual and who deeply regretted the "nostalgia" felt about Canada even by some sovereigntists (47). But unless federalist Quebecers rallied strongly behind the Yes, it is difficult to believe that an amended bill could have passed the assembly within a week or two.

30 Arguments that a "misinformed" or "confused" Yes vote should not be accepted often rest on a very tight exercise in logic, one advanced by some analysts in the "impossible secession" school of prognostication. This argument reasons that because some Yes voters thought that a Yes would not actually bring "separation" but would lead to some new arrangement with Canada, either within the existing constitutional order or as two sovereign states, then their votes were misinformed and should be discounted. Not only does this impose a very high standard of information on the democratic voter – What question is put to the electorate in an election campaign? – and not only would it mask the failure of the No side to get across its message about "separation," but it is also tautological. If Ottawa refused to enter negotiations, for example, and instead put some new

constitutional proposals before the country in a referendum, then a
Yes vote could very well have produced exactly the result that
purportedly justified ignoring it!

See, for instance, Monahan, *"Cooler Heads Shall Prevail,"* 6. His flow
chart of options after a Yes result starts with Quebec setting a date for
declaring independence, and this is followed by "Square 1,"
"constitutional negotiations begin." The subsequent alternatives
include: (1) "Agreement reached whereby Quebec will remain within
Canada; secession avoided"; (2) "Agreement reached on terms of
Quebec's secession from Canada" (some subpaths of which lead back
to Square 1); and (3) "Negotiations reach impasse" (again with some
subpaths leading back to Square 1). After a Yes is rejected by ROC, in
fact, most paths lead to Quebec staying within Canada through some
form of constitutional agreement. Some of these scenarios would
involve heavy costs indeed, but it is hard to see how anyone believing
in them could reject Yes voters as uninformed on the grounds that
they thought their Yes would produce precisely the same results as
those foreseen by Monahan. The agency problem makes this interpretation contestable, but the bottom line is that sophisticated anti-
sovereigntists could not predict the outcome of a Yes vote, and some of
the results they envisaged did coincide with those expected by the Yes
voters whose ballots would be discounted on grounds of "ignorance."

31 See, for example, the *Globe and Mail* editorial, "What Yes and No
Might Bring," 27 October 1995, and Jeffrey Simpson, "The Federalist
Forces Seize the Magic Wand from the Secessionists," *Globe and Mail*,
26 October 1995.

32 The notion that Quebec could prop up the Canadian dollar for very
long with $17 billion is ludicrous.

33 See Young, "'Maybe Yes, Maybe No,'" 54–5.

34 See for example, Robert Sheppard, "A Loopy, Messy Federalism,"
Globe and Mail, 25 October 1995, and Andrew Coyne, "How to
Respond if Quebeckers Vote Yes: First Do Nothing," *Globe and Mail*, 30
October 1995.

35 See, for example, McRoberts, "After the Referendum," 414.

36 White, "Speech."

37 Mr Black is an historian of Quebec and the owner of many Canadian
newspapers. See his "Hope for a No, but See the Opportunities in a
Yes," *Globe and Mail*, 27 October 1995. In this piece he stated, "If
Quebec votes Yes, it is voting for sovereignty. It is a sophisticated
electorate that knows perfectly well the implications of this vote."

38 Dion, "The Dynamic of Secessions," 548–50; *Globe and Mail*, 30
October 1995.

39 *Maclean's*, 1 July 1995, 14.

40 Ibid. 73% of people in ROC expected a No vote.

41 While several secession referendums elsewhere have carried by wide margins, very important decisions have been sanctioned by narrow ones. These include referendums in Sweden on entry into the EU (carried by 52.2%), the Irish referendum on divorce (decided by 50.2%), and the Newfoundland referendum on church-run schools that led to a proposed constitutional amendment in 1996. This last vote, on a very obscure question, broke 54 to 46% on a turnout of only 52% of the eligible voters.

42 *Le Devoir*, 23–4 September 1995, reporting a Créatec poll done for the No committee.

43 One prominent commentator, for example, criticized Mr Chrétien's insistence that the 1995 referendum question had been misleading, in very harsh terms. Barbara Amiel wrote that "his statement is wishful thinking and insulting to those who voted Yes. While there is no question that Lucien Bouchard and Jacques Parizeau attempted to fudge the consequences of a vote for sovereignty, it is also true that a Yes vote would have clearly empowered them to negotiate it. By the day of the vote, any Quebecer who did not know this must have spent his life with his head in a paper bag" (*Maclean's*, 20 November 1995).

44 Québec, Directeur général, *Rapport des résultats officiels du scrutin*, 193.

45 Quebec, Directeur général, *Rejected Ballot Papers – Unity Rally*, 2, and appendix 1: the Honourable Alan B. Gold to the Director General, 9 May 1996: "I confirm that my inquiry gave no reason to believe that there had been a nationally orchestrated conspiracy."

46 Ibid., appendix 3.

47 Quebec, Chief Electoral Officer, press releases of 13 May and 7 June 1996.

48 Directeur général, *Rejected Ballot Papers – Unity Rally*, 32, 35.

49 See *Globe and Mail*, editorial, "Mysterious Doings on Referendum Night," 9 November 1995, and *Globe and Mail*, 10 November 1995. The editorial raised the possibility that there had been a "deliberate attempt to reduce the No vote" and that this could have involved the "foot soldiers" on the ground or the "generals" of the campaign.

50 The voting irregularities were also noted abroad: see the editorial in the *Washington Times*, 7 November 1995.

CHAPTER FOUR

1 This is very different from saying that every secession is unique. Stéphane Dion, in particular, has tried to argue that all other cases of peaceful secession are irrelevant to the Quebec-Canada situation because they involved bipartite federations, or were not welfare states, or were not fully democratic. Hence, "we are left with no

precedent" ("The Dynamic of Secessions," 549). Of course, every case is unique, but to insist too strongly on this is simply to deny all possibility of comparative study. *In extremis* we are told that one cannot compare apples and oranges. In reality, of course, apples and oranges are both spherical fruits; they roll when placed on an inclined plane; if they hit an object, they will both split (though in ways that vary with their different rinds and internal composition); and so on. If important commonalities are found in very different cases, this suggests that they should be taken into account when thinking about any comparable situation. Not to do so – to insist on the uniqueness of every case – is to demand a licence to make whatever predictions seem reasonable, congenial, or useful.

2   See *Globe and Mail*, 25 April 1997, for the trend over time.

3   *The Gallup Poll*, 27 November 1995; *Globe and Mail*, 24 February, 26 March, and 20 June 1996.

4   *Globe and Mail*, 1 February 1997.

5   This is sensitive to the question posed, however. Throughout 1995, about 70% agreed that Quebec had the right to separate (Lachapelle, "La souveraineté partenariat," 60, fig. 1). In 1996, 68% agreed with the proposition that Quebecers are "free to take charge of their own destiny" (*Globe and Mail*, 25 May 1996). However, only 46% thought the National Assembly could make a UDI, while 40% thought it could not (*Globe and Mail*, 23 October 1996).

6   *Globe and Mail*, 23 October 1996; the Yes vote would drop from 45 to 39%. Almost one-half of Yes supporters claimed that their vote would secure "a good deal" from Canada, while 53% sought a new country (Montreal *Gazette*, 12 May 1997).

7   See, for example, *Globe and Mail*, 4 December 1996. The federal minister responsible had stated that native territory is not Quebec territory; see *Globe and Mail*, 14 February 1996.

8   *Globe and Mail*, 2 November 1996.

9   Some of these groups and their activities are described in Trent, "Post-Referendum Citizen Group Activity."

10   *Globe and Mail*, 5 February 1996; *London Free Press*, 10 June 1996.

11   *Toronto Star*, 31 December 1995.

12   *Globe and Mail*, 25 March 1997. See also *Globe and Mail*, 13 November 1996, and Robert Libman and Tommy Schnurmacher, "A Case for Partitioning Quebec," *London Free Press*, 30 June 1996.

13   Tom Kierans, "Is Quebec Partition an Idea Worth Pursuing?" *Globe and Mail*, 25 March 1997. See also Don MacPherson, "Opening Up Partition's Can of Worms," *London Free Press*, 24 January 1996, and Jeffrey Simpson, "How Quebec's English Population Views the Secessionists," *Globe and Mail*, 13 September 1996.

14   William Johnson, "A New Anglo Leadership," Montreal *Gazette*, 2 August 1996; *Le Devoir*, 2 August 1996.

15 *Globe and Mail*, 8 August 1996.

16 Montreal *Gazette*, 3 August 1996.

17 National unity, usually cited as "the most important problem facing this country today" by fewer than 10% of respondents between 1985 and 1995, rose to 25% after the referendum (*The Gallup Poll*, 20 November 1995). On support for distinct society recognition, see *The Gallup Poll*, 27 November 1995, and the Angus Reid poll reported in the *London Free Press*, 4 November 1995.

18 *Globe and Mail*, 2 December 1995.

19 *Vancouver Sun*, 13 November 1995.

20 Allan Gregg, "Can Canada Survive?" *Maclean's*, 25 December 1995 – 1 January 1996, 17. Intriguingly, the proportions in Quebec were 45% and 46%.

21 Ibid., 17.

22 Anthony Wilson-Smith, "Future Imperfect," *Maclean's*, 30 December 1996 – 6 January 1997, 46, 41.

23 *London Free Press*, 28 December 1995. Another 35% supported Ottawa's current (mixed) approach.

24 *Globe and Mail*, 16 November 1996.

25 Anthony Wilson-Smith, "Future Imperfect," *Maclean's*, 30 December 1996 – 6 January 1997, 41. Outside Quebec, there was a narrow margin in favour of the view that a "tougher stand" would make Quebec more willing (32%) rather than less (25%) to negotiate a deal with ROC. But fully 39% thought it would make no difference; presumably, this group includes many people who support the harder stand on principle.

26 See *Globe and Mail*, 19 September 1995, and the SOM/Environics poll reported in the *London Free Press*, 2 October 1995.

27 In early 1995, 67.6% in ROC thought Quebecers would not vote Yes, and during that summer 73% thought they would not (*Globe and Mail*, 8 February 1995; Anthony Wilson-Smith, "A Quiet Passion," *Maclean's*, 1 July 1995, 13). At the end of 1995, only 33% in ROC thought Quebecers would vote Yes if another referendum were held within five years (calculated from data in Allan Gregg, "Can Canada Survive?" *Maclean's*, 25 December 1995 – 1 January 1996, 14–33).

28 Cairns, "Looking Back from the Future," 79.

29 Milne, "Past and Future: Reflections after the Referendum," 83.

30 These expressions are found in the Halifax *Chronicle-Herald*, 1 November 1995; *Vancouver Sun, Calgary Herald, Toronto Star*, and St John's *Evening Telegram*, all 3 November 1995.

31 *Globe and Mail*, 22 December 1995. In ROC, 46% of respondents to a Canadian Facts poll thought that Quebec would not separate, while 40% saw separation as inevitable; however, 81% thought it important for ROC to "establish its conditions for Quebec separation."

32 *London Free Press*, 28 December 1995.

33 Monahan and Bryant, *Coming to Terms with Plan B*, 3. Apart from two "principles" concerning the substance of partition and Aboriginal rights, the authors concentrated on matters of process, including the need to clarify the legality of secession, maintain the rule of law, set the requirements for referendums, and establish the required majority.

34 *Globe and Mail*, 9 July 1996.

35 *Globe and Mail*, 5 July 1997.

36 See, for example, Jeffrey Simpson, "With No Clear Thinking, Canada Was Ill Prepared for Its Dismemberment," *Globe and Mail*, 8 November 1995.

37 See, for example, Rowlands, "International Aspects of the Division of Debt Under Secession". New rounds of studies are also forthcoming from various think tanks.

38 *Globe and Mail*, 26 February 1996.

39 *Globe and Mail*, 28 May 1997.

40 *Globe and Mail*, 4 December 1996. See Gibson, *Renewing the Federation: Options for British Columbia*, esp. 9–42.

41 *Globe and Mail*, 20 November 1996.

42 Milne, "Past and Future," 83.

43 *London Free Press*, 3 May 1997.

44 David Bercuson and Barry Cooper, "An Idea Whose Time Has Not Yet Come: B.C. Separation," *Globe and Mail*, 24 May 1997.

45 Cairns, "Looking Back from the Future."

46 See, for example, Gibson, *Renewing the Federation: Options for British Columbia*, 33: "Any deal with Quebec that is implemented according to law will require a constitutional amendment, and therefore the consent of the provinces. It is obvious that the negotiating structure must fully involve the provincial level at every stage – not simply on an informational basis, but on a full decision-making basis." Decisions to be taken would include the debt burden, "moral and practical questions," and the shape and future of ROC. More generally on the linkage, see William Thorsell, "Speak Softly and Carry a Big Torch for Lucien Bouchard," *Globe and Mail*, 23 March 1996, and Jeffrey Simpson, "Legal or Illegal, Canada Will Defend Its Interests with Quebec," *Globe and Mail*, 15 May 1996.

47 See Jockel, "And If Quebec Secedes?"; Black, "Canada's Continuing Identity Crisis."

48 See, for example, Peter Brimelow, "Canadian Roulette," *Forbes*, 25 September 1995; William C. Symonds, "Would Quebec Survive Sovereignty?" *Business Week*, 30 October 1995, and "Shaking Canada," *Economist*, 21 October 1995.

49 Parizeau, "The Case for a Sovereign Quebec"; Johnson, "The Case for a United Canada."

50 See Cooper, "Quebec Sovereignty." Jockel, "And If Quebec Secedes?"

51 See, for example, the New Orleans *Times-Picayune*, 2 November 1995; *San Francisco Chronicle*, 1 November 1995; *Tulsa World*, 1 November 1995; *Philadelphia Inquirer*, 1 November 1995; and *Washington Post*, 1 November 1995. Occasionally, editorialists called for a more robust American approach to the issue, given the stakes for the United States; see, for example, the Newark *Star-Ledger*, 1 November 1995.

52 *Globe and Mail*, 11 June 1996. Mr Juppé reaffirmed France's position of non-indifference but non-interference, and also acceptance of Quebecers' right to self-determination. As he put it at a banquet for Mr Bouchard, "Our country has always been anxious to accompany Quebec on its path and it does so by scrupulously respecting your orientations, your decisions, because it is you who clearly hold your destiny in your hands" (*Globe and Mail*, 12 June 1996).

53 It is most unlikely that French recognition would have influenced the United States. As one State Department official exclaimed when the former premier's book was released, "Just the notion! *France?* France! Come on!" (*Globe and Mail*, 22 May 1997).

54 James Reed, "Will Americans Finally Train Lenses on Canada?" *Christian Science Monitor*, 15 December 1995, and David R. Henderson, "If Quebec Separates, Almost Everybody Wins," *Wall Street Journal*, 19 January 1996.

55 Doran, "Will Canada Unravel?"

56 Ibid., 104.

57 Ibid., 98.

58 Ibid., 107.

59 Ibid., 109.

60 For a reply to a scenario that left him "almost at a loss for words," see Thomas d'Aquino (president of the Business Council on National Issues), "The Case for Canada."

61 Fry, "Quebec's Sovereignty Movement"; Tom Campbell, "Statement."

62 United States, Committee on International Relations, *The Issue of Quebec's Sovereignty*, 1–27.

63 Ibid., 11 (Christopher Sands).

64 Jones, "An Independent Quebec: Looking into the Abyss," 21.

65 Ibid., 22, 35.

66 Ibid., 33.

67 Ibid., 33; United States, Committee on International Relations, *The Issue of Quebec's Sovereignty*, 27; Jockel, "Prepared Statement," 53.

68 See United States, Committee on International Relations, *The Issue of Quebec's Sovereignty*.

69 See, for example, S. Neil MacFarlane, *Sovereignty and Stability*.

70 See, for example, Lawson, "No Canada?" As well, the top-rated morning news show, *Good Morning America*, devoted a week of broadcasts to a cross-Canada tour in 1996, during which interviews with Mr Chrétien and Mr Bouchard about the process of secession

exposed their strong antipathy; see *Globe and Mail*, 14 May 1996, and *Maclean's*, 27 May 1996.

71 In the crudest form, this involves a bilateral trade flow of over $300 billion (U.S.) and direct investment in Canada of over $80 billion; see Fry, "Quebec's Sovereignty Movement."

72 See, for example, the "between the lines" interpretation of Charles Doran's article by a seasoned observer: George F. Bain, "How to Prepare for Life Without Quebec," *Globe and Mail*, 19 September 1996.

CHAPTER FIVE

1 *Globe and Mail*, 21 November 1995.

2 *Globe and Mail*, 22 November 1995 and 17 January 1996.

3 *Globe and Mail*, 22 November 1995.

4 *Globe and Mail*, 27 and 29 January 1996; *Ottawa Citizen*, 28 January 1996. See also Québec, Assemblée nationale, *Journal des débats*, 25 March 1996, 11. Mr Bouchard, in his "discours d'ouverture," noted that Quebecers had voted in referendums and elections in every year since 1992, and he declared, "Cette année, nous allons gouverner à plein temps" ("This year, we will govern full time").

5 As Mr Bouchard put it, "We need a reconciliation of all the components of Quebec society. We must embark together upon the path of recovery; business people with the unions; the public sector in concert with the private sector; women and men, academics and workers, the elderly and the young, anglophones, allophones and native people working side-by-side with francophones" (Barry Came, "Taking the Plunge," *Maclean's*, 4 December 1995, 30).

6 *Globe and Mail*, 9, 20, and 21 March 1996. The working groups were to examine "the economy and jobs," "enterprises and jobs," "the social economy," and "the *relance* of Montreal." With the exception of the third, they were led by prominent businesspeople. Also established was a commission to study taxation, with a view to eliminating the provincial debt, along with task forces on educational reform and income security. See *Le Journal de Montréal*, 4 May 1996, for a progress report.

7 See Québec, National Assembly, 2nd session, 35th Legislature, Bill 3, *An Act Respecting the Elimination of the Deficit and a Balanced Budget*. The deficit was to be at a maximum of $3,275,000,000 in fiscal year 1996–97 and was to fall to zero by 1999–2000, after which "no deficit shall be incurred."

8 *Globe and Mail*, 2 November 1996. At the close of the summit, Mr Bouchard declared, "No one can say we are doing nothing for social democracy." For an analysis of representation at the summit and a

critique of its decisions, see Belleau, "Le sommet de l'emploi et de l'économie." Even stauchly federalist businessmen admitted that the government had "consolidated its relations with the business community" and that Mr Bouchard had demonstrated "the hand of a master" (*Toronto Star*, 2 November 1996). Most notably, the government decided to slow the implementation of pay equity, a major irritant for business (*Globe and Mail*, 9 October and 8 November 1996). It also began to warn that wage rollbacks for public-sector workers would be necessary to reach the deficit targets (*Globe and Mail*, 13 November 1996). Generally, see Tremblay, "Zero Deficit."

9 See Cameron, "Does Ottawa Know It Is Part of the Problem?"

10 As Mr Johnson expressed this view, "He's soon going to face a reality check. And once he gets around to the actual business of managing, I think the public's perception of the man is going to change" (Barry Came, "Taking the Plunge," *Maclean's*, 4 December 1995, 30).

11 *Globe and Mail*, 22 November 1996. Over 43% felt that Mr Bouchard would be the best premier, as opposed to 21.4% for Mr Johnson.

12 The text of his speech is in the *Globe and Mail*, 13 March 1996.

13 *Toronto Star*, 31 October 1996, and *Globe and Mail*, 14 November 1996.

14 Globe and Mail, 23 January 1997.

15 *Globe and Mail*, 4 April, 8 August, and 14 November 1996. See also Desjardins, "Lucien Bouchard at the Helm," 82–5.

16 *Globe and Mail*, 23 January 1997.

17 *Le Devoir*, 12 February 1997, and *Globe and Mail*, 13 February 1997.

18 *Globe and Mail*, 16 April 1997, and Government of Canada, Privy Council Office, News Release, 22 April 1997. See also *Globe and Mail*, 19 June 1997, on the restructuring bill.

19 *Globe and Mail*, 19 November and 16 December 1997.

20 *Globe and Mail*, 20 December 1997. The motion of the National Assembly stated, on the one hand, that the constitutional amendment in no way represented a recognition of the Constitution Act, 1982, and, on the other, that the assembly reaffirmed the established rights to publicly funded English-language instruction under the Charter of the French Language (see Quebec, Assemblée Nationale, *Journal des débats*, 15 April 1997, 6245–7).

21 *London Free Press*, 8 June 1996.

22 *Globe and Mail*, 20 June and 28 November 1996.

23 *Globe and Mail*, Report on Business Magazine, August 1997, 55–9. Mr Bouchard's government had been restructured to create a minister responsible for "La métropole" who would coordinate initiatives affecting the Greater Montreal area. On the strategic importance of the Montreal economy for Canadian unity, see Côté, "Adapting or Breaking: Corporate Strategies for the Future of Canada," 22–3.

24 *Globe and Mail*, 5 December 1995 and 1 March 1996.
25 *La Presse*, 31 May 1996. In this very complex field, the general offer made to the provinces had been designed to be salable in Quebec; see *Globe and Mail*, 29 May 1996, and *Le Devoir*, 31 May 1996 (the latter reporting that Mr Johnson had been consulted about the package).
26 *Globe and Mail* and *London Free Press*, 22 April 1997. The agreement paralleled others signed with New Brunswick, Alberta, Newfoundland, and Manitoba.
27 *Globe and Mail*, 6 August 1997 and 7 January 1998.
28 *Globe and Mail*, 10 December 1997.
29 Desjardins, "Lucien Bouchard at the Helm," 84–5.
30 First appearing in *Le Devoir*, the translated article was published in the *Globe and Mail*, 31 October 1996.
31 See *Globe and Mail*, 23 April 1996 (on the platform) and 9 and 23 November 1996.
32 *Globe and Mail*, 25 November 1996.
33 *Globe and Mail*, 27 and 28 November, 10 and 17 December 1996.
34 *Globe and Mail*, 19 February, 7 and 19 March 1997.
35 *La Presse*, 23 August 1997 ("to the detriment of the citizens"). See also *Globe and Mail*, 6 December 1997.
36 *Globe and Mail*, 1 February 1997. Some 45.9% were dissatisfied or very dissatisfied with the government.
37 *Globe and Mail*, 1 and 29 March 1997.
38 *Globe and Mail*, 5, 1, and 23 May 1997.
39 Claude Castonguay, "It's Five Minutes to Midnight," *Globe and Mail*, 2 May 1997.
40 *London Free Press*, 1 February and 20 December 1996, 3 April 1997.
41 See polls reported in *Globe and Mail*, 24 May 1996, 29 March and 12 April 1997. Mr Chrétien's popularity was sliding sharply, and Mr Charest's image was improving, especially in Quebec.
42 *Bank of Canada Review*, autumn 1997, table G-1.
43 Ibid., table F-1, and *Bank of Canada Review*, autumn 1995, table F-1.
44 Ibid., table A-1. The figures are in constant prices, the 1997 figures being for the second quarter.
45 Ibid., table F-1.
46 Ibid., table H-5.
47 See, for example, Thomas J. Courchene, "The Implications of the No Vote," *Globe and Mail*, 31 October 1995; Group of 22, *Making Canada Work Better*; Business Council on National Issues, "Today and Tomorrow"; Conway, *Debts to Pay*, 238–54.
48 See, for example, Richards, *Language Matters*; Kenneth McRoberts, "What Do Canadians outside Quebec Want?" *Globe and Mail*, 31 October 1995; McRoberts, *Misconceiving Canada*, 245–76; Elton, "Canada 1996: The Reconfederation Challenge"; Burelle, "Pour un fédéralisme partenarial"; and Hawkes, "Reconfederating Canada."

49 *Globe and Mail*, 2 November 1995.
50 Right after the referendum, the western premiers were meeting, and Mr Charest and Mr Chrétien met separately with Mr Harris, but to little avail (*Globe and Mail*, 2 and 3 November 1995).
51 *Globe and Mail*, 14 November 1995.
52 Canada, House of Commons, *Debates*, 29 November 1995, 16971.
53 The text was "Whereas the People of Quebec have expressed the desire for recognition of Quebec's distinct society;
  (1) the House recognize that Quebec is a distinct society within Canada;
  (2) the House recognize that Quebec's distinct society includes its French-speaking majority, unique culture and civil law tradition;
  (3) the House undertake to be guided by this reality;
  (4) the House encourage all components of the legislative and executive branches of government to take note of this recognition and be guided in their conduct accordingly" (ibid.)
54 Ibid., 16961, 16975, and 16980.
55 Ibid., 16962, 16982–4. Reform proposed three amendments to the effect that the resolution would not confer any new powers on Quebec, diminish the rights of Quebec residents, or be interpreted "as denying that Canada constitutes one nation."
56 All provinces have a veto over those matters laid out in section 41 of the Constitution Act, 1982, and matters affecting one or more but not all provinces require the consent of those affected. Amendments under the general amending formula (section 38) that diminish provincial powers do not apply where the provincial legislature has opposed them. Hence, the new veto would be used to block amendments that do not derogate from provincial powers but that fall under the general formula. Some of these matters are laid out in section 42, and they are important, especially those concerning the establishment of new provinces and the powers, selection, and distribution of members of the Senate. Recognition of Quebec as a distinct society would fall into this class of matter.
  As for "consent," the minister, Allan Rock, stated that "it will be up to the federal government to determine what this phrase means every time a new situation arises." This could mean an expression by a provincial government, a resolution of a legislative assembly, or "a direct expression of the population's agreement through a referendum." Ottawa's pledge was "that we will use our veto to oppose any change that, in the opinion of Quebecers or people from any other region, goes against their best interests" (Canada, House of Commons, *Debates*, 30 November 30 1995, 17002, 17000).
57 *Globe and Mail*, 29 November 1995. An influential open-line radio host predicted that the measure would help ignite a B.C. separatist movement, and stated, "I don't think there is any hope any more for British Columbia within the Canadian federation."

58 See Canada, *Statutes*, 1996, c. 1 For a thorough analysis, see Heard and Schwartz, "The Regional Veto Formula." In essence, the change makes constitutional amendments more difficult to achieve, and it widens the disparities in power among provincial governments while rendering the power of individual citizens more nearly equal.

59 *Globe and Mail*, 14 December 1995, reporting on a motion by the Reform Party to provide for the removal of a prime minister "who fails to uphold the Constitution of Canada or fails to protect the Canadian interest in any dealings with a provincial government committed to secession."

60 *Globe and Mail*, 8 and 9 November 1995. The committee was led by Marcel Massé, minister of intergovernmental affairs.

61 *Globe and Mail*, 26 January 1996. Mr Massé moved to Treasury Board (but remained the "political minister" for Quebec), and Mme Robillard shifted to Citizenship and Immigration. See Greenspon and Wilson-Smith, *Double Vision*, 349–70.

62 Part of Mr Dion's statement and Mr Chrétien's remarks are in the *Globe and Mail*, 26 January 1996.

63 Canada, House of Commons, *Debates*, 27 February 1996, 4. Provinces not participating in any new program would be compensated, "provided they establish equivalent or comparable initiatives."

64 Hence, the initiatives were attacked by Quebec nationalists as centralizing. See the editorial by Michel Venne, "Un gouvernement central fort," *Le Devoir*, 28 February 1996. For a thorough review of the social-policy framework, see Courchene, *Social Canada in the Millennium* and *Redistributing Money and Power*.

65 *Globe and Mail*, 31 May 1996; Bakvis, "Federalism, New Public Management, and Labour-Market Development"; Haddow, "Federalism and Training Policy in Canada."

66 *Maclean's*, 11 March 1996.

67 As Mr Massé explained the pamphlet, "Our conclusion is that it is the role of the federal government to make sure that its message goes through and that it goes through with the real facts, and that the real story is given" (*Globe and Mail*, 19 January 1996). As well, federal departments cooperated to produce twelve one-hour "infomercials" to inform Quebecers about their services (*London Free Press*, 2 January 1997).

68 *Globe and Mail*, 3 and 10 July 1996.

69 *Globe and Mail*, 24 July 1996.

70 *Globe and Mail*, 19 and 22 October 1996. This type of initiative flowed from a Throne Speech commitment to assist the aerospace, biotechnology, and environmental technologies sectors.

71 *Globe and Mail*, 21 May 1997. These investments included $33 million for the Lachine Canal, $56 million for small- and medium-sized business, and $781 million for research and development in Quebec.

72 *Globe and Mail*, 22 June 1996; see also 11 and 14 June 1996.
73 *Globe and Mail*, 22 June 1996.
74 Ministerial Council on Social Policy Reform and Renewal, *Report to Premiers*.
75 *Globe and Mail*, 20 August 1996, and Courchene, *ACCESS*. The Courchene paper proposed two models for setting social-policy principles and standards, one that was primarily federal-provincial and another that relied on interprovincial coordination. See also Biggs, *Building Blocks for Canada's New Social Union*, and Institute of Intergovernmental Relations, *Assessing ACCESS*.
76 *Globe and Mail*, 23 August 1996, The Quebec government refused to be associated with this initiative, because it would have implied acceptance of a federal role in areas of provincial jurisdiction. Nevertheless, the premiers pressed Ottawa to proceed without Quebec (*Globe and Mail*, 27 September 1996).
77 See the speech by the province's minister of intergovernmental affairs, reported in the *Globe and Mail*, 31 October 1996. Ontario received a smaller share of retraining funds than its numbers of unemployed would dictate, less than its per capita entitlement of transfers for social programs, and less unemployment insurance money than its citizens contributed.
78 Ibid. The minister stated, "The time for the grand gesture of the past is long gone. Our government wants to see some non-constitutional successes before embarking on any constitutional changes." Earlier, the minister had gone even further: "If the federal government doesn't change the way we do business and recognize that the status quo isn't good enough they may have some other provinces that are seriously considering doing business outside of Canada" (*London Free Press*, 29 August 1996).
79 *Globe and Mail*, 21 and 28 November 1996, and, on Mr Pettigrew's approach, 1 February 1997.
80 *Globe and Mail*, 13 February 1997. Ottawa increased funding for immigrant settlement in Alberta, British Columbia and Ontario, compensated British Columbia for eliminating its social-assistance residency requirement, and finally signed an infrastructure cost-sharing agreement with Ontario (*Globe and Mail*, 24 February, 6 March, and 3 May 1997).
81 *Globe and Mail*, 16 and 31 May 1997. The minister of health objected to the opening of a for-profit hospital in Calgary.
82 See, for example, Rose, "Some Reflections on Social Entitlements," Broadbent, "Post-referendum Canada," Young, "Defending Decentralization," and Whitaker, "Cruising at 30,000 Feet."
83 *Globe and Mail*, 28 August 1997.
84 *Globe and Mail*, 27 November 1995.
85 Parisella, "Is the Quebec Liberal Party Still Relevant?"

86 See, for example, White, "The Political Future of Quebec Francophones."

87 See Daniel Johnson's statements in the *Globe and Mail*, 12 February 1996 (on a bitter exchange of letters between Mr Trudeau and Mr Bouchard), 11 March 1996 (on the partitionists), and 11 February 1997 (on a hard-line Quebec federalist challenge to distinct society proposals).

88 *Globe and Mail*, 16 December 1995, 6 January, 15 and 16 April 1996.

89 *Globe and Mail*, 16 May 1996. See also 28 and 30 September 1996 on the Supreme Court reference and the referendum question.

90 *Globe and Mail*, 30 September, 11 October, 7 and 9 December 1996. As a leading QLP member put it, "The nail in the coffin of the Parti Québécois is the recognition of Quebec's uniqueness in the Constitution. This would be the stake that we could drive through the heart of the separatists" (*Globe and Mail*, 11 October 1996).

99 *Globe and Mail*, 5 and 10 March 1997. This constitutional position is in Quebec Liberal Party, *Recognition and Interdependence*.

92 *Globe and Mail*, 20 June and 24 August 1996.

93 See, for example, Dion, "Building Bridges to National Reconciliation" and "The Challenges of the Canadian Economic Union."

94 *Globe and Mail*, 10 and 19 December 1996.

95 *Globe and Mail*, 5 April 1997. The premier continued on to say that "Liberals, Conservatives, the Toronto Star, all the elites, labour leaders, academics, all said the right policy was appeasement for Quebec and they were all wrong. They were proven wrong."

96 Gordon Gibson, "Why B.C. Won't Agree to a 'Distinct Society' Clause," *Globe and Mail*, 24 June 1997.

97 See, for example, typical condemnations of distinct society recognition as "inherently nationalist, or racist" by Robert Mason Lee and Stephen Harper (*Globe and Mail*, 20 April 1996, and Montreal *Gazette*, 2 August 1996). Mr Manning intervened in the Alberta campaign to ask whether a Klein administration would accept distinct society (*Globe and Mail*, 27 February and 9 May 1997).

98 Conrad Black, "Abandon the National Effort to Accommodate Quebec," *Globe and Mail*, 7 November 1995; Andrew Coyne, "The Case for Unapologetic Federalism," *Globe and Mail*, 18 November 1995, and Breton, "A Minimalist Strategy." For a more sustained analysis of the limitations of the incremental Plan A strategy, see Gibbins, *Time Out*.

99 William Johnson, "Ottawa Must Set Rules for Separation," *London Free Press*, 15 November 1995. See also Andrew Coyne, "Suppose They Held a Referendum and Nobody Came," *Globe and Mail*, 13 November 1995: "It is beyond belief that an entire generation of national leaders could have subscribed to the idea that a single question, posed only to the people of Quebec, worded to the

maximum advantage of the Parti Québécois, proposing institutional arrangements that were known to be impossible, should have any force or validity."

100 Thomas Berger, "What about Quebec's Next Referendum?" *Globe and Mail*, 9 November 1995; Jeffrey Simpson, "Federalists Need a Plan B to Show to Secessionists in the Future," *Globe and Mail*, 5 December 1995. In Simpson's view, Plan B would prevent the sovereigntists "from arrogating unto themselves the right to interpret what the rest of Canada would think and do faced with its own dismemberment."

101 Robertson, "Contingency Legislation for a Quebec Referendum"; Monahan and Bryant, *Coming to Terms with Plan B*; Richard Gwyn, "Canadians Must Start Dealing with the Unthinkable," *Toronto Star*, 18 February 1996.

102 Reform Party of Canada, *Reform Responses to the Twenty Questions*. See also *Globe and Mail*, 1 December 1995 and 18 January 1996. Among other principles, the party favoured partition and dividing the debt according to population, and it rejected joint citizenship and any special trade arrangements.

103 *Globe and Mail*, 20 January 1996. He said that "failure is not an option. Rather than contemplate how the country will fail, all our energy and time should be dedicated to finding answers on how we can change things."

104 Whitaker, "Managing Quebec," 8.

105 F.L. Morton, "Jean Chrétien Is Playing Constitutional 'Chicken,'" *Globe and Mail*, 6 February 1996.

106 *Globe and Mail*, 2 November 1995.

107 *Globe and Mail*, 29 June 1996. This committee was later expanded to include Ms Copps and Mr Axworthy, both of whom were less inclined to support decentralization and perhaps more willing to take a confrontational attitude towards the sovereigntists (*Globe and Mail*, 28 September 1996).

108 *Globe and Mail*, 30 January 1996.

109 *London Free Press*, 2 February 1996.

110 *Ottawa Citizen*, 28 January 1996.

111 *Globe and Mail*, 30 January 1996.

112 *Globe and Mail*, 30 January 1996; Lysiane Gagnon, "A Badly Coached Rookie Named Dion Takes to the Ice," *Globe and Mail*, 3 February 1996.

113 *London Free Press*, 1 February 1996.

114 See the comments by José Woehrling, professor of law at l'Université de Montréal, in *Le Devoir*, 8–9 February 1996.

115 Montreal *Gazette*, 8 February 1996.

116 One poll found that francophone Quebecers were strongly opposed to partition but that the issue had little effect on how they would vote in a referendum on sovereignty (*L'Actualité*, 15 May 1996, 37-42).

Another, later, using an unusual technique involving "discussion" throughout the interview, found that the issue did benefit the federalist side because awareness of it reduced the propensity of Yes voters to hold to their position (*London Free Press*, 14 May 1997). A later poll found that a majority of Quebecers believed there is "a real risk" of partition, and 60% agreed that regions that wished to remain in Canada should have the right to do so (*Globe and Mail*, 13 September 1997).

117 In a major speech in Quebec, the president of the C.D. Howe Institute warned partitionists that while their supporters in ROC "may be willing to hold your coat as you prepare to fight, they will not be there, or representative of anybody else outside of Quebec, in the event of a decision by Quebecers to separate" (Kierans, *President's Digest*, 1). See also Bashevkin, "Myths and Rebuttals." As the editorialists of the *Globe and Mail* put it, "There is ample doubt that Canadians outside Quebec would materially support partitionists in the face of clear victory for independence, but the scope for conflict within Quebec over partition certainly exists" (13 August 1997). For an American view of the issue, see Sands, "Quebecium est dividae in partes tres," 3: "For us the debate over Quebec's borders is like the difference between a haircut and a lobotomy. Where you make the cut will have a decisive influence on the client's ability to repay."

118 Conrad Black, "Quebec Partition: The Critical Questions," letter to the editor, *Globe and Mail*, 12 February 1997.

119 *Globe and Mail*, 7 August 1997.

120 The letter was reprinted in the *Globe and Mail*, 12 August 1997.

121 *Globe and Mail*, 13 and 28 August 1997.

122 *London Free Press*, 13 August 1997. Under section 43 of the Constitution Act, 1982, changes to "boundaries between provinces" require the consent of the legislative assemblies of the affected provinces. The sovereigntists generally argue that this provision guarantees that Quebec's borders would remain intact throughout a secession; the federalists reply that the provision holds only so long as Quebec remains a province within Canada, covered by the constitution.

123 *London Free Press*, 28 August 1997.

124 When the issue first surfaced, the federal minister of Indian affairs stated that the Quebec government should clarify whether "they would use force to keep the Mohawks or other aboriginal interests in Quebec" (*Globe and Mail*, 31 January 1996). Later, Quebec's intergovernmental affairs minister insisted that a Quebec becoming sovereign would "exercise effective control over all of the territory" and that if federalist municipalities refused to accept a majority decision, "the state would see to it that the laws be enforced" (*Globe and Mail*,

30 January 1997). Still later, in a typical thrust, Mr Dion suggested that the PQ government should renounce the use of force during a secession (*Toronto Star*, 20 November 1997).

125 *Globe and Mail*, 27 August 1996.

126 *Globe and Mail*, 30 August 1996.

127 *Le Devoir*, 2 August 1996. ("The struggle of francophone, anglophone, and native minorities is unending. One of the functions of the federal government is to make certain that people have the means to defend their rights under the Canadian constitution.")

128 Montreal *Gazette*, 2 August 1996.

129 Canada, House of Commons, *Debates*, 27 February 1996, 5.

130 *Globe and Mail*, 16 May and 1 October 1996.

131 *Globe and Mail*, 28 September 1996.

132 Mr Dion stated, "The National Assembly has a perfect right to ask any question it wants. But to accomplish secession requires a question on secession. If you pose a question that is confused and leads to other possibilities, you are not in a situation where you are able to negotiate secession" (*Globe and Mail*, 1 October 1996).

133 *Globe and Mail*, 21 December 1995. There were also suggestions that an unclear question or a sovereignty bill based on one could be blocked through the lieutenant-governor's powers of reservation and disallowance (*London Free Press*, 24 January 1997).

134 Montreal *Gazette*, 12 May 1997. Mr Dion stated, "We will not negotiate secession if we do not have the certainty that it's what people want. We do demand the right to have a clear question established. We hope to establish it in relation with Mr Bouchard, rather than in a unilateral manner." See also *London Free Press*, 16 May 1996, reporting Mr Chrétien: "If ever we have a referendum by any province I hope that there will be a discussion before to make sure that the rules are known by both sides."

135 *Globe and Mail*, 11 and 21 December 1995, 31 January 1996.

136 *Globe and Mail*, 31 January 1996.

137 *Globe and Mail*, 16 May 1996.

138 Monahan and Bryant, *Coming to Terms with Plan B*, 29–31. See also Jeffrey Simpson, "Two Quebec Pen Pals Have Different Definitions of Democracy," *Globe and Mail*, 15 August 1997.

139 *London Free Press*, 2 September 1995.

140 *Globe and Mail*, 6 September 1995. An official in the Prime Minister's Office said, "I wouldn't touch that with a 10-foot pole" (Globe and Mail, 9 September 1995).

141 *Bertrand v. Québec (Procureur Général)*, 127 *Dominion Law Reports*, 408–32, 428. He concluded by holding that "Bill 1, entitled an *Act respecting the future of Québec*, introduced by Prime Minister Jacques

Parizeau in the National Assembly on September 7, 1995, which would grant the National Assembly of Québec the power to proclaim that Québec will become a sovereign country without the need to follow the amending procedure provided for in Part V of the *Constitution Act, 1982*, constitutes a serious threat to the rights and freedoms of the plaintiff guaranteed by the *Canadian Charter of Rights and Freedoms*, in particular in ss. 2, 3, 6, 7, 15, and 24(1)" (ibid., 432). The cited sections of the Charter refer to freedom of peaceful assembly, the right to vote for federal representatives, mobility rights within Canada, "security of the Person," equality rights, and the right to seek redress in the courts for rights violations.

142 *Globe and Mail*, 9 September 1995, quoting the Quebec justice minister.

143 Montreal *Gazette*, 28 October 1995.

144 Guy Bertrand and Angeline Fournier, "The Rules of the Game," Montreal *Gazette*, 25 January 1996.

145 Quebec's lawyers argued that Mr Bertrand's demand "est irrecevable parce qu'il concerne des questions non justiciables et sur lesquelles cette cour n'a pas juridiction"; and, referring to the Universal Declaration of Human Rights, that because "la volonté des peuples est le fondement de l'autorité des pouvoirs publics," then "le processus d'accession du Québec à la souveraineté a pour fondement le principe démocratique et il s'agit d'un question qui ne relève pas de la juridiction des tribunaux" (Quebec, Attorney General, *Reqête déclinatoire*, sections 12, 14). (The request "cannot be entertained because it concerns questions that are nonjusticiable and over which this court has no jurisdiction"; and because "the will of peoples is the basis of governmental authority," then "the process of Quebec's accession to sovereignty is based on the democratic principle and involves a question that is beyond the jurisdiction of the courts.")

146 Canada, Attorney General, *Synopsis of the Position of the Attorney General*, section 16 (emphasis in original). The attorney general had been named as a third party by Mr Bertrand.

147 *Toronto Star*, 10 May 1996; *Globe and Mail*, 11 May 1996.

148 *Globe and Mail*, 14 May 1996.

149 *Globe and Mail*, 15 May 1996.

150 *Globe and Mail*, 18 May 1996; *Toronto Star*, 17 May 1996.

151 *Globe and Mail*, 14 May 1996.

152 *Globe and Mail*, 18 May 1996; *Toronto Star*, 10 May 1996.

153 Canada, Attorney General, News Media Advisory, "Summary of the Argument of the Attorney General of Canada in the Bertrand Case (Quebec's Motion to Dismiss)," 2.

154 *Globe and Mail*, 31 August 1996.

155 Canada, House of Commons, *Debates*, 26 September 1996, 4709.

156 Ibid., 4708.

157 *London Free Press*, 27 September 1996.

158 *Globe and Mail*, 12 May 1997.

159 *Globe and Mail*, 15 and 16 July 1997. See also *La Presse*, 28 December 1996. The lawyer was André Joli-Coeur.

160 *La Presse*, 27 September 1996.

161 *Globe and Mail*, 12 May 1997.

162 *La Presse*, 27 September 1996; *Toronto Star*, 29 September 1996.

163 *Globe and Mail*, 27 September 1996; *Toronto Star*, 29 September 1996. This argument, which has potential legal consequences as well as political implications, is a long-standing one, hotly debated among Quebec intellectuals. In brief, sovereigntists tend to maintain that the constitution was patriated without the consent of the National Assembly and that it both reduced the assembly's powers, in part by making them subordinate to the Canadian Charter of Rights and Freedoms, and eliminated the province's veto, which it traditionally possessed as the homeland of one of Canada's two founding peoples. The federalist position, essentially, is that Quebec members of Parliament and many members of the National Assembly voted for the new constitution, and that Premier Lévesque negotiated away any conventional veto possessed by Quebec. For background, see Laforest, *Trudeau and the End of a Canadian Dream*, 125–49, and McRoberts, *Misconceiving Canada*, 136–75; for an example of how the "imposition" can legitimize sovereignty, see Les intellectuels pour la souveraineté, "Oui au changement"; for a debate on the issue, see Pierre Trudeau, "J'accuse," *Ottawa Citizen*, 4 February 1996, and Lucien Bouchard, "Trudeau's 'I accuse' Smacks of Déjà Vu," *Globe and Mail*, 12 February 1996; and for the critical exchange of letters on the matter between Mr Trudeau and Mr Lévesque in 1981–82, see Hurley, *Amending Canada's Constitution*, appendices 11–16.

164 Lise Bissonnette, "Un an plus tard, la clarté," editorial, *Le Devoir*, 17 September 1996 ("un carcan").

165 *London Free Press*, 19 December 1997 (Jacques Brassard).

166 Lysiane Gagnon, "Court's Friend Draws Anger of Sovereigntists," *Globe and Mail*, 26 July 1997.

167 The minister of justice said, "Of course we'd use that, nationally and internationally" (*Globe and Mail*, 28 September 1996).

168 As the new minister of justice put it after the 1997 election, Canada can no longer be held "hostage" by the sovereigntists (*London Free Press*, 25 June 1997).

169 Montreal *Gazette*, 12 May 1997.

170 In his letter to Bernard Landry, Mr Dion insisted on a process that would be clear, legal, and fair for Quebecers and all Canadians: "If we

are all to agree on such a procedure, we must discuss it calmly and in a level-headed manner, as our fellow citizens wish us to do" (*Globe and Mail*, 28 August 1997).

171 Lise Bissonnette, "Un an plus tard, la clarté," editorial, *Le Devoir*, 17 September 1996.
172 *London Free Press*, 25 June 1997.
173 *Globe and Mail*, 10 June 1996.
174 Preston Manning, "An Open Letter to the Federal Tories," *Globe and Mail*, 22 August 1996; Susan Delacourt, "A Pre-campaign Visit with the Boys in the Backrooms," *Globe and Mail*, 1 March 1997; *London Free Press*, 4 March 1997.
175 *Globe and Mail*, 28 April 1997.
176 *Toronto Star*, 8 February 1997, reporting an interview with Mr Chrétien. See also *Le Devoir*, 10 February 1997.
177 See the Angus Reid poll reported in the *London Free Press*, 26 April 1997.
178 Jeffrey Simpson, "Like an Unwelcome Guest, the Issue of Unity Just Won't Go Away," *Globe and Mail*, 2 April 1997; David Bercuson and Barry Cooper, "National Unity Will March onto the Agenda," *Globe and Mail*, 3 May 1997.
179 *Toronto Star*, 26 January and 20 April 1997.
180 *Globe and Mail*, 29 and 30 April 1997.
181 *Toronto Star*, 2 May 1997.
182 *Toronto Star*, 20 April 1997. See the poll results reported in the *Globe and Mail*, 29 March, 12 and 29 April 1997.
183 *London Free Press*, 29 January 1997.
184 *London Free Press*, 26 April 1997; *Globe and Mail*, 1, 15, and 26 May 1997.
185 Reform Party of Canada, *A Fresh Start for Canadians*, 20–1. Reform supported negotiations to protect Canada's interests, the right of dissident Quebecers to petition to remain in Canada, the requirement that Quebec assume its population share of the national debt, the revocation of passports from those remaining in Quebec, full rights of passage across Quebec, and approval of the terms of secession through a Canadian referendum.
186 *Toronto Star*, 2 May 1997.
187 *Globe and Mail*, 3 May 1997.
188 *Globe and Mail* and *London Free Press*, 5 May 1997.
189 *Globe and Mail*, 9 May 1997. Mr Dion argued that "if Quebecers want an additional demonstration of the reasons which led us to the Supreme Court, well, Mr Parizeau gave it to us."
190 *Globe and Mail*, 12 May 1997.
191 *Globe and Mail*, 9 May 1997.
192 *Globe and Mail*, 15 May 1997.
193 *Globe and Mail*, 9 May 1997.

194 *London Free Press*, 9 May 1997; *Globe and Mail*, 17 and 19 May 1997.
195 See the polls by Léger & Léger and Environics reported in the *Globe and Mail*, 12, 17, and 19 May 1997. Mr Charest was by far the most popular federal leader in the province, and vote intentions were divided almost equally among the Bloc, the Liberals, and the Progressive Conservatives.
196 *Globe and Mail*, 15 May 1997.
197 *Globe and Mail*, 9 and 17 May 1997.
198 *Globe and Mail*, 20 May 1997 (former leader Michel Gauthier). Along with Mr Duceppe and Mr Bouchard, the leading campaigners were Mr Parizeau and Yves Duhaime, a contender for the Bloc leadership, who waged a bitter campaign against Mr Chrétien in his home riding of Shawinigan.
199 See the Léger & Léger poll reported in the *Globe and Mail*, 24 May 1997.
200 *Globe and Mail*, 21 May 1997; *London Free Press*, 23 May 1997.
201 *London Free Press*, 20 May 1997; *Globe and Mail*, 21 May 1997.
202 *Globe and Mail*, 21 May 1997.
203 *London Free Press* and *Globe and Mail*, 21 May 1997.
204 *Globe and Mail*, 23 May 1997.
205 *London Free Press*, 24 May 1997; *Globe and Mail*, 20 May 1997.
206 *Globe and Mail*, 26 May 1997. In the televised French-language leaders' debate on 13 May, one journalist had just asked whether Mr Chrétien would accept a 50.4% Yes margin when the moderator slumped unconscious to the floor. In a subsequent special French-language debate on the national unity issue, the question was not explicitly posed.
207 *London Free Press*, 27 May 1997.
208 *Globe and Mail*, 28 May 1997. As the head of a Quebec polling firm put it, "People vote for the Bloc because they are voting against something. Until now, the Bloc has failed to give them that. Now, the Bloc has been given a reason on a silver platter to vote against something."
209 *Globe and Mail*, 5 June 1997. The campaign director said, "There was an instant polarization in that province and only room for one federalist side and one separatist side and that's what he drove it to – total polarization and we paid the price for that." On the polls, see *Globe and Mail*, 29 May 1997.
210 *Globe and Mail*, 27 May 1997.
211 Ibid. See also Michel Venne, "La majorité, c'est simple," editorial, *Le Devoir*, 27 May 1997.
212 *Globe and Mail*, 28 May 1997.
213 *Globe and Mail*, 31 May 1997.
214 *London Free Press*, 20 and 30 May, 1997.
215 Complete results are in the *Globe and Mail*, 4 June 1997.

216 Jeffrey Simpson, "Vote Failed to Patch Fractured System," *Globe and Mail*, 4 June 1997. For a pessimistic reflection on the party system, see Meisel, "An Echo," 247–8. See also Marzolini, "The Regionalization of Canadian Electoral Politics."
217 *Globe and Mail*, 3 May and 6 August 1997.
218 See, for example, *Globe and Mail*, 7 June 1997.
219 *Globe and Mail*, 15 May, 9 June, and 2 May 1997; Montreal *Gazette*, 2 March 1997.
220 *Globe and Mail*, 30 May, 8 and 10 July 1997. See also *Maclean's*, 28 July 1997.
221 Business Council on National Issues, "Memorandum for the Honourable Frank McKenna." The statement is found in the *Globe and Mail*, 31 July 1997. The National Assembly was to "exercise the powers that fall within its jurisdiction," and the unique character of Quebec was "expressed through its language, culture, institutions and civil law tradition." The BCNI was careful also to state that "French-speaking Canadians" have been and are "essential partners" in creating the Canadian identity.
222 *Globe and Mail*, 31 July 1997.
223 See *Globe and Mail*, 30 July and 7 August 1997.
224 The discussion centred around a paper presented by the Provincial/Territorial Council on Social Policy Renewal, *New Approaches to Canada's Social Union*.
225 *Globe and Mail*, 7 and 8 August 1997.
226 *Globe and Mail*, 8 August 1997. Mr Bouchard said, "Once again, it seems to me there has been a demonstration here that there is no solution" (*London Free Press*, 8 August 1997).
227 *Globe and Mail*, 9 August 1997.
228 *London Free Press*, 31 July 1997, and *Globe and Mail*, 7 August 1997. Mr Klein had suggested that Ottawa scrap its entire post-referendum approach, including the resolution about distinct society and the bill conferring regional vetoes (*Globe and Mail*, 23 July and 9 August 1997).
229 *London Free Press*, 31 July 1997.
230 Stein, Cameron, and Simeon, *Citizen Engagement in Conflict Resolution*; Stein, "Improving the Process of Constitutional Reform."
231 *London Free Press*, 9 August 1997; Jeffrey Simpson, "A Resolute Unwillingness to Tackle the Unity Issue," *Globe and Mail*, 8 August 1997; Lysiane Gagnon, "Populist Ideology Reaches the Silly Stage," *Globe and Mail*, 16 August 1997.
232 *Calgary Herald*, 30 August and 4 September 1997; *Globe and Mail*, 20 August, 5, 10, and 11 September 1997.
233 Tom Flanagan and Steven Harper, "Dear Premiers ... It's Time to Oppose – Not Appease – Separatism," *Calgary Herald*, 13 September 1997.

234 *Le Soleil*, 22 August 1997, reporting the remarks of Senator Jean-Claude Rivest; *Globe and Mail*, 23 August 1997. Also, Mr Johnson insisted that recognition of Quebec's distinct society was essential – it was "non-negotiable" (*Le Devoir*, 23–4 August 1997).

235 *Globe and Mail*, 13 September 1997.

236 See, for example, Gordon Gibson, "There's No Time to Lose," *Globe and Mail*, 9 September 1997; and *Edmonton Journal*, 11 September 1997, reporting a speech by the president of the BCNI.

237 *Calgary Herald*, 15 September 1997; *Globe and Mail*, 30 August 1997.

238 *Globe and Mail*, 16 September 1997; Preston Manning, "Solution to Unity Woes Is in Our Hands," *Calgary Herald*, 27 December 1997. As the Reform Party leader put it, because any powers granted to Quebec would be available to all provinces, "at last, special status is dying, and the concept of equality is replacing it."

239 *Globe and Mail*, 16 September 1997; Daniel Johnson, "The Separatists Are Truly Worried," *Globe and Mail*, 11 December 1997.

240 Michel Auger, "No Thanks to Equality of the Provinces," and Jeffrey Simpson, "The Ghost of 'Distinct Society' Is Still Clanking Its Chains," *Globe and Mail*, 16 September 1997.

241 *Globe and Mail*, 16 September 1997 (Jacques Brassard).

242 *Globe and Mail*, 17 September 1997.

243 *London Free Press*, 17 September 1997.

244 *Globe and Mail*, 1 October 1997.

245 *Globe and Mail*, 15 October 1997.

246 Ibid. See also the poll results in *Globe and Mail*, 8 December 1997: support for the declaration was higher than 60% in every province, including Quebec.

247 Alberta, Dialogue on Unity, *My Canada Is ...*

248 Alberta, Dialogue on Unity, *My Canada Is ... Albertans Speak Out on Unity.*

249 Ibid., 5. Overall, 76% supported the package. But whereas 47% particularly liked the provincial-equality provision and only 8% found it a matter of concern, a mere 12% especially liked the unique-society provision and 33% were concerned by it. Similarly, an Environics poll of Albertans found that 33% of respondents did not think Quebec is unique (*Edmonton Journal*, 8 December 1997).

250 The actual motion was carefully hedged, as were those passed by some other provincial legislatures. It resolved "that the Legislative Assembly of Alberta be guided by the input received from Albertans during the public consultation process, Dialogue on Unity, and on behalf of the people of Alberta concur with the principles embodied in the elements of the Calgary framework, recognizing that the Calgary framework is not an amendment to the Constitution Acts of 1867 to 1982 and that the specific wording of any amendment to those

with the Constitution Referendum Act" (Alberta, Legislative Assembly, *Alberta Hansard*, 8 December 1997, 1313–14.)

251 *Globe and Mail*, 18 and 19 November 1997.
252 *Ottawa Citizen*, 21 November 1997.
253 *Globe and Mail*, 25 September and 26 November 1997.
254 *Globe and Mail*, 17 September 1997, and Joan Bryden, "Battle over Social Policy Threatens Unity Declaration," *Edmonton Journal*, 8 December 1997.
255 *Globe and Mail*, 28 August and 9 December 1997. See Canada, House of Commons, *Debates*, 23 September 1997, 5–12.
256 *Globe and Mail*, 13 December 1997.
257 Lysiane Gagnon, "Why Bouchard Was Wise to Refuse Ottawa," *Globe and Mail*, 20 December 1997.

CHAPTER SIX

1 Note, however, that even this depends on the course of events. After the Meech Lake Accord failed to be ratified, the QLP was profoundly divided; and after the Bélanger-Campeau Commission reported, it was Robert Bourassa's Liberal government that decided to hold a referendum.
2 *Maclean's*, 16 June 1997, 20.
3 The most striking case is the Great Coalition of 1864 between George Brown's Reformers and the Conservatives under John A. Macdonald and George-Etienne Cartier. This powerful combination pressed for a federal solution to the deadlock in the united Canada. I am indebted to Peter Neary for consistently drawing this to my attention.
4 *Globe and Mail*, 29 October 1996: according to a prominent Quebec political scientist, some hard-line sovereigntists suspect that Mr Bouchard does not want independence, but rather a "new union with Canada where Quebec would be recognized as a nation."
5 *Globe and Mail*, 22 November 1995.
6 *Globe and Mail*, 29 November 1995.
7 *Globe and Mail*, 1 February 1996.
8 Canada, House of Commons, *Debates*, 29 November 1995, 16981.
9 *Globe and Mail*, 8 August 1997.
10 *Globe and Mail*, 11 March 1996.
11 Canada, House of Commons, *Debates*, 29 November 1995, 16977.
12 "Explaining Quebec Nationalism," 97–110.
13 Lemieux, "Le référendum de 1995," 66.
14 As noted above, there is by no means universal support – even among francophones – for the view that Quebec has the right of self-determination, and some poll results indicate that a large minority of Quebecers consider Quebec to be a province like the others. See 168n5 and 169n20 above.

15 See, for instance, his reply to the federal government's post-referendum initiatives: "My personal wish, in the interests of Quebec and of Canada, although I am aware that it is harder to convince Canada of this than Quebec, is that one day a premier of Quebec will find himself across the table from his federal counterpart, precisely for the purpose of discussing political systems ... But from now on, the situation will be different, because the Premiers [of Quebec] who come to talk about the Constitution and political arrangements will come with a mandate from the people of Quebec. They will not be out to retaliate, to be aggressive, to be negative. No. They will come with respect but confident, with the confidence of a prime minister, a head of state, who has received a mandate for sovereignty from the people. In other words, we will negotiate as equals, and then we will be able to agree, and only then. As long as Quebec comes here as a province like the others we will never be able to agree" (Canada, House of Commons, *Debates*, 29 November 1995, 16981).

16 See Young, *The Secession of Quebec*, chapter 15.

17 After taking on the PQ leadership, Mr Bouchard remarked, "I'm provoking English Canada only by breathing, so I'm used to it" (*Globe and Mail*, 17 January 1996).

18 Pierre Bourgault advocated this strategy in order to eliminate the possibility of voting No while keeping the sovereignty option alive for the future. It was not dismissed by Quebec's minister of intergovernmental affairs, who said, "It's not an idea without interest. Are we going to say it as clearly as Mr Bourgault? That remains to be seen" (*Toronto Star*, 16 March 1997).

19 See Cairns, *Looking into the Abyss*.

20 See Young, *The Secession of Quebec*, 48–59, 231–6.

21 Ibid. 184–91, and Monahan, *"Cooler Heads Shall Prevail."*

22 Dion, "The Dynamic of Secessions," 545–6.

23 For a sensible treatment of many issues involved in the ratification of a sovereignty agreement, including constitutional amendments, see Russell and Ryder, *Ratifying a Postreferendum Agreement*. These authors suggest, notably, that the rules might be bent *in extremis*, but only when a referendum had carried in all five regions. The major provinces could still block ratification, of course.

24 See Young, *The Secession of Quebec*, 119–20, treating Lamont's *Breakup*.

25 Here it is worth recalling the massive public support within ROC for the imposition of the War Measures Act during the FLQ crisis of 1970.

26 See Diane Francis, "Mouvement Growing Much Bolder," *London Free Press*, 4 December 1997. Raymond Villeneuve, leader of the Mouvement de libération nationale du Québec, whose adherents have been involved in scuffles with partitionists, has said, "On est prêts à se battre jusqu'au bout pour l'indépendance" ("We are ready to fight to the end for independence"), *Le Devoir*, 12 December 1997.

27 Ontario sovereignty is also possible. For an account of the province's shift in economic linkages towards the United States and of its governments' growing alienation from the federal system of which traditionally it was the keystone, see Courchene, *From Heartland to North American Region State*. See also William Christian, "And now ... Ontario Separatism," *Globe and Mail*, 2 October 1997.

28 The Economic Council's Confederation of Regions model had Ottawa responsible for the debt, currency, defence, tariffs and the customs union, external trade, and international relations, with shared responsibility for the environment, transportation, communications, taxation, culture, and policing and justice (*A Joint Venture*, fig. 5-1).

29 Ibid., 83–4. See also Leslie, *The European Community* and *The Maastricht Model*.

30 McCallum, "The Canadian Economic Union after Breakup," 79.

31 Gordon Gibson, "Largesse, He Says," *Globe and Mail*, 7 October 1997.

32 This is why some commentators have written off the option. See Leslie, "Options for the Future of Canada," 136–7.

POSTSCRIPT

1 *Toronto Star*, 22 February 1998.

2 *Globe and Mail*, 23 February 1998.

3 *Globe and Mail*, 3 March 1998.

4 *Globe and Mail*, 26 March 1998. The polls indicated that sovereignty support would also drop sharply. Partly as a result of his performance in the 1997 election campaign, and partly because of unpopular measures taken by Mr Bouchard's government, Mr Charest was rivalling the premier in public esteem by the end of 1997; see *Globe and Mail*, 3 March 1998.

5 *Le Devoir*, 27 March 1998.

6 *Le Devoir*, 28 March 1998.

7 *London Free Press*, 1 and 15 August 1998; *Globe and Mail*, 15 August 1998.

8 *Globe and Mail*, 3 February 1998.

9 *Globe and Mail*, 18 February 1998.

10 *Globe and Mail*, 21 February 1998. At a large sovereigntist rally, Mr Parizeau declared that "the judges can decide what they want. It has no importance. We will never live under the threat of decisions taken by others."

11 Canada, Supreme Court, *Reference re Secession of Quebec*.

12 See the remarks of pollster Jean-Marc Léger, *London Free Press*, 21 August 1998.

13 *Globe and Mail*, 21 August 1998.

14 Ibid.

15 *Globe and Mail*, 22 August 1998.

16 Jean Lapierre, "How to Design a 'Winnable' Referendum," *Globe and Mail*, 25 August 1998.

17 Josée Legault, "How to Deny Quebec's Right to Self-Determination," *Globe and Mail*, 21 August 1998. This piece appeared in a longer version in *Le Devoir*, yet the editorial in that newspaper suggested that the PQ should "forget convoluted referendum questions" (*Globe and Mail*, 22 August 1998).

18 See the remarks of Stephen Harper, *Globe and Mail*, 24 August 1998.

19 Canada, Press Release, "Declarations by the Honourable Anne McLellan and the Honourable Stéphane Dion," 20 August 1998.

20 Quebec, "Notes for a preliminary statement by the Prime Minister of Québec, Mr. Lucien Bouchard, the day following the opinion of the Supreme Court of Canada on the reference by the federal government," Quebec City, 21 August 1998.

21 *Globe and Mail*, 25 August 1998; *Le Devoir*, 26 August 1998; Canada, Privy Council Office, letter from Stéphane Dion to Mr Lucien Bouchard, 25 August 1998.

22 Canadian Intergovernmental Conference Secretariat, News Release, First Ministers' Meeting, Ottawa, Ontario, 11 and 12 December 1997 (ref: 800-036/06).

23 Ibid.

24 Québec, Cabinet du ministre délégue aux affaires intergouvernmentales canadiennes, "Avis aux médias: Déclaration du ministre Brassard à l'occasion de la réunion fédérale-provinciale des ministres responsables de l'entente-cadre sur l'union sociale," Toronto, 17 April 1998.

25 *Globe and Mail*, 19 and 24 June 1998. See also the provincial responses to Ottawa's February 1998 Speech from the Throne, which announced the Millenium Scholarship Endowment Fund (*Globe and Mail*, 26 February 1998).

26 Mr Chrétien met with Mr Romanow, the host of the premiers' conference, shortly before it convened (*London Free Press*, 30 July 1998).

27 Canadian Intergovernmental Conference Secretariat, News Release, "Framework Agreement on Canada's Social Union," 39th Annual Premiers' Conference, Saskatoon, Saskatchewan, 5–7 August 1998 (ref: 850-070/10).

28 *Globe and Mail*, 7 August 1998.

29 Ibid.

Selected Bibliography

Alberta, Dialogue on Unity. *My Canada Is ...* [pamphlet]. 2 October 1997.

– *My Canada Is ... Albertans Speak Out on Unity* [pamphlet]. December 1997.

Allaire Report (Report of the Constitutional Committee of the Quebec Liberal Party). *A Québec Free to Choose*. For submission to the 25th Convention, 28 January 1991.

Archer, Keith, and Faron Ellis. "Opinion Structure of Party Activists: The Reform Party of Canada." *Canadian Journal of Political Science* 27, no. 2 (1994): 277–308.

Bakvis, Herman. "Federalism, New Public Management, and Labour-Market Development." In Patrick C. Fafard and Douglas M. Brown, eds., *Canada: The State of the Federation 1996*, 135–65. Kingston: Institute of Intergovernmental Relations 1996.

Bashevkin, Sylvia. "Myths and Rebuttals." In Trent, Young, and Lachapelle, eds., *Québec-Canada*, 35–9.

Belleau, Josée. "Le Sommet de l'emploi et de l'économie: À soleil trompeur, une participation sans illusions." Société québécoise de science politique, *bulletin* 6, no. 1 (1996): 7–11.

Bercuson, David Jay, and Barry Cooper. *Deconfederation: Canada without Quebec*. Toronto: Key Porter 1991.

Biggs, Margaret. "Building Blocks for Canada's New Social Union," Canadian Policy Research Networks, Working Paper no. F[02], 1996.

Black, Conrad. "Canada's Continuing Identity Crisis." *Foreign Affairs* 17, no. 2 (1995): 99–115.

Blais, André. "Quebec: Raising the Stakes." Paper presented at the annual meeting of the Canadian Political Science Association, Calgary, 12 June 1994.

Blais, André, and Richard Nadeau. "To Be or Not to Be Sovereignist: Quebeckers' Perennial Dilemma." *Canadian Public Policy* 18, no. 1 (1992): 89–
103.

Blais, André, Richard Nadeau, and Pierre Martin. "Pourquoi le Oui a-t-il
fait des gains pendant la campagne référendaire?" In Trent, Young, and
Lachapelle, eds., *Québec-Canada*, 71–6.

Bloc québécois. *Proposition pour un Partenariat économique et politique entre le
Québec et le Canada.* Rapport du Groupe de travail sur l'union économique
et les institutions communes. Montreal: Bloc québécois, 8 June 1995.

Boadway, Robin W., Thomas J. Courchene, and Douglas D. Purvis, eds. *Economic Dimensions of Constitutional Change.* 2 vols. Kingston: John Deutsch
Institute 1991.

Bookman, Milica Zarkovic. *The Economics of Secession.* New York: St Martin's
Press 1993.

Boothe, Paul, ed. *Alberta and the Economics of Constitutional Change.* Western
Studies in Economic Policy no. 3. Edmonton: Western Centre for Economic Research 1992.

Breton, Albert. "A Minimalist Strategy to Deal with Quebec Secessionism."
Paper presented at the Seventh Villa Colombella Seminar, Rome, 6 September 1996.

Brimelow, Peter, "Canadian Roulette." *Forbes,* 25 September 1995, 46–8.

Broadbent, Edward. "Post-Referendum Canada." In Trent, Young, and
Lachapelle, eds., *Québec-Canada*, 271–80.

Brown, Douglas M. "Thinking the 'Unthinkable.'" In Patrick C. Fafard and
Douglas M. Brown, eds., *Canada: The State of the Federation 1996*, 23–44.
Kingston: Institute of Intergovernmental Relations 1996.

Buchanan, Allen. *Secession: The Morality of Political Divorce from Fort Sumter
to Lithuania and Quebec.* Boulder: Westview Press 1991.

Buchheit, Lee C. *Secession: The Legitimacy of Self-Determination.* New Haven:
Yale University Press 1978.

Burelle, André. *Le mal canadien.* Montreal: Fides 1995.

– "Pour un fédéralisme partenarial à la canadienne." In Trent, Young, and
Lachapelle, eds., *Québec-Canada*, 283–92.

Burns, R.M., ed. *One Country or Two?* Montreal: McGill-Queen's University
Press 1971.

Business Council on National Issues. "Today and Tomorrow: An Agenda
for Action." Ideas and recommendations of the Confederation 2000 Conference participants, 3–4 May 1996.

– "Memorandum for the Honourable Frank McKenna, Premier of New
Brunswick and Chairman-Designate, Council of Premiers." 15 July 1997.

Cairns, Alan C. "Looking Back from the Future." In Trent, Young, and
Lachapelle, eds., *Québec-Canada*, 77–80.

– *Looking into the Abyss: The Need for a Plan C.* Commentary no. 96. Toronto:
C.D. Howe Institute 1997.

Cameron, David. "Does Ottawa Know It Is Part of the Problem?" In Trent, Young, and Lachapelle, eds., *Québec-Canada*, 293–8.

Campbell, Tom. "Statement." In United States, House of Representatives, *The Issue of Quebec's Sovereignty and Its Potential Impact on the United States*, 29–31. Washington: U.S. Government Printing Office 1996.

Canada. Attorney General. *Synopsis of the Position of the Attorney General of Canada on the Motion to Dismiss*, filed in Quebec Superior Court, *Bertrand v. Bégin*, case no: 200-05-002117-955, 22 May 1996.

– Department of Justice. *A Consolidation of the Constitution Acts 1987–1982*. Ottawa: Minister of Supply and Services 1983.

– House of Commons, Office of the Leader of the Opposition. "Discours de l'honorable Lucien Bouchard, député de Lac-Saint-Jean, chef de l'opposition officielle et chef du Bloc québécois." Prononcé lors de l'ouverture du Congrès national du Bloc québécois, Palais des Congrès, Montreal, 7 April 1995.

– Supreme Court. *Reference re Secession of Quebec*. File No.: 25506. 16, 17, 18, 19 February and 20 August 1998.

Cloutier, Édouard, Jean H. Guay, and Daniel Latouche. *Le virage: L'évolution de l'opinion publique au Québec depuis 1960*. Montreal: Québec/Amérique 1992.

Coleman, William. *The Independence Movement in Quebec, 1945-1980*. Toronto: University of Toronto Press 1984.

Conway, John F. *Debts to Pay: A Fresh Approach to the Quebec Question*, 2nd ed. Toronto: Lorimer 1997.

Cooper, Mary H. "Quebec Sovereignty." *The CQ Researcher* 5, no. 37 (1995): 873–95.

Côté, Marcel. *La rêve de la terre promise: Les coûts de l'indépendance*. Montreal: Stanké 1995.

– "Adapting or Breaking: Corporate Strategies for the Future of Canada." Unpublished manuscript, February 1996.

Côté, Marcel, and David Johnston. *If Québec Goes ... The Real Cost of Separation*. Toronto: Stoddart 1995.

Courchene, Thomas J. *Social Canada in the Millennium*, The Social Policy Challenge no. 4. Toronto: C.D. Howe Institute 1994.

– *Redistributing Money and Power: A Guide to the Canada Health and Social Transfer*. Observation no. 39. Toronto: C.D. Howe Institute 1995.

– "ACCESS: A Convention on the Canadian Economic and Social Systems." Working paper prepared for the Ministry of Intergovernmental Affairs, Government of Ontario, August 1996.

Courchene, Thomas J., with Colin R. Telmer. *From Heartland to North American Region State: The Social, Fiscal and Federal Evolution of Ontario*. Toronto: Centre for Public Management, University of Toronto 1998.

Covell, Maureen. *Thinking about the Rest of Canada: Options for Canada without Quebec*. Study no. 6, Background Studies of the York University

Constitutional Reform Project. North York: York University Centre for Public Law and Public Policy 1992.

d'Aquino, Thomas. "The Case for Canada: A Perspective on Canada's Political and Economic Future." Address to the Paul H. Nitze School of Advanced International Studies, Centre of Canadian Studies, Johns Hopkins University, Washington, February 1997.

Derriennic, Jean-Pierre. *Nationalisme et démocratie.* Montreal: Boréal 1995.

Desjardins, Marc. "Lucien Bouchard at the Helm: An Assessment of the Premier's First Six Months in Power." In Patrick C. Fafard and Douglas M. Brown, eds., *Canada: The State of the Federation 1996,* 77–95. Kingston: Institute of Intergovernmental Relations 1996.

Dion, Stéphane. "Explaining Quebec Nationalism." In R. Kent Weaver, ed., *The Collapse of Canada?* 77–121. Washington: Brookings Institution 1992.

– "The Importance of the Language Issue in the Constitutional Crisis." In Douglas Brown and Robert Young, eds., *Canada: The State of the Federation 1992,* 77–88. Kingston: Institute of Intergovernmental Relations 1992.

– "The Dynamic of Secessions: Scenarios after a Pro-Separatist Vote in a Quebec Referendum." *Canadian Journal of Political Science* 28, no. 3 (1995): 533–51.

– "Why Is Secession Rare? Lessons from Quebec." *British Journal of Political Science* 26, no. 2 (1996): 269–83.

– "Building Bridges to National Reconciliation." Notes for an address to the Annual Social Studies Council Conference of the Alberta Teachers' Association, Lethbridge, 18 October 1996.

– "The Challenges of the Canadian Economic Union." Notes for an address to the Canadian Chemical Producers' Association, Ottawa, 20 November 1996.

Doran, Charles. "Will Canada Unravel?" *Foreign Affairs* 75, no. 5 (1996): 97–109.

Drache, Daniel, and Roberto Perin, eds. *Negotiating with a Sovereign Québec.* Toronto: James Lorimer 1992.

Economic Council of Canada. *A Joint Venture: The Economics of Constitutional Options,* Twenty-Eighth Annual Review. Ottawa: Minister of Supply and Services 1991.

Elton, David, "Canada 1996: The Reconfederation Challenge." In Trent, Young, and Lachapelle, eds., *Québec-Canada,* 299–307.

Freeman, Alan, and Patrick Grady. *Dividing the House: Planning for a Canada without Quebec.* Toronto: HarperCollins 1995.

Fry, Earl H. "Quebec's Sovereignty Movement and Its Implications for the U.S. Economy." In United States, House of Representatives, *The Issue of Quebec's Sovereignty and Its Potential Impact on the United States,* 59–67. Washington: U.S. Government Printing Office 1996.

Gagnon, Alain-G., and Guy Lachapelle. "Québec Confronts Canada: Two Competing Societal Projects Searching for Legitimacy." *Publius* 26, no. 3 (1996): 177–91.

Gagnon, Alain-G., and François Rocher, eds. *Répliques aux détracteurs de la souveraineté du Québec.* VLB éditeur 1992.

Gibbins, Roger. *Time Out: Assessing Incremental Strategies for Enhancing the Canadian Political Union.* Commentary no. 88. Toronto: C.D. Howe Institute 1997.

Gibson, Gordon. *Plan B: The Future of the Rest of Canada.* Vancouver: Fraser Institute 1994.

– *Renewing the Federation: Options for British Columbia.* Prepared for the National Unity Project, British Columbia. Vancouver: Queen's Printer 1997.

Grady, Patrick. *Economic Consequences of Quebec Sovereignty.* Vancouver: Fraser Institute 1991.

Granatstein, J.L., and Kenneth McNaught, eds. *"English Canada" Speaks Out.* Toronto: Doubleday 1991.

Grand Council of the Crees (of Quebec). *Sovereign Injustice: Forcible Inclusion of the James Bay Crees and Cree Territory into a Sovereign Quebec.* Nemaska, Quebec: Grand Council of the Crees 1995.

Greenspon, Edward, and Anthony Wilson-Smith. *Double Vision: The Inside Story of the Liberals in Power.* Toronto: Doubleday (Seal Books) 1997.

Group of 22. *Making Canada Work Better.* N.p. 1 May 1996.

Haddow, Rodney. "Federalism and Training Policy in Canada: Institutional Barriers to Economic Adjustment." In François Rocher and Miriam Smith, eds., *New Trends in Canadian Federalism,* 338–68. Peterborough: Broadview Press 1995.

Hartt, Stanley H., et al. *Tangled Web: Legal Aspects of Deconfederation.* Canada Round Series no. 15. Toronto: C.D. Howe Institute 1992.

Hawkes, David C. "Reconfederating Canada." In Trent, Young, and Lachapelle, eds., *Québec-Canada,* 309–16.

Heard, Andrew, and Tim Swartz. "The Regional Veto Formula and Its Effects on Canada's Constitutional Amendment Process." *Canadian Journal of Political Science* 30, no. 2 (1997): 339–56.

Hogg, Peter W. *Constitutional Law of Canada,* 2nd ed. Toronto: Carswell 1985.

Hurley, James Ross. *Amending Canada's Constitution.* Ottawa: Minister of Supply and Services Canada 1996.

Institute of Intergovernmental Relations. *Assessing ACCESS.* Kingston: Institute of Intergovernmental Relations 1997.

Jockel, Joseph. "And if Quebec Secedes? A View from The United States." *Current History* 94, no. 590 (1995): 127–30.

– "On Watching, from across the Border, the Canadian Game of Chicken." In Charles F. Doran and Ellen Reisman Babby, eds., *Being and Becoming*

Canadian. Vol. 538 of *The Annals of the American Academy of Political and Social Science,* 16–26. Thousand Oaks: SAGE Periodicals Press 1995.

– "Prepared Statement." In United States, House of Representatives, *The Issue of Quebec's Sovereignty and Its Potential Impact on the United States,* 43–58. Washington: U.S. Government Printing Office 1996.

Johnson, Daniel. "The Case for a United Canada." *Foreign Policy* 99 (1995): 78–88.

Johnston, Richard, et al. "The People and the Charlottetown Accord." In Ronald L. Watts and Douglas M. Brown, eds., *Canada: The State of the Federation 1993,* 19–43. Kingston: Institute of Intergovernmental Relations 1993.

Jones, David T. "An Independent Quebec: Looking into the Abyss." *Washington Quarterly* 20, no. 2 (1997): 21–36.

Kierans, Tom. *President's Digest.* Toronto: C.D. Howe Institute 1997 (March).

Lachapelle, Guy. "La souveraineté partenariat: Donnée essentielle du résultat référendaire et de l'avenir des relations Québec-Canada." In Trent, Young, and Lachapelle, eds., *Québec-Canada,* 41–63.

Laforest, Guy. *Trudeau and the End of a Canadian Dream.* Montreal: McGill-Queen's University Press 1995.

Lamont, Lansing. *Breakup: The Coming End of Canada and the Stakes for America.* New York: W.W. Norton 1994.

Lawson, Guy. "No Canada?" *Harper's Magazine,* April 1996: 67–78.

Lemieux, Vincent. "Le référendum de 1995: Quelques pistes d'explication." In Trent, Young, and Lachapelle, eds., *Québec-Canada,* 65–9. Ottawa: University of Ottawa Press 1996.

Lemieux, Vincent, and Robert Bernier. "L'électorat flottant francophone en août 1995." In Maurice Pinard, Robert Bernier, and Vincent Lemieux, *Un combat inachevé,* 215-57. Sainte-Foy: Les Presses de l'Université du Québec 1997.

Les intellectuels pour la souveraineté (IPSO). "Oui au changement." In Michel Sarra-Bournet, ed., *Manifeste des intellectuels pour la souveraineté,* 15-21. Montreal: Fides 1995.

Leslie, Peter. "Options for the Future of Canada: The Good, the Bad, and the Fantastic." In Ronald L. Watts and Douglas M. Brown, eds., *Options for a New Canada,* 122–40. Toronto: University of Toronto Press 1991.

– *The European Community: A Political Model for Canada?* Ottawa: Minister of Supply and Services Canada 1991.

– *The Maastricht Model: A Canadian Perspective on the European Union.* Research Paper no. 33. Kingston: Institute of Intergovernmental Relations 1996.

McCallum, John. "The Canadian Economic Union after Breakup." *Inroads* 1 (1992): 68–79.

McCallum, John, and Chris Green. *Parting as Friends: The Economic Consequences for Quebec.* Canada Round Series no. 5. Toronto: C.D. Howe Institute 1991.

MacFarlane, S. Neil. *Sovereignty and Stability: The Domestic and Regional Security Implications of Québec Separation.* Occasional paper. Hanover, New Hampshire: Dickey Center, Dartmouth College 1997.

McRoberts, Kenneth. "After the Referendum: Canada with or without Quebec." In McRoberts, ed., *Beyond Quebec,* 403–32. Montreal: McGill-Queen's University Press 1995.

– *Misconceiving Canada: The Struggle for National Unity.* Toronto: Oxford University Press 1997.

– ed. *Beyond Quebec: Taking Stock of Canada.* Montreal: McGill-Queen's University Press 1995.

McRoberts, Kenneth, and Patrick J. Monahan, eds. *The Charlottetown Accord, the Referendum, and the Future of Canada.* Toronto: University of Toronto Press 1993.

Martin, Pierre. "Association after Sovereignty? Canadian Views on Economic Association with a Sovereign Quebec." *Canadian Public Policy* 21, no.1 (1995): 53–71.

Marzolini, Michael. "The Regionalization of Canadian Electoral Politics." In Alan Frizzell and Jon H. Pammett, eds., *The Canadian General Election of 1997,* 193–205. Toronto: Dundurn Press 1997.

Matalin, Mary, and James Carville, with Peter Knobler. *All's Fair.* New York: Random House 1994.

Meisel, John. "An Echo of Ghiţa Ionescu's Reading Notes: Travails of the Canadian State." *Government and Opposition* 32, no. 2 (1997): 234–50.

Milne, David. "Past and Future: Reflections after the Referendum." In Trent, Young, and Lachapelle, eds., *Québec-Canada,* 81–3.

Ministerial Council on Social Policy Reform and Renewal. "Report to Premiers." December 1995.

Monahan, Patrick J. *"Cooler Heads Shall Prevail": Assessing the Costs and Consequences of Quebec Separation.* Commentary no. 65. Toronto: C.D. Howe Institute 1995.

Monahan, Patrick, and Michael J. Bryant, with Nancy C. Coté. *Coming to Terms with Plan B: Ten Principles Governing Secession.* Commentary no. 83. Toronto: C.D. Howe Institute 1996.

Morrison, Alex, ed. *Divided We Fall: The National Security Implications of Canadian Constitutional Issues.* Toronto: Canadian Institute of Strategic Studies 1991.

Nemni, Max. *Canada in Crisis and the Destructive Power of Myth.* Université Laval, Laboratoire d'études politiques et administratives. Cahier 92-10. November 1992.

Ontario, Office of the Premier. "Notes for an Address by the Honourable Mike Harris, Premier of Ontario." The Canadian Club, Toronto, Ontario, 12 October 1995.

Page, Benjamin J. *Choices and Echoes in Presidential Elections*. Chicago: University of Chicago Press 1978.

Parisella, John. "Is the Quebec Liberal Party Still Relevant?" Unpublished manuscript. March 1996.

Parizeau, Jacques. "The Case for a Sovereign Quebec." *Foreign Policy* 99 (1995): 69–76.

– *Pour un Québec souverain*. Montreal: VLB éditeur 1997.

Parti québécois. *Le Québec dans un monde nouveau*. Montreal: VLB éditeur et le Parti québécois 1993.

Pinard, Maurice. "The Dramatic Reemergence of the Quebec Independence Movement." *Journal of International Affairs* 45, no. 2 (1992): 471–97.

– "The Secessionist Option and Quebec Public Opinion, 1988–1993." *Opinion Canada* 2, no. 3 (June 1994): 1–5.

– "Le cheminement de l'opinion publique." In Pinard, Bernier, and Lemieux, *Un combat inachevé*, 261-76.

– "Le contexte politique et les dimensions sociodémographiques." In Pinard, Bernier, and Lemieux, *Un combat inachevé*, 277–315.

– "Les déterminants psychosociaux." In Pinard, Bernier, and Lemieux, *Un combat inachevé*, 317-53.

Pinard, Maurice, Robert Bernier, and Vincent Lemieux. *Un combat inachevé*. Sainte-Foy: Les Presses de l'Université du Québec 1997.

Poole, Greg B., and David Westerterp. "Financial Markets and Instability: Market Response to the Quebec Referendum." Unpublished fourth-year honours paper, Department of Economics, University of Western Ontario, April 1996.

Provincial/Territorial Council on Social Policy Renewal. *New Approaches to Canada's Social Union: An Options Paper*. 29 April 1997.

– "Progress Report to Premiers." Report no. 2. July 1997.

Québec, Assemblée nationale. Avant-projet de loi. *Loi sur la souveraineté du Québec*. Québec: Éditeur officiel du Québec 1994.

– *Bill 1 An Act respecting the Future of Québec*. Québec: Québec Official Publisher 1995.

– Bill 3 *An Act respecting the Elimination of the Deficit and a Balanced Budget*. Quebec: Quebec Official Publisher 1996.

– Commission d'étude des questions afférentes à l'accession du Québec à la souveraineté. *Draft Report*. Quebec 1992.

Québec, Attorney General. *Requête déclinatoire et en irrecevabilité*, filed in the Superior Court of Quebec, *Bertrand v. Bégin*, case no: 200-05-002117-955, 12 April 1996, by Saint-Laurent, Boucher, Gagnon, Martineau, Walker on behalf of the Attorney General of Quebec.

Québec, Commission sur l'avenir politique et constitutionnel du Québec (Bélanger-Campeau Commission). *Report of the Commission on the Political and Constitutional Future of Quebec.* Quebec, March 1991.

– *Les avis des spécialistes invités à répondre aux huit questions posées par la Commission.* Working Paper no. 4. Quebec, 1991.

Québec, Conseil exécutif, Commission nationale sur l'avenir du Québec. *Rapport.* Quebec: Éditeur officiel du Québec 1995.

Québec, Directeur général des élections du Québec. *Referendum Act: Special Version of the Election Act for the Holding of a Referendum.* Quebec 1995.

– *Rapport des résultats officiels du scrutin: Référendum du 30 Octobre 1995.* Quebec 1995.

– *Rejected Ballot Papers – Unity Rally: Report of the Chief Electoral Officer.* Sainte-Foy: Directeur général des élections du Québec 1996.

Quebec Liberal Party, Committee on the Evolution of Canadian Federalism. *Recognition and Interdependence: Quebec's Identity and Canadian Federalism.* Montreal: Quebec Liberal Party 1996.

Reform Party of Canada. *Reform Responses to the Twenty Questions Posed to the Prime Minister on June 8, 1994.* Press release, December 1995.

– *A Fresh Start for Canadians.* Calgary: Reform Party 1997.

Richards, John. *Language Matters: Ensuring That the Sugar Not Dissolve in the Coffee.* Commentary no. 84. Toronto: C.D. Howe Institute 1996.

Riker, William. *The Art of Political Manipulation.* New Haven: Yale University Press 1986.

Ritchie, Gordon, et al. *Broken Links: Trade Relations after a Quebec Secession.* Canada Round Series no. 4. Toronto: C.D. Howe Institute 1991.

Robertson, Gordon. "Contingency Legislation for a Quebec Referendum." Unpublished manuscript. 26 February 1996.

Rocher, François. "Les aléas de la stratégie pré-référendaire: Chronique d'une mort annoncée." In Douglas M. Brown and Jonathan W. Rose, eds., *Canada: The State of the Federation 1995*, 19-45. Kingston: Institute of Intergovernmental Relations 1995.

Roh, Charles E. Jr. *The Implications for U.S. Trade Policy of an Independent Quebec.* Decision Quebec Series, Centre for Strategic and International Studies and Centre for Trade Policy and Law. Washington and Ottawa, 1995.

Rose, Jeff. "Some Reflections on Social Entitlements, Social Cohesion and National Unity." Occasional Paper, Faculty of Law, University of Toronto, 22 April 1996.

Rowlands, Dane, "International Aspects of the Division of Debt under Secession: The Case of Canada and Quebec." *Canadian Public Policy* 23, no.1 (1997): 40–54.

Russell, Peter H. *Constitutional Odyssey: Can Canadians Become a Sovereign People?* Toronto: University of Toronto Press 1992.

Russell, Peter, and Bruce Ryder. *Ratifying a Postreferendum Agreement on Quebec*

Sovereignty. Commentary no. 97. Toronto: C.D. Howe Institute 1997.

Sands, Christopher. "Quebecium est dividae in partes tres." Paper presented to the Conference on Sovereignty and Stability, Dartmouth College, 1–2 April 1996.

Shum, Pauline M. "Stock Market Response to Political Uncertainty: Evidence from the 1992 Constitutional Referendum." *Canadian Journal of Economics*, 29, special issue (1996): S213-18.

Simeon, Richard, "Scenarios for Separation." In Richard Simeon, ed., *Must Canada Fail?* 189–203. Montreal: McGill-Queen's University Press 1977.

Simeon, Richard, and Mary Janigan, eds. *Toolkits and Building Blocks: Constructing a New Canada*. Toronto: C.D. Howe Institute 1991.

Stein, Janice Gross, David R. Cameron, and Richard Simeon, with Alan Alexandroff. *Citizen Engagement in Conflict Resolution: Lessons for Canada in International Experience*. Commentary no. 94. Toronto: C.D. Howe Institute 1997.

Stein, Michael B. "Improving the Process of Constitutional Reform in Canada: Lessons from the Meech Lake and Charlottetown Constitutional Rounds." *Canadian Journal of Political Science* 30, no. 2 (1997): 307–38.

Symonds, William C. "Would Quebec Survive Sovereignty?" *Business Week*, 30 October 1995: 54–5.

Tremblay, Miville. "Zero Deficit by the Year 2000." *Inroads*, 6 (1997): 7–18.

Trent, John E. "Post-Referendum Citizen Group Activity." In Patrick C. Fafard and Douglas M. Brown, eds., *Canada: The State of the Federation 1996*, 45–76. Kingston: Institute of Intergovernmental Relations, 1996.

Trent, John E., Robert Young, and Guy Lachapelle, eds. *Québec-Canada: What Is the Path Ahead?* Ottawa: University of Ottawa Press 1996.

Turp, Daniel. "Réponses aux questions posées par la commission sur l'avenir politique et constitutionnel du Québec." In Québec, Commission sur l'avenir, *Les avis des spécialistes*, Working Paper no. 4, 1057–1116. Quebec 1991.

United States. House of Representatives. Hearing before the Subcommittee on the Western Hemisphere of the Committee on International Relations, One Hundred Fourth Congress, Second Session. *The Issue of Quebec's Sovereignty and Its Potential Impact on the United States*, 25 September 1996. Washington: U.S. Government Printing Office 1996.

Valaskakis, Kimon, and Angéline Fournier. *Le piège de l'indépendance*. Montreal: L'Étincelle 1995.

Watts, Ronald L., and Douglas M. Brown, eds. *Options for a New Canada*. Toronto: University of Toronto Press 1991.

Wells, Paul. "Be Vewy, Vewy Quiet." *Saturday Night*, September 1995, 17–21.

Whitaker, Reg. "Managing Quebec: The Mackenzie King Model." *Literary Review of Canada* 6, no. 1 (1996).

– "Cruising at 30,000 Feet with a Missing Engine: The Chrétien Government in the Aftermath of the Quebec Referendum." In Gene Swimmer, ed., *How Ottawa Spends 1997–98*, 51–83. Ottawa: Carleton University Press 1997.

White, Peter G. "The Political Future of Quebec Francophones." Occasional paper, Council for Canadian Unity. Montreal 1996.

White, Robert. "Speech by Robert White, President, Canadian Labour Congress, to the Québec Federation of Labour's Special Meeting on the Québec Referendum." Montreal, 21 February 1995.

Young, Robert. "Le Canada hors Québec: Voudra-t-il coopérer avec un Québec souverain?" In Alain-G. Gagnon and François Rocher, eds., *Répliques aux détracteurs de la souveraineté du Quebec*: 392–407. VLB éditeur 1992.

– *The Breakup of Czechoslovakia*. Research Paper no. 32, Kingston: Institute of Intergovernmental Relations 1994.

– "The Political Economy of Secession: The Case of Quebec." *Constitutional Political Economy* 5, no. 2 (1994): 221–45.

– "How Do Peaceful Secessions Happen?" *Canadian Journal of Political Science* 27, no. 4 (1994): 773–92.

– *The Secession of Quebec and the Future of Canada*. Montreal: McGill-Queen's University Press 1995.

– "'Maybe Yes, Maybe No': The Rest of Canada and a Quebec 'Oui.'" In Douglas M. Brown and Jonathan W. Rose, eds., *Canada: The State of the Federation 1995*, 47–62. Kingston: Institute of Intergovernmental Relations 1995.

– "Secession, Games and Strategic Discourse." Paper presented to the Seventh Villa Colombella Seminar, Rome, 5 September 1996.

– "Defending Decentralization." *Policy Options* 18, no. 2 (1997): 42–4.

Index

Aboriginal peoples, 6; and Aboriginal rights, 147; Canadian fiduciary obligations to, 110; after a future Yes vote, 130–1, 134, 137–9; and impact of 1995 referendum, 74–5, 79, 102; and Quebec policies, 14; and right of self-determination and secession, 29; in 1995 referendum, 14, 29–30; after a 1995 Yes vote, 64, 67–8, 71
ACCESS proposals, 98
Action démocratique du Québec (ADQ), 11, 13, 21-2, 124, 155n52. *See also* Dumont, Mario
Act Respecting the Sovereignty of Quebec, 15–16
Alberta, 78, 100; and Calgary Declaration, 120–1
Allaire, Jean, 157n93
Alliance Québec, 75
amicus curiae, 108
Amiel, Barbara, 167n43

Armed forces: after a future Yes, 136–7, 139; in secession negotiations, 6; vote in 1995 referendum, 164n27; after a 1995 Yes vote, 65–6
Assembly of First Nations, 152n3
Assets of Canada: in secession negotiations, 6
Atikamekw, 152n2. *See also* Aboriginal peoples
Attorney general of Canada, 107
Austria-Hungary, 5
Auto Pact, 34
Axworthy, Lloyd, 179n107

Bagotville, 164n27
Beaudoin, Laurent, 29
Bélanger, Michel, 18
Bélanger-Campeau Commission, 9, 188n1
Bertrand, Guy, 106
Bill 1 (An Act Respecting the Future of Quebec),

24–6, 49, 65, 71
Bill 101. *See* Charter of the French Language
Bill C-110, 95–6
Black, Conrad, 67
Blais, André, 40–1
Bloc québécois (BQ), 10, 28; constitutional position of, 19–20; leadership of, 73; in 1995 referendum, 14, 54; in 1997 election, 92, 111–16. *See also* Bouchard, Lucien
Bombardier, 29, 97
Borders of Quebec: after a future Yes vote, 131–2; in Plan B, 102–3; in secession negotiations, 6; in 1995 referendum, 29–30. *See also* Aboriginal peoples; Partition
Bouchard, Lucien:
–General: 10-13; Quebec attitudes towards, 15, 24
–In 1995 referendum: 13, 15, 19, 35, 38; and campaign discourse,

43–59; as chief negotiator, 31–2, 39–40; impact of, 39–42; and partnership, 19–23, 25; and *virage*, 19–21, 43, 56
–After a 1995 Yes vote: 65–6
–As premier of Quebec: 7, 73, 87–92, 146; and Calgary Declaration, 120; and Plan A, 95; and Plan B, 102–3, 108–10; and social union, 149-50; and strategy about next referendum, 87–92, 123–8; and Supreme Court reference, 147–8; in 1997 election, 112–15. *See also* Bloc québécois
Bourassa, Robert, 9, 188n1
Bourgault, Pierre, 189n18
Brassard, Jacques, 147, 180n124, 183n165
Britain, 141
British Columbia, 73; and attitudes towards Quebec, 76; and contingency planning, 79–80; and its secession, 81, 140, 142
Bush, George, 34
Business Council on National Issues, 117

Cairns, Alan C., 77, 80
Caisse de dépôt et placement du Québec, 65, 164n24
Calgary Declaration, 8, 100, 117–21, 127
Campeau, Jean, 152n1
Canada. *See* Rest of Canada (ROC)
Canada Health Act, 98
Canadian Charter of Rights and Freedoms, 8, 106, 181n141
Canadian Information

Office, 97
Canadian Labour Congress, 67
Canam Manac, 29
Castonguay, Claude, 64–5, 117
C.D. Howe Institute, 180n117
Charest, Jean, 11; and Calgary Declaration, 119; and Plan B, 146; in 1995 referendum, 18, 36, 161n32; as Quebec Liberal leader, 145–6; in 1997 election, 111–17
Charlottetown Accord, 9, 97, 118
Charter of the French Language (Bill 101), 9
Chirac, Jacques, 34
Chomedey, 269–70
Chrétien, Jean:
–General:11; constitutional position of, 28
–In 1995 referendum: 17, 23–4, 37; campaign discourse, 43–59; constitutional promises, 35–6; democracy, 27; strategy, 17–18, 24
–After a 1995 Yes vote: 64, 66–9
–Strategy about next referendum: 73, 94–110; distinct society, 84–6, 118; economic policy, 93; job creation, 90; legality of UDI, 105–9; majority required, 105, 115; partition, 102–3; Plan A, 87, 93–100, 120; Plan B, 87, 94, 101–10, 124; prenegotiation about, 105, 109–10; social union, 149; referendum question, 104–5; in 1997 election, 111–17. *See also* Liberal Party of Canada
Christopher, Warren, 34–5

Churchill Falls power contract, 80
Citizens' Committee for a New Province, 75
Citizenship, in secession negotiations, 6; in 1995 referendum campaign, 26, 50
Clark, Glen, 73, 118
Clark, Joe, 117
Cliche, David, 152n2
Clinton, Bill, 34, 158n118
Commercial and economic relations, Canada and Quebec: options about, 5; in secession negotiations, 6; in 1995 referendum campaign, 30
Confédération des syndicats nationaux, 154n33
Conseil du patronat du Québec, 18
Constitution Acts, 8; amending formulae in, 95–6; application to Quebec, 116–19, 183n163; patriation of, 8; section 49 review, 97
Constitution of Canada. *See* Constitution Acts
Coon-Come, Chief Matthew, 29, 152n3
Copps, Sheila, 17, 179n107
Council for Canadian Unity, 18
Courchene, Thomas J., 98
Cree, 29–30. *See also* Aboriginal peoples
CROP Inc., 41
Currency: in secession negotiations, 6
Czechoslovakia, polarization in, 5; separation of Slovakia and the Czech Republic, 5, 27–8

d'Aquino, Thomas, 171n60

Debt. *See* National debt
Decentralization: and
 Plan A, 96–8, 117, 121
Desmarais, Paul, 29
Dion, Stéphane: and
 distinct society, 96,
 100, 118; and majority
 required in
 referendum, 105; and
 partition, 102–3; and
 prenegotiation about
 next referendum, 109–
 10, 148; and
 referendum question,
 104–5; and referendum
 scenarios, 61–2, 127,
 134, 167n1; and
 school-board reform,
 90; and UDI, 107. *See
 also* Chrétien, Jean
Discourse, 23; in 1995
 referendum campaign,
 39–59
Distinct society clause,
 25–6, 45–6, 74, 76–7,
 94–5, 100, 112–13
Dollard-des-Ormeaux, 75
Doran, Charles, 83–4,
 142, 172n72
Duceppe, Gilles, 73, 92,
 112–16. *See also* Bloc
 québécois
Duhaime, Yves, 185n198
Dumont, Mario, 11, 13,
 19–21, 44, 124
Dutil, Marcel, 29

Economic Council of
 Canada, 190n28
Economist, 33
Election, federal of 1997,
 111–17
Employment training
 programs, 90–96
Environmental issues: in
 secession negotia-
 tions, 6
European Union (EU),
 22, 44, 140
Federal government. *See*
 Chrétien, Jean
First Ministers'

Conference, 148–9
First Nations. *See*
 Aboriginal Peoples
France: and recognition
 öf Quebec, 14, 34, 65,
 71, 83, 165n29
Francophonie, La, 65, 96

G-7, 50
Gauthier, Michel, 73,
 185n198
Gold, Justice Alan B.,
 167n45
Good Morning America,
 171n70
Great Coalition of 1864,
 188n3
Great Whale hydroelec-
 tric project, 14

Hampstead, 75
Harris, Mike, 73; and
 distinct society, 100;
 and Ontario demands,
 98, 117; in 1995
 referendum, 30, 45
Hébert, Chantal, 31
Hull, 58
Hydro-Québec, 164n24

Institute for Research on
 Public Policy, 155n50
Inuit, 29, 74–5. *See also*
 Aboriginal peoples
Ireland, 161n41

Johnson, Daniel, 11; and
 constitutional renewal,
 74, 97, 99, 118–9,
 187n234; and Plan B,
 105; and referendum
 campaign discourse,
 46, 50–1, 54; in 1995
 referendum, 17–18, 24,
 29–30, 35–6, 56, 83,
 163n68; and
 resignation, 145–6;
 after a 1995 Yes vote,
 64. *See also* Quebec
 Liberal Party
Joli-Coeur, André,
 183n159

June 12 agreement, 21–3,
 25
Juppé, Alain, 171n52

Klein, Ralph, 45, 78; and
 distinct society, 95, 100

Lachapelle, Guy, 41
La Chaudière-
 Appalaches, 18
L'Actualité, 20
Landry, Bernard, 14, 49,
 65, 103, 125, 153n14
Language rights: in
 Quebec, 25, 76, 104.
 See also Linguistic
 minorities
Laurier-Dorion, 69
Léger & Léger, 40, 160n6
Le Hir, Richard, 27
Lemieux, Vincent, 39
Le Point, 154n35
Liberal Party of Canada,
 constitutional position
 of, 11. *See also*
 Chrétien, Jean
Liberal Party of Quebec.
 See Quebec Liberal
 Party
Lincoln, Abraham,
 160n17
Lincoln-Douglas debates,
 114
Linguistic minorities: in
 Quebec, 14; and
 impact of 1995
 referendum, 75–6, 104;
 and Lucien Bouchard,
 89; in secession
 negotiations, 6. *See also*
 Language rights
Lisée, Jean-François,
 153n10

McGill Law School, 75
Makavik, 29
Manitoba, 120
Manning, Preston, 11;
 and Calgary
 Declaration, 118–19;
 and Plan A, 95, 118; in
 1995 referendum, 30–1,

45, 55–6; in 1997
election, 74, 111–17.
See also Reform Party
of Canada
Margeurite-Bourgeoys,
69–70
Marois, Pauline, 45
Martin, Paul, 32, 51
Martin, Pierre, 40–1
Massé, Marcel, 17, 102,
176n60, 176n61,
176n67
Meech Lake Accord, 9,
10, 47, 120, 127, 130
Millenium Scholarship
Endowment Fund,
191n25
Milne, David, 77
Mobility of population:
in secession
negotiations, 6
Mohawk, 180n124. *See
also* Aboriginal
peoples
Monahan, Patrick,
165n30
Montagnais, 152n2. *See
also* Aboriginal
peoples
Montreal, 16, 37; and
language rights, 76, 89,
91
Montreal International, 90
Mouvement de libération
nationale du Québec,
189n26
Mulroney, Brian, 117

Nadeau, Richard, 40–1
NAFTA. *See* North
American Free Trade
Agreement
National Commission on
the Future of Quebec,
16, 20
National debt: in
secession negotiations,
6, 81, 142–3
Neary, Peter, 188n3
New Brunswick, 73
New Democratic Party
(NDP): in 1997

election, 111, 114, 116
Newfoundland and
Labrador, 120, 167n41
New York, 34
North American Free
Trade Agreement
(NAFTA), Quebec's
accession to, 32, 34–5;
Quebec's exposure
under, 137. *See also*
United States
Norway-Sweden,
separation of, 5
Nova Scotia, 73

October 27 Group, 75
Olympics, 44
Olympic Stadium, 139
Ontario, 120; interests of,
73, 79; secession of,
177n78; union with
Quebec, 140
Outaouais, 37

Paré, Jean, 20
Parizeau, Jacques, 10, 13,
91; in polarization
strategy, 27, 153n8;
referendum campaign
discourse, 44, 47–50,
57; referendum
strategy, 15–16; in 1995
referendum, 13–14, 19,
23, 27–8, 38, 83; and
Supreme Court
reference, 147; after a
1995 Yes vote, 63–6,
165n29; in 1997
election, 93, 113–14.
See also Parti québécois
Parti québécois, 8–10;
constitutional position
of, 91; divisions
within, 19, 91–2, 125;
in 1995 referendum,
13–38.
Partition (of Quebec), 71,
75–6, 79, 102–3, 131–2.
See also Borders of
Quebec
Pettigrew, Pierre, 73, 96,
98

Pinard, Maurice, 40–2
Place du Canada, 36
Plan A, 7–8, 94–100;
defined, 87
Plan B, 7–8, 101–110;
defined, 87
Polarization, political: in
Czechoslovakia, 5;
after a future
referendum, 128, 138–
9; and impact of 1995
referendum, 76–7, 80;
in 1995 referendum,
27–8; in 1997 election,
112–16
Power Corporation, 29
Prince Edward Island, 73
Privy Council Office, 18,
161n32
Pro-Canada rally, 35–6,
70, 159n134
Progressive Conservative
Party of Canada, 11; in
1997 federal election,
111–17. *See also*
Charest, Jean
Public service: in
secession negotiations,
6

Quebec: identification
with Canada in, 40–2,
46–8; public opinion
about sovereignty in,
9–10; recent policy in
87–92; 1980
referendum in, 8; 1995
referendum in, 13–38.
See also Quebec
secession
Quebec Business Council
for Canada, 18
Quebec Committee for
Canada, 75
Quebec Federation of
Labour, 92
Quebec Liberal Party, 11;
constitutional position
of, 74, 98–9; and a
future referendum,
124, 135; in 1995
referendum, 17–18;

after 1995 referendum, 74, 88, 98–9; after a 1995 Yes vote, 64–5, 71. *See also* Johnson, Daniel; Charest, Jean

Quebec Political Action Committee, 75

Quebec secession:
–Background and possible effects of: constitutional and political background of, 8–11; constitution-ality of, 105–9, 146–8; studies of, 5; and possible economic relations with ROC, 15, 21–3, 48–52; and possible political relations with ROC, 19–23; and public opinion about, 9–10; and right of Quebec to secede, 104–9, 127, 147; scenarios of, 61–2, 128–43
–The event of secession: acceptance by ROC, 5–6, 60–3, 147; international recognition of, 82–6, 109; political autonomy in, 4; probable peaceful nature of, 61–2; public support for (polls), 13, 18, 23–4, 32, 40–2, 74, 92, 99, 120; rationality in, 14, 48–52; and referendum about, 13–38; role of foreign powers in, 82–6; uncertainty in, 5, 48–52; uniqueness of, 72–3, 167n1
–The aftermath of secession: and Canadian reconstitu-tion, 80, 131; economic effects of, 5; and long-term relations with ROC, 143–4;

negotiations about with ROC, 80–2; outcomes of negotiations about, 6 (*see also subject heads*); and Quebec constitution, 25–6; timetable for, 25
–The 1995 referendum campaign: 13–38; Bill 1, 24–6; and business, 28–9; and campaign organizations, 155n56; Declaration of Sovereignty, 16, 24–5; and economic uncertainty, 33–4; and electoral fraud, 60, 69–71; polarization in, 27–8; and public consultation, 16, 18; and referendum law, 23–4; and referendum question, 10, 16, 26, 54–7, 66–9, 104, 165n30; results, 37
–Discourse in the 1995 referendum campaign: 7, 39–59; the constitution, 43–6; democracy, 52–9; economic implications, 48–52; national identification, 45–8; the partnership, 21–3, 45
–After a 1995 Yes victory: 7, 60–71; economic uncertainty, 62–3; electoral fraud, 69–71
–Impact of the 1995 referendum: 7, 72–86; on foreign countries, 82–6; on future negotiations, 80–2; on the process of secession 78–9; on terms of secession, 79–80
–Post-referendum strategies about secession: 87–122 (*see*

also Chrétien, Jean, and Bouchard, Lucien)
–A future secession: 123–44; the campaign, 126–8; determining factors, 144; pre-negotiation about, 126, 131–3; pre-referendum compromise, 124–6; and ROC-Quebec institutions, 132, 141, 143; scenarios of, 128–43; and Supreme Court judgment about, 146–8; UDI in, 134–43, 147. *See also* Transition to sovereignty; Rest of Canada

Quebec Superior Court, 106–7

Racine, Serge, 157n93
Rae, Bob, 30, 153n9
Rae, John, 157n86
Reform Party of Canada, 11; and Plan B, 101, 105; in 1995 referendum, 18, 45, 55–6; after a 1995 Yes vote, 67; in 1997 election, 111–17. *See also* Manning, Preston
RESPEQ, 64
Rest of Canada (ROC): defined, 4
–Quebec secession and ROC: in a future secession, 128–43; impact of 1995 referendum on, 76–82, 129–30; and polarization *vis-à-vis* Quebec, 27–8, 139–42; process of reconstitution of, 131; secession negotiations with Quebec, 79–82; substance of reconstitution of, 80–2; in 1995 referendum, 28–31, 35–6, 46–52; after a 1995 Yes vote,

66–71. *See also* Quebec
    secession
Riker, William, 42
Rivest, Jean-Claude,
    187n234
Robillard, Lucienne, 18,
    46, 54, 176n61
Rock, Allan, 102, 175n56
Romanow, Roy, 191n26
Ryan, Claude, 64, 146

Saguenay floods, 97
Saint Hubert, 164n27
Saint Jean, 164n27
School board reform, 90–1
Secession: generaliza-
    tions about, 5, 72–3,
    167n1
Senate, reform of, 121
Simard, Jacynthe, 157n93
Simpson, Jeffrey, 31
Singapore-Malaysia,
    separation of, 5
Social union, 148–50;
    background to, 97–8
Société Saint-Jean
    Baptiste de Montréal,
    154n33
Sovereignty: meaning of
    in Quebec, 9–10. *See
    also* Quebec secession
Sovereignty-association,
    3–8. *See also* Quebec
    secession
Spending power, 96, 121,
    149

Stability, 75
State Department (USA),
    85–6
Succession to treaties by
    Quebec: in secession
    negotiations, 6; in 1995
    referendum campaign,
    32
Supreme Court of
    Canada, 9; and
    reference re Quebec
    secession, 71, 106–10,
    127–8, 131, 146–8
Sûreté du Québec, 137,
    139
Sweden 167n41

Team Canada trade
    missions, 90, 93
Tobin, Brian, 73, 80, 98
Toronto Stock Exchange,
    33, 62
Toronto Sun, 156n72
Transition to sovereignty:
    importance of, 72
Tremblay, Arthur, 157n93
Trudeau, Pierre, 8,
    183n163
Turp, Daniel, 20, 155n45,
    155n52

Unilateral declaration of
    independence (UDI):
    after a future Yes vote,
    134–41; legality of,
    105–9, 127, 146–8; in

post-referendum
    strategy, 105; by
    Quebec, 25, 61; in
    ROC, 140–3; after a
    1995 Yes vote, 66, 71
United Nations, 44, 130
United Quebec
    Federalists, 75
United States: and
    absorption of Canada,
    84–6; intervention
    after a future Yes vote,
    138–40; policy about
    Quebec secession, 34–
    5, 83–6; policy about
    recognition of Quebec,
    65, 85, 171n53; Quebec
    accession to treaties
    with, 34–5, 84–5
Universal Declaration of
    Human Rights, 182n145

Valcartier, 164n27
Vieille souche, 48
Venault, Denise, 157n93
Verdun, 36, 58–9
Veto, constitutional, of
    Quebec, 95–6, 183n163
Villeneuve, Raymond,
    189n26

Wells, Clyde, 45–6, 73
Western provinces, 11;
    and constitutional
    veto, 96
Woehrling, José, 179n114